A New Look At
Black Families

THIRD EDITION

A NEW LOOK AT BLACK FAMILIES
THIRD EDITION

GENERAL HALL, INC.
5 Talon Way
Dix Hills, New York 11746

Publisher: Ravi Mehra
Consulting Editor: Anand Sinha
Composition: *Graphics Division,* General Hall, Inc.

LIBRARY OF CONGRESS CATALOG CARD NUMBER: 88–82177
ISBN: 0–930390–91–1 [paper]
    0–930390–92–X [cloth]

Manufactured in the United States of America

A NEW LOOK
AT BLACK FAMILIES

THIRD EDITION

Charles Vert Willie
Harvard University

GENERAL HALL, INC.
Publishers
5 Talon Way
Dix Hills, New York 11746

This book is dedicated to my
parents and students,
who have taught me
many wonderful things.

Contents

Part III
Black Families And
The Social System

Part IV
Conclusion

Preface

By way of 18 case studies, this book answers the question of what it is like to be black in the United States. The stories of these families as told to our interviewers provide a window through which we can see patterns of variation in the life-style of affluent or middle-class, working-class, and poor black households.

Analysis of the way of life of black families, using the case method, is particularly effective in overcoming stereotypes. A comparison of adaptations by social class reveals both strengths and weaknesses that are associated with each status level.

This is a study of black families today and the situations in which they find themselves. It is not a study of the past, although there are brief references to history and slavery, that peculiar institution. A chapter on the continuing significance of race presents new data having to do with the 1980s, in this Third Edition.

A unique aspect of this investigation into black family life is that it combines a descriptive analysis and a theoretical explanation of behavior patterns. The application of social theory to the study of family life reveals the specific areas of similarity and difference between minority and majority populations and enhances our understanding of race relations.

The comparative analysis of black and of white families is introduced but is not comprehensive. It relies upon the studies of blacks presented in this book and an analysis of the adaptations of white families that is found in the literature. The conclusions from this brief investigation indicate the need for a full comparison of case studies of white as well as of black households. This book presents a partial revelation of the rich material and profound insights that can be derived from a comparative analysis by race and social class.

This book also analyzes situation of black families in the total social system and what blacks have contributed to the

1

society that is unique. Particular attention is given to male and female roles in the society at large. This chapter is presented for the first time in the Third Edition.

The case studies of black families have been accumulated over the decades by participants in a course on The Black Family at Syracuse University and a course on Adaptation and Learning in Majority and Minority Families at the Harvard Graduate School of Education.

The names and geographic locations of families have been disguised to protect their privacy. These are fictitious; but the ways of life of the households reported in this book — including their joys and sorrows, their hard times and good times — are vivid and real.

Acknowledged with appreciation are all families that co-operated and the students who faithfully reported their interview conversations with sympathy and sincerity. Contributions included in this book were prepared by Dennis Ashby, Karin Caruso, Beryl M. Dakers, Jill Kirschner Katz, Daniel G. Lowengard, Judy Mesinger, Nancy Martin, Kathleen Dickinson Rockwood, Edward Sloan, Donna Willey Schum, Carol Blanck Tannenhauser, Michael Rettig, Nanalee Raphael, and Marshall T. Young, who attended Syracuse University. Additional interviews were prepared by Kristen Haggman Mitchell, Alan Haymon, Susan Kluver, William A. Mason, and Levi Moore, who attended Harvard University. Editorial assistance of high professional quality was rendered by Dorothy Sickles and Katharine Parker. The manuscript was skillfully typed by Mary Walsh, Jane Frost, Betty Blake, and Jacqueline Kennedy. My wife, Mary Sue, and our three offspring — Sarah Susannah, Martin Charles, and James Theodore — comforted and consoled me during the inevitable periods of frustration that are associated with attempts at creation.

Acknowledged also is the Maurice Falk Medical Fund which provided a grant to assist with the publication of the Third Edition. Some of the material in chapter 1 was first published in my book, *Five Black Scholars,* Abt Books and University Press of America in 1986. Chapter 4 is the modification of an article which I prepared for the 1988 volume of *The State of Black*

America, published by the National Urban League. Chapter 10 first appeared as an article in the *Journal of Family Issues* vol. 5, No. 3, September, 1984, pp. 291-306, issued by Sage Publications. I am grateful to the organizations mentioned for the privilege of using materials which appeared in their publications.

C.V.W.
Harvard University
Cambridge, Massachusetts
September, 1988

PART I

Concepts, Data, and Methods

1 INTRODUCTION: CONCEPTS &
ANALYTICAL PERSPECTIVES

THE BLACK FAMILY IN HISTORY

The black family is still around; it has not broken down.
The miracle of the black family is that it has survived and grown
stronger over the years. As psychiatrist Robert Coles says,
"there's sinew in the black family" (Coles 1965:El). It had, for
one thing, to survive the family breakups resulting from the internal slave trade. It is interesting, as background for this study
of conditions today, to see what Frederick Douglass, born in
slavery in 1817, has to say in his autobiography.

> The reader must not expect me to say much of my family. My first ex-
> perience of life, as I now remember it, ... began in the family of my grandmother
> and grandfather. ... The practice of separating mothers from their children and
> hiring them out at distances too great to admit of their meeting, save at long in-
> tervals, was a marked feature of the cruelty and barbarity of the slave system. ...
> It had no interest in recognizing or preserving any of the ties that bind families
> together or to their homes.
>
> My grandmother's five daughters [one of whom was my mother] were hired
> out in this way, and my only recollections of my own mother are of a few hasty
> visits made in the night on foot, after the daily tasks were over, and when she was
> under the necessity of returning in time to respond to the ... call to the field in early
> morning.
>
> Of my father I know nothing. Slavery had no recognition of fathers. ...
>
> Old master ... only allowed the little children to live with grandmother for a
> limited time; ... as soon as they were big enough they were promptly taken away. ...
>
> The time came when I must go. ... I was seven years old (Douglass
> 1962:27-33).

Frederick Douglass was an ingenious man. By the age of 21
years he had escaped from slavery. In disguise, he traveled from
Maryland to New York and immediately sent for his fiancee,
Anna Murray, who was a free woman. They were married and

lived together as husband and wife 44 years until Mrs. Douglass died in 1882 (Douglass 1962:20, 204-205).

Booker T. Washington, born in slavery in 1858 or 1859, presented a similar statement of family separation. He said:

> I was born in a typical log cabin. ... In this cabin I lived with my mother and a brother and sister till after the Civil War, when we were all declared free. Of my ancestry I know almost nothing. ... I have been unsuccessful in securing any information that would throw any accurate light upon the history of my family beyond my mother. ... In the days of slavery not very much attention was given to family history and family records — that is, black family records. Of my father I know even less than of my mother, I do not even know his name. ... (Washington 1965: 15-16).

> My mother's husband, who was the stepfather of my brother John and myself, did not belong to the same owner as did my mother. In fact, he seldom came to our plantation. I remember seeing him there perhaps once a year, that being about Christmas time (Washington 1965:30).

Washington reported that during the war, by running away and following the federal soldiers, his stepfather found his way into the new state of West Virginia. "As soon as freedom was declared, he sent for my mother to come to the Kanawha Valley, in West Virginia. ... My stepfather had already secured a job at a salt-furnace, and he had also secured a little cabin for us to live in. ... (Washington 1965:30-31).

These excerpts from *The Life and Times of Frederick Douglass* and *Up from Slavery* by Booker T. Washington tell us two things: first, there was limited opportunity for experiencing full family life among black slaves; second, former slaves were nevertheless capable of forming enduring family unions. The first fact is usually remembered; the second fact, frequently forgotten.

For years there has been a great debate over where the story of black families in America should begin—on the shore of the United States or in Africa. Wade Nobles believes there is parallelism between African tribalism and the black family unit in America. Specifically, he refers to "the strong kinship bonds found in black extended families" as "positive functional reflections of the sense of Africanity in black communities" (Noble, 1978:22). Yet there are many other ancient customs of African origin that seem to have no vestiges in contemporary black families in America. Particularly in West Africa, the area from which Kunta Kinte (the ancestor of Alex Haley) came, the Moslem influence was strong. A Council of Elders consisting only of men settled the affairs of the community when there were disputes, including disputes within families. Haley said that in Kunta's village, men could charge that their wives failed to respect them, were unduly lazy, were unwilling to make love when their turn came (some West African men had two, three, or four wives). Unless an accused wife presented a strong counter argument, Haley said, the Council of Elders would rule that the aggrieved husband could divorce such a wife. The husband could do this simply by setting any three of his wife's possessions outside her hut and "then uttering toward those possessions, three times, with witnesses present, the words, 'I divorce you!'" (Haley, 1976:114-117). The absence of any semblance of a custom of supreme male authority in contemporary black families in this society causes me to cast doubt on hypotheses of the African origin of most cultural practices among American blacks.

Some social scientists have tried to explain the higher proportion of broken families among blacks than among whites as a direct outgrowth of the slave experience. For example, Andrew Billingsley has said:

the slave system had a crippling effect on the establishment, maintenance, and growth of normal patterns of family life among Negro people. ... This crippled the development not only of individual slaves, but of families, and hence of the whole society of Negro people. ... The consequences these conditions wrought for Negroes under the slave system were direct and insidious. The consequences for succeeding and even modern generations of Negroes are, perhaps, less direct, but no less insidious (Billingsley 1968:68-69).

Daniel Patrick Moynihan attempts to specify the consequences: "In essence, the black community has been forced into a matriarchal structure which, because it is so out of line with the rest of American society seriously retards the progress of the group as a whole." He called this matriarchal structure and its alleged limitations the "fearful price" the black American community has paid "for the incredible mistreatment to which it has been subjected over the past three centuries" (U.S. Department of Labor 1965:29).

But the facts do not jibe with the assertions. The black family is not basically a matriarchal system (Jackson 1973: 186,199). Most black children grow up in households in which a mother and a father are present. The hypothesis that the slavery heritage has contributed to both a high rate of family instability and a matriarchal system fails to recognize that among intact families (the prevailing pattern) many blacks have grandparents or great-grandparents who were born as slaves. These contemporary two-parent households are stable, although some of their ancestors were not free or able to form enduring marriages.

The history of the black family in the United States must be viewed as a miraculous movement from more or less nothing to something. After slavery, black people continued to experience severe handicaps. The higher rate of family instability among blacks compared with whites probably is more a function of contemporary situations and circumstances than of the historic condition of slavery or the African origin of blacks. For example, an indirect association has been found to exist between family income and family instability: as the family income decreases, the proportion of families headed by one parent tends to increase. Inadequate income today resulting from racial discrimination is the "fearful price" for being black and is the "incredible mistreatment" that "seriously retards the progress of the group as a whole," a fact missed by Moynihan, who tried to blame the contemporary circumstances of blacks on their group's past experiences of slavery. Poverty, racial discrimination, and family instability are linked. Poverty, of course, can be eradicated, and so can discrimination. Those interested in further stabilizing the black family could be of much help by working for the elimination of racial discrimination in employment and income.

By and large the 18 case studies indicate that the students, though inexperienced in interviewing, awkward and naive in their approach, established honest and trusting relationships with the families and obtained basic facts and elicited information about some important feelings. Reported are the results of a guided conversation. Because all students asked similar questions of all families, the opportunity for comparative analysis is presented. I believe that the students have rendered good reports of a range of adaptations among black families in the United States.

BLACK PARENTS TODAY

Too frequently in the past, the description and analysis of black family life has emphasized that which is unique, exotic, and different. The interview schedule designed for this study was for the purpose of getting at the everyday happenings in the lives of black people. We were trying to understand a style of life, a way of life — the habits of family members, the customs and conventions of the group. Researchers had to be sensitive to the variety of life-styles among blacks and the situational determinants of different family forms and patterns of adaptation. A summary of situational differences of black families by social class follows.

Affluent black families tend to be nuclear households consisting of husband and wife and two or three children. Working-class black families tend to be nuclear households, too, consisting of husband and wife and children. However, the working-class black family is likely to be larger, with five or more children present. Also, there is the possibility that a relative or boarder may be part of the working-class household. Working-class black families are broken more often than are those that are affluent, with illness and death frequently among the reasons for the absence of the male spouse. Poor black families are likely to be one-parent households more often than are families in the other class levels. Some are extended families consisting of grandmother, mother, and children. Among the poor, desertion and divorce are chief causes for family disruption. One-parent households are not always without a male presence, however; a boyfriend may visit frequently, help support the mother, and be attentive to her children.

All blacks — affluent, working-class, and poor — are so deeply involved in work that they seldom have much time for voluntary community activity. Nevertheless, there are some interesting variations by social class. Affluent black parents tend to be active participants in church affairs, mainstays of the Parent-Teacher Association or a school-community group, and possibly members of a social club. Black working-class parents tend to attend church worship services regularly; the mother may periodically go to meetings of the school-community group; and that is about all the family can do. Poor black families tend to be univolved in community affairs and may or may not be church members. Those who are faithful in church attendance are likely to be completely enveloped by the religious system, but many have no church affiliation and no other organized community participation. Visiting with family members and a few friends is about all that they do as a leisure-time activity outside the home.

Thus, we see different and distinct styles of life among blacks of different class levels associated with family composition, child-rearing, and community participation. A fuller discussion of these differences is presented in Part II.

These case studies should help lay to rest for all time the tendency to stereotype blacks. This study of black families by social class indicates the diversity within the race. Despite the diversity there are some common responses among families with similar resources and opportunities. This is the story of 18 families who are both similar to and different from other blacks and all families in the United States.

I have reviewed the lives of several outstanding scholars in my book, Five Black Scholars (1986). Their accomplishments are illustrative of how some families function today. These scholars grew up under conditions not unlike circumstances that other blacks have experienced.

John Hope Franklin, a famous black historian, Professor Emeritus of the University of Chicago, was born in Rentiesville, Oklahoma, an all-black town of 200 people. His father moved there to protect his family from the outrageous experience of racial discrimination. Franklin's father was a lawyer and his mother a school teacher. Franklin earned a Doctor of Philosophy degree in history at Harvard University. He grew up in a family of professionals who were college graduates.

Kenneth B. Clark, a famous black psychologist, is Professor Emeritus of City College of the City University of New York. He was born in the Panama Canal Zone to immigrant parents from Jamaica. When his parents separated, his mother moved to New York's Harlem in search of a better education for her young children. As a single parent she worked in the garment industry to support her family. She insisted that her children pursue academic subjects in high school, get good grades, and go to college. Meanwhile, Clark's mother went to school at night while her children were being educated during the day. She eventually earned a high school diploma and Clark eventually was awarded a Ph.D. degree by Columbia University. Kenneth Clark grew up in a single-parent, working-class family in a big-city ghetto.

W. Arthur Lewis, a famous black economist, is Professor Emeritus of Princeton University. He was born in the British West Indies. Both his father and mother completed two years of college, which is all they needed then to obtain a license to teach in school. Lewis's father died when he was only seven years old. His mother, who had retired from teaching to nurture her young family, had to return to the labor force to support her children. This she did as a self-employed businesswoman who operated a small dry goods enterprise. With income derived from this source, she supported and educated her sons. W. Arthur Lewis was sent from St. Lucia Island to London where he earned a doctorate degree at the London School of Economics. W. Arthur Lewis came of age in a family that was broken by the premature death of a parent.

Of the three scholars I have mentioned, all came from families with modest means. Parents were college graduates in one; they attended but did not finish college in another; and the mother did not go beyond high school in the third. These scholars were reared in different family forms. One was a two-parent household. The others were single-parent families in which the father was absent due to death or divorce. Regionally, these scholars came of age in the North, the South, and in the West Indies. Despite their variations in life-circumstances, all were outstanding and high academic achievers. All earned a doctorate degree. All taught in great universities. All had distinguished careers of research, and public service also. Two were elected to Phi Beta Kappa; one was knighted by the United Kingdom. Despite their high achievements, their backgrounds, as we have seen, were not very different from the life-experiences of many other blacks.

A common experience in the lives of these men is the support they received from their mothers. With or without husbands, their mothers sacrificed and suffered to support them. Young Franklin was frequently in the company of his mother who took him to school where she taught and sat him on the back bench to play. There was no day-care in those days. He learned to read as she taught older children, and kept a watchful eye on him. From his mother, Franklin said, he got a headstart decades before there was such a national program. Clark's mother insisted that he be placed in high school academic courses and not steered into vocational education as was customary for minorities in the days of his youth. Clark said, his mother was not awed by authority; and, according to him, her daring ways saved him and his sister. His mother gave full support and worked to put him and his sister through college. Of his mother, W. Arthur Lewis said, "I never found out how she managed to establish and support us; but she did on the income from the business." Law, medicine, and economics were among the careers her sons pursued.

And what of fathers? They too support and sustain their offspring, especially their daughters. A book about *The Managerial Woman* (1976) authored by Margaret Hennig and Anne Jardim looks at the life and career histories of twenty-five women who had reached top management positions in business and industry. These authors discovered that successful white women in business and industry "had extremely close relationships with their fathers" (Hennig and Jardim, 1976:99). These daughters of high achievement had fathers who would take them places, teach them athletic skills, praised them, encouraged them and instructed them never to let others impose limits on their level of achievement (Hennig and Jardim, 1976:100-108). These women of success had fathers who believed that they could do much more than others of their gender had done in the past, even as the men of success had mothers who believed that they could succeed.

Mothers and fathers who hold such beliefs and behave as these parents have expand their children's definition of themselves as persons. With such support, their children become individuals of achievement. Quite possibly, these contemporary findings about black mothers and their sons and white fathers and their daughters are models for all families in our times. These are hypotheses worthy of studying.

BLACK CHILDREN TODAY

The social science information on black children is mixed. In *Brown* v. *Board of Education,* the U.S. Supreme Court said, "To separate [children in grade and high schools] from others of similar age and qualifications solely because of their race generates feelings of inferiority as to their status in the community that may affect their hearts and minds in a way unlikely ever to be undone." The Court based its finding on what it called "amply ... modern authority."

Two items that support the Court's contention are found in the 1978 *Annual Report* of the Children's Defense Fund:

- One Black child drops out of school for every two who graduate. Black children are more than twice as likely to be suspended from school and to receive corporal punishment in school than white children. They are three times as likely to be placed in classes for the educable mentally retarded, but are less than half as likely to be placed in gifted classes as their white peers.
- A Black college graduate has the same chance of being unemployed as a white high school dropout.

A Black high school graduate has the same chance
of being unemployed as a white grade school dropout. Black teenagers are unemployed at almost
three times the white rate.

This is the educational condition of black children a generation after the *Brown* decision.

At the midpoint of the twentieth century, an appendix to
the appellant's briefs in *Brown* vs. *Board of Education* sum-
marized the mental health arguments for desegregating the
schools. The statement was prepared by Floyd Allport of Syracuse
University and indicated that:

As children learn the inferior status to which they
are assigned—as they observe the fact that they are
almost always segregated and kept apart from
others who are treated with more respect by the
society as a whole—they often react with feelings of
inferiority and a sense of personal humiliation.
Many of them become confused about their own
personal worth. ... Almost nowhere in the larger
society do they find their own dignity as human beings respected by others .... The minority child is
thrown into a conflict with regard to his feelings
about himself and his group. He wonders whether
his group and himself are worthy of no more respect
than they receive. This conflict and confusion leads
to self-hatred and rejection of his own group.
(Allport, 1952:166-184).

In *The Mark of Oppression,* Abram Kardiner and Lionel
Oversey report the case of an adolescent who is black whom
they describe as having "keen insight into both the familial and
societal origins of her low self-esteem." The female patient said,
"I wish my people would think twice before they start raising a
family. I mean the [blacks] as a whole ... I wish they wouldn't. It
would save them a lot of headaches. Yesterday, as I walked
through Harlem, I looked at the people and the buildings and I

realized that if you weren't optimistic you would do one of two things: either kill yourself or drink yourself to death. Now I understand why they do that sort of thing." This is the testimony of a black teenager in therapy who had experienced parental rejection. Kardiner and Oversey observe that her "added awareness of being black finished whatever chance she had for an effective social adaptation" (Kardiner and Ovesey, 1962:282-283).

The Carnegie Council on Children and its report (*All Our Children,* New York: Harcourt Brace Jovanovich, 1977) said that "survey after survey has shown that blacks with the same education constantly earn far less than whites." The report continues, "Of course black children, ... do not read these statistics— ... they don't have to. The most crucial facts for them are daily experiences. And when daily experience shows a black ... child that the adults with whom he lives, no matter how capable, have difficulty in gaining education and work, what can he conclude about his own future? Why should he remember what he learns in school when the process has no real use for him?" (Carnegie Council, 1977:35).

According to these discussions by competent authorities, the picture for the black child is grim. Yet there is something unrealistic about these discussions. We know children who came of age in environments that discriminated against them, but who nevertheless made it.

Too often, analysis of the adaptations of black children and other minority-group children has focused on the negative consequences of life for a black person in a racist society. Little attention has been given to the multitude of possible responses to racism, including those that may be classified as positive. Fortunately James Comer, a black psychiatrist, has begun to bring these alternative responses into focus. His professional experience taught him that the "constant daily reminder that it's tough to be black caused many youngsters enough discomfort to turn off or turn away." Then he remembered his personal experience in a family where his parents always said, "You never let race stop you from doing what you want to do." Comer concluded that the formula worked. He went to school—"hurt feelings or no hurt feelings"—got an education, and got ahead. When his self-esteem was battered, his parents patched it up and sent him back into the battle (Comer, 1972:23).

Comer has become a psychiatrist and a member of the faculty of the Yale University Medical School. The professional and personal experience of Dr. Comer illustrates the principle that adversity can both turn one off or turn one on. It turned him on.

I also think of Martin Luther King, Jr. Without ever occupying an official position, he had a moral impact upon the way of life of this nation that can only be classified as massive. Think for a moment about his background. During childhood he experienced the worst of racial segregation.

Historian L. D. Reddick, who prepared the history of the Montgomery Bus Boycott, noted that King was born in Atlanta, Georgia, January 15, 1929. Reddick further said in his book *Crusader Without Violence* that, "Any environment in which a person spends virtually the first two decades of his life would leave an indelible impression on him." The Atlanta in which King spent his first twenty years had segregated schools, a Klan that paraded and demonstrated until, in the 1940s, masking was outlawed. In general, Reddick characterized the Atlanta in which King grew up as "Southern and Jim Crow but not absolutely or rudely so" (Reddick, 1959:26, 30). According to Reddick, Martin Luther King, Jr. regarded the American South "as a land of terror and painful anxiety" (Reddick, 1959:22).

King's education was in segregated schools. He was separated from white children solely because of his race in grade school, high school, and college; yet he did not feel inferior as the Supreme Court said he would. Such separation did not adversely affect King's heart and mind as the Supreme Court said it would. King was not confused about his personal worth as Floyd Allport said he might be because he was kept apart from whites during his schooling. King continued his education and obtained a Ph.D. degree despite the fact that he saw all around him black educated people improperly regarded.

King, Comer, and a host of other blacks who came of age during the days of legally-enforced racial segregation are clear and present examples that adversity can stimulate the desire to transcend and overcome it. Psychologist Curtis Banks said that the negative judgments of society about racial minorities sometimes have less impact upon minorities than the white social scientists believe because blacks tends to discount the source. Many blacks believe whites are not appropriate judges of their character. Thus, their negative attitudes about the black race are discounted.

A recent study of Vietnamese refugees conducted by a research team associated with the Department of Psychiatry and Behavioral Science at the University of Washington in Seattle is revealing some interesting results about successful adaptations to adverse environments. Minota Masuda, a member of the research team, said this in an interview with the *New York Times:* "... aggressive attitudes of refugees, involving either severe criticism or anger at the host society ... had often proved to be a successful adaptive style. Many of these more aggressive refugees made better progress and fared better in their new environment than their more passive and benign fellows," he said. "'They may be awakening themselves to the fact that they're oppressed,'" he said. Then they become angry and their emotional arousal helps them to seek out and find ways to get along better and overcome their problems (Webster, *New York Times,* 1979: C1-C2).

Joyce Ladner, in *Mixed Families,* states that "every child is entitled to a *permanent* home and parents." Moreover, she states that "the permanency that the home offers enables the child to develop a secure sense of self, a stable identity, and the confidence that will enhance his or her ability to function, to perform adequately, and to meet the challenging tasks in life" (Ladner, 1978:139, 282). This is what families do for black children despite the discrimination that they encounter.

The problem with most of our studies of black children is that the researchers and the practitioners ask the wrong questions and make the wrong assumptions. Most researchers ask questions either about how well blacks adapt to the dominant culture or why they deviate from it. This, of course, is the wrong question. The wrong assumption that most researchers and practitioners make is that black families and their children are passive and deviant. Actually, the family is the first line of defense against a discriminating culture.

REFERENCES

Allport, F.H. 1952. "The Effect of Segregation and the Consequences of Desegregation: A Social Science Statement." In *Prejudice and Your Child,* edited by K.B. Clark, Boston: Beacon Press, 1963, pp. 164. 184.

Billingsley, Andrew. 1968. *Black Families in White America.* Englewood Cliffs, N.J.: Prentice-Hall.

Carnegie Council on Children. 1977. *All Our Children,* New York: Harcourt Brace Jovanovich.

Coles, Robert. 1965. "There's Sinew in the Negro Family." Background paper for White House Conference on Civil Rights, Washington, D.C., November 1965. Reprinted from the *Washington Post*, October 10, 1965.

Comer, James. 1972. *Beyond Black and White,* New York: Quadrangle Books.

Douglass, Frederick. 1962. *Life and Times of Frederick Douglass.* New York: Macmillan (first published in 1892).

Haley, Alex. 1976. *Roots.* Garden City: Doubleday.

Heiss, Jerold. 1975. *The Case of the Black Family.* New York: Columbia University Press.

Hennig, Margaret, and Anne Jardim. 1976. *Managerial Women.*

Jackson, Jacquelyn Johnson. 1973. "Black Women in a Racist Society." In *Racism and Mental Health,* edited by C.V. Willie, et. al., Pittsburgh: University of Pittsburgh Press.

Kardiner, Abram and Lionel Ovesey. 1962. *The Mark of Oppression,* Cleveland: World Publishing Co.

Ladner, Joyce. 1978. *Mixed Families,* New York: Anchor.

Merton, Robert K. 1949. *Social Structure and Social Theory.* New York: Free Press.

Noble, Wade. 1978. "Africanity: Its Role in Black Families." In *The Black Family,* edited by Robert Staples, Belmont: Wadsworth.

Reddick, L.D. 1959. *Crusader Without Violence,* New York: Harper.

U.S. Department of Labor. 1965. *The Negro Family.* Washington, D.C.: U.S. Government Printing Office.

Washington, Booker T. 1965. *Up From Slavery.* New York: Dell.

Webster, Bayard. 1979. "Studies Report Refugees Plagued by Persistent Stress," *New York Times* (Sept. 11), pp. C1-2.

Willie, Charles V. 1986. *Five Black Scholars,* Cambridge: Abt Books.

2 DATA, HYPOTHESES, AND
THEORIES OF ADAPTATION

Many investigators approach the study of the black family today with predetermined attitudes, often stereotyped and inflexible. They often focus on the poor which is only one sector of the black population and is not representative of the whole. Even when this error is not committed, the black family is described as a deviant adaptation from an "ideal type"—the family form that alledgely exists among most whites.

Jerold Heiss states that "an indictment has been handed down against the black family." He states that "the key aspect of the accusation claims that blacks would be 'better off' if the differences in family form did not exist" (Heiss 1975:3). Thus many investigators are not so much concerned about discovering how black families cope as they are concerned with explaining why they are different from white families.

Such approaches overlook the significant reference groups for many blacks, groups that consist of other blacks. Sanctions, norms, and standards are generated by these groups — these associations in black communities in which many black persons act out their roles and relationships. In daily interactions with others of their race, black family members engage in a wide range of behaviors that may have little, if anything, to do with whites. Yet the white society is a context with which blacks must contend. Affirmation of oneself and one's group is an activity that differs from confirmation by others. Blacks must affirm themselves.

In his classic essay "Social Structure and Anomie," Robert Merton identified several kinds of adaptations that individuals make to social organization. Three that seem to be helpful in explaining the adaptations of different kinds of black families are *conformity, innovation,* and *rebellion.* The conformists acknowledge the legitimacy of societal goals and also accept the means that are prescribed for achieving them. The innovationists

19

believe in the socially sanctioned goals but discover that the acceptable means for their achievement are not available and that they must improvise new and novel methods. Or the innovationist may follow the socially sanctioned methods but develop new goals. The rebels reject both the societal goals and the sanctioned means for their achievement and seek to change the existing cultural and social structure rather than accommodate to it (Merton 1949:133,379). Rebellion involves a range of adaptations from passive resistance to violent rejection. The Mertonian theory of adaptation in social organization suggests that individuals in all families in this society share and participate in a common system of values.

My hypothesis is that these values, though shared in common, are adapted to differentially by race and by social class. And thus, the participation of all families in social organization in the United States is influenced by these circumstances of dominance or subdominance in the community's power structure.

To test the Mertonian theory, I will examine that which is significant in the life of black families of different social classes, according to their own definition of significance. This means that black families in different social class positions will be analyzed not as deviants from any predetermined ideal type.

Part I of this book presents concepts about race and social class in our society. Using the case method, I will analyze in depth black families of different social classes in Part II. Part III is devoted to a macro-sociological analysis of blacks and the social system. And the concluding chapter summarizes what has been found in this analysis and discusses theoretical implications for research on black families.

DATA

During the past years, I have examined case studies of more than 500 black families. These have been prepared by students, using a standard schedule of questions developed by me. The families interviewed reside in northern and southern sections of the United States, although most are northern residents who migrated from the South. Household composition varies from extended, to two-parent, to one-parent units. There are small households and families with many children. The case studies have been obtained, as an assignment, by students enrolled in my courses.

An assignment that requires direct contact with families is a meaningful pedagogical technique. The responsibility for locating a family to interview was that of each student. Some interviewed families in the community of the college or university of their enrollment. Others interviewed families in their hometowns. Some interviewed families who were friends, referred to them by friends, referred by a social service agency, or selected at random by knocking on the door of a stranger. When possible, the interview was conducted in the home of a family.

The interview schedule requested specific information about family customs, aspirations of parents for children, and patterns of authority within the family (see Appendix A).

Interviewers were undergraduate and graduate students of different racial and ethnic backgrounds. Out of the 500 or more case studies 18 have been selected for detailed analysis in this book as representative of three social class levels — the affluent, the working class, and the poor. There are 6 families in each of 3 social class categories. The economic resources of a family are the primary basis for assigning families to each class level. Affluent, or middle-class, families have annual family incomes at or above the national median. Working-class families have incomes that range from above the official federal poverty line up to the national median. Poor families are those below the official poverty line. Roughly, about one-third of all black families is affluent; one-third, working-class; and one-third, poor. Families have been disguised in name, occupation, and geographic area to protect their privacy.

Because blacks are often referred to in the literature as if they were a homogeneous group, 18 families of the same race but of different income levels are analyzed to determine if, in fact, their ways of life, customs, and practices are similar. This study thus has a very limited goal of ascertaining the presence or absence of a common way of life among black families of similar and different income levels. Generalizations about the frequency of certain behavior forms within the total black population is not our goal. Although I do not claim that the 18 families are representative of all blacks, their ways of life are illustrative of adaptations in varying social classes.

THE INTERVIEWERS

Before undertaking the interview, many black students tended to project the experiences of their home life upon other blacks and assumed that they behaved in similar ways. Stereotyping may apply to an Ingroup as well as an Outgroup. Black students especially were likely to stereotype all blacks as leading a common way of life because of their common experience of racial oppression in the United States. According to this view, the struggle against racism is all-consuming, demanding unity and commitment toward a common cause and, therefore, levels all differences among blacks. This study will determine the truthfulness or falsity of this assumption.

Initially, the black students resisted the assigment for other reasons too. They insisted that blacks had been studied too often and that no good could come from prying around in the private affairs of other black people. I held firmly to the assignment and insisted that it would enhance the students' understandings and insights. I admitted, however, that blacks have been studied often but tried to point out that seldom has the black family been observed and analyzed as an integrated and adaptive system, that most observers have considered it to be a deviant form. Thus black students were urged to carry through with the interview for the value they would derive from an intimate understanding of a family other than their own, and as a way of helping to set the record straight. They developed excellent case studies, as you will see, using a common interview schedule.

The white students also were reluctant to follow through with the interview. Some white students were embarrassed to ask the blacks to share intimate information with them. A few whites were annoyed with the prospect of having to beg blacks to grant them an interview. Others were fearful of calling on blacks in a black neighborhood. Many whites confessed that they did not know any blacks and did not know how to go about contacting a black family. They were worried about how they would be received. The assignment was unsettling.

Again, I held firmly to the requirements of the course. The white students had to transcend their fears. They did this in various ways and prepared case studies that were excellent. After the interview experience, the students were ecstatic in commenting upon their new insights, which had freed them from lifetime stereotypes of the black family. They had thought of the black family as poor and disorganized. They found some black families poor and some black families disorganized. But most were stable and sound.

MARXIST AND COLONIALIST THEORIES OF ADAPTATION

Of the more popular theoretical explanations of race relations in the United States, the Marxist explanation of labor exploitation and the colonialist thesis have gained much attention. The Marxists contend that capitalists created slavery or semi-slavery as a system of cheap labor and as a way of subduing potential white competitors by splitting the labor force along racial lines. The colonialists classify ghettoes or contained communities of blacks and other racial minorities as colonies that are deliberately left underdeveloped and that are dominated socially, politically, and economically by outsiders or whites. The school, an important institution in black and other communities, is described by Samuel Bowles and Herbert Gintis as "foster[ing] types of personal development compatible with the relationship of dominance and subdominance in the economic sphere" (Bowles and Gintis 1976:11).

As evidence that the alleged conspiracy of white capitalists has worked, white workers are described as not being allies of the black revolution but indeed enemies of it (Boggs 1969: 54-

55). To indicate how black ghettoes are under outside control, Joseph Lohman has stated that minority groups view the law as not of their making and not in their interest, but as a foreign power. Moreover, he said that they view the police as an army of occupation (Altshuler 1970:41).

There are several difficulties with these theoretical perspectives for analyzing the black community. First, they do not account for variations within the black population. In Stephen Birmingham's book *Certain People,* the life-styles of several black millionaires are described (Birmingham 1977). These individuals have prospered by developing products and services especially for but not limited to the black community. They, therefore, are not part of a white capitalist conspiracy to perpetuate cheap labor. Indeed, these blacks have prospered by providing a service for blacks.

Also there is evidence that less affluent blacks and less affluent whites have united in common causes more frequently than have more affluent blacks and more affluent whites. For example, blue-collar white workers and blacks have teamed up often, but not always, in presidential elections (Newman 1978:17-31). Specifically, Dorothy Newman and her associates point out that "the greatest power blacks have over public policy is in their numbers in places where, from lack of choice in housing or neighborhoods, they make up a majority or an important swing vote in the electorate."

Thomas Pettigrew reminds us that "the American racial scene has always been highly complex, varied, and inconsistent, defying facile generalizations." He points out that some white workers may oppose school desegregation and yet never think of the interracial neighborhood in which they live as strange or unusual (Pettigrew 1971:264). Only recently has the residential integration of affluent blacks with affluent whites begun to catch up with that which has characterized lower-income blacks and lower-income whites in the past (Simkus 1978: 81-93). Karl and Alma Taeuber report that economic differentials such as occupational rank have diminished between the races but that "residential segregation persists." In fact, they conclude that "it is implausible to attribute the high degrees of residential segregation of Negroes from whites to differences in the ... value of the homes they own." This conclusion led them to predict that "improving the economic status of blacks is unlikely by itself to alter prevailing patterns of racial residential segregation" (Taeuber and Taeuber 1969:94-95). The studies of blacks in cities by these researchers reveal clear and present evidence of resistance of affluent whites to accepting affluent blacks in their neighborhoods.

The school desegregation effort in Corpus Christi, Texas raises serious questions about the alleged antagonism between the working class of different races because of their competition for scarce jobs. Already it has been shown that less separation exists between working-class blacks and whites in residential neighborhoods than between the affluent of both races. In Corpus Christi, expenses for litigating the school desegregation case that created great racial tension were paid for by an organization that represents working-class people of different races — the United Steel Workers of America, a labor union (Cirilo-Medina and Purdy 1981:140). It is not possible to explain such happenings as these by Marxist principles. In higher-income levels where resources are plentiful and there is allegedly less competition between the races, there is more separation. In lower-income levels where there are scarce resources and allegedly more competition between the races, there is relatively more cooperation and desegregation.

The Marxist perspective, which treats social differentiation and discrimination by race as an economic variable, fails to explain why there is greater segregation between the affluent of different races than between the working-class or poor people of different races. Also Marxist principles do not explain why white capitalists give the white poor with limited education better paying jobs than the black poor who are similarly educated. Because numerically there are more poor whites than poor blacks (they outnumber blacks three to one), the capitalists, in terms of Marxist ideology, ought to have favored black workers over white workers, if race relations were economic in origin — so that the former could be coerced to conform because of the larger pool of available cheap white labor that could displace nonconforming blacks. But clearly, the white poor have been favored over the black poor in capitalistic America. Some factor other than the economics of the situation is operating. Some people call that factor racism.

The colonialist perspective also has limitations, one of which is that it treats racial minorities as if their way of life was totally dominated by the majority. It is doubtful that any group can fully dominate the social life of another group. All ghetto-ized populations everywhere have maintained their folk beliefs and values despite external pressure to conform to the dominant group. These beliefs and values sustain the subdominant group and enable its members to endure. The spirituals, for example, emerged out of a common experience of black folk that no dominant group could suppress. The major limitation of the colonialist perspective is that it does not acknowledge the inevitable interdependency that develops between two populations that share a common setting. When two groups coexist in the same area, their fates become intertwined (whether or not they acknowledge it) so much so that one group cannot destroy the other without ultimately destroying itself.

The proponents of the colonialist theory emphasize the exploitation of the subdominant group by the dominant group and tend to ignore the veto power of subdominants over the dominants and ultimately over the whole society. The colonialist theory is an appropriate explanation of the relationships between dominant and subdominant racial populations only when the two groups do not share a common area.

SITUATIONAL ANALYSIS

Twentieth-century Nazi Germany is evidence that the fate of dominant and subdominant racial or ethnic populations that occupy a common territory is intertwined. When Nazi Germans tried to destroy Jewish people who dwelt among them, they contributed ultimately to the destruction of the German nation, which is now divided into two separate countries.

The veto power of subdominants has not been a popular theme of analysis among social scientists of the colonialist orientation, whose theory of race relations has focused largely on the strategies of control by the dominants. Although the Marxist social scientists have paid more attention to the subdominants than have the colonialists, their race-relations theory is defective in that it does not explain the absence of oppressive practices toward the black working class by affluent blacks, and the presence of cooperative behavior between some members of both the black and the white working classes despite the scarce resources available to these groups. Another defect of these two theoretical explanations is that they portray subdominants always as passive, reacting to the initiatives of others. This, of course, is an inappropriate characterization. Finally, they erroneously describe subdominants as people without choice.

Rather than rely upon global theories that contribute to stereotypes or distorted pictures, a more appropriate analysis of blacks in American society, and particularly black families, might flow from situational sociology, which assumes that the behavior of most people is structured by particular situations. This assumption may be extended to include race relations that tend to be shaped, according to Pettigrew, by "specific situational norms" (Pettigrew 1971:264-265).

"In order to comprehend some of the complexity of American racial patterns," Pettigrew said, "it becomes necessary to examine separately some of the major institutions of American society" (Pettigrew 1971:267). This book analyzes the specific situational norms that guide and govern the behavior of affluent, working-class, and poor black families. A particular benefit of situational analysis is that it protects against the tendency to project findings pertaining to the adaptation of one group that experiences a certain set of circumstances upon another group whose circumstances may be different. Also it helps overcome ethnocentric interpretations.

In situational analysis, all social relationships in human society are matters of choice, and all human beings are free to seek a set of relationships different from those that exist. Moreover, a different set of relationships is possible theoretically in each new situation despite the pattern of social interaction that existed between the participants of a system in the past. For example, people in subdominant positions of power in a social system may be oppressed but they can choose not to cooperate in their own oppression. They can rebel. Rebellion is the exercise of veto power, an ever-present option even in coercive systems.

The act of rebellion is a choice, as is the decision to abide by the requirements of a coercive system. Choice, of course, is an action that is possible only by one who essentially is free. Even in a system of coercion, the freedom of each participant is ever present, the freedom to participate or not to participate in such a system and, of course, to experience the negative or positive consequences of such action.

Individuals in human society arrive at definitions of their situations and determine appropriate action in terms of their self-interest. Self-interest is the fundamental basis of decisions and choices. One can determine why a system is organized as it is by determining which individuals are in charge and what is their self-interest. Thus, change in a social system primarily is a function of change in the definition of self-interest by the participants. Neither change nor stability is taken for granted in situational sociology; each is a function of human decision in a given situation.

Self-interest is not the same as selfishness. Selfishness is the act of seeking one's own good at the expense of others. Total selfishness, of course, ultimately is a logical impossibility, for none can continue to exist without the goodwill of some who will guarantee one's safety and security. Safety and security cannot be self-determined completely. Thus, one can be selfish in some but not all human situations if one expects to survive. Self-interest is seeking one's own good by seeking that which is good for others on whom one is dependent and with whom one must interact. The fulfillment of self-interest appears to be paradoxical but in essence is a complex activity of complementarity. One obtains and maintains the benefits of social organization for oneself by finding ways of sharing the opportunities and obligations of social organization with others. Self-interest is prudent and calculating. In its purest form, self-interest is manifested in a double victory in which one fulfills oneself by fulfilling another, resulting in mutual enhancement.

Self-interest is emphasized in situational sociology because social organization is effected through individuals, and individuals have their being through social systems. "There is neither the loss of oneself by participation ... [nor] the loss of one's [society] by individualization" (Tillich 1959:187). Both the self and society are taken seriously in situational sociology.

Situational analysis, then, is based on the premise that action is tailored to fit objective circumstances — the situation (Fletcher 1966:14). Situational sociology is an attempt to describe social systems in terms of attitudes, behavior, and social settings. Situational sociology involves the construction of social system models that explain discontinuities as well as continuities in the process of human interaction and asymmetries as well as symmetries in the structure of social relations. In situational sociology, all kinds of exchange relationships are examined as real.

A study of the American black family from the perspective of situational sociology is a study of power relationships between majority and minority populations. Power is the capacity to influence others to behave in a prescribed way; it is derived either from the prerogatives of one's nominal position or the rank of one's graduated position in society, or from a combination of both. Thus, power may be a function of the independent and joint effects of prestige and privilege (Blau 1977:31).

Privilege or authority has to do with prerogatives within a group or parameter. Conceptually, these may be dichotomized into responsibilities and obligations that are interdependent but mutually exclusive. A symbiotic relationship exists between those who are responsible for and obligated to each other. The nominal parameter is castelike, with the various ascriptive groups such as age, sex, and race coexisting along the horizontal axis. However, none of the positions within these groups — majority or minority, male or female, older or younger — is more or less significant in the viability of the social system. Responsibility and obligation are linked and both are essential;

one without the other is incomplete. In other words, a majority needs a minority, males need females, and older people need younger people. Dominant people cannot go it alone without help and assistance from subdominants. These ascriptive characteristics, conceptually, are arrayed side by side because there is no intrinsic basis for classifying race, sex, age, or any other ascriptive characteristic as being more or less valuable.

Prestige and esteem exist in a continuous range of multiple ranks within a group or parameter, arrayed along the vertical axis. The parameter is classlike because of the continuous range of differentiated ranks within it. These ranks are higher or lower or they consist of more or less of something such as income, occupation, or education. That which is higher obviously is related to that which is lower, and so is that which is more related to that which is less. One category cannot exist without the other. In a society of limited resources, some people have more only because other people have less. High and low, more or less are inextricably linked and in a symbiotic way.

The achievement of prestige and esteem by some individuals over others in society because of their education, occupation, or wealth need not be detrimental in a just society. Rawls states that "The social system is not an unchangeable order beyond human control but a pattern of human action. In justice as fairness [people] agree to share one another's fate." From the standpoint of common sense, Rawls has said, the benefits of one individual should contribute to the welfare of others (Rawls 1971:102-104).

There are four forms of justice in a properly functioning human society: commutative or one-to-one, distributive or many-to-one, contributive or one-to-many, and corporative or many-to-many (Fletcher 1966:90). When these forms of justice are implemented according to requirements of the situation, they can affect populations and social relationships of the vertical and horizontal dimensions of the social system to such an extent that all accept and fulfill their obligations and responsibilities, or give to and receive from each other in ways that are fair.

There is social pathology when a society responds to a nominal parameter as if it were a graduated parameter and a graduated parameter as if it were a nominal parameter. This is precisely what has happened in our contemporary society. People of low-education, low-occupation, and low-income rank are accommodated by the society at large as if their levels of achievement in these graduated parameters were an unchangeable function of ascription. Poor whites, members of the majority race, have been led to believe that their low estate is ascriptive or is due to the presence of racial minorities, also an ascriptive group, when in essence their problem is due to a blocked opportunity system in the graduated parameter and an unjust distribution of resources. Thus their circumstances and conditions of life are inappropriately described as intractable and are attributed to structural deficits.

People of racial minority, of female, and of younger-age status are treated sometimes as invisible groups, as persons for whom the racial majority, men, and the older age group of the nominal parameter have no responsibility. To further complicate the situation, these nominal groups are sometimes identified as part of the vertical dimension of the social system. When these misidentifications are accepted, individuals such as those in black families who experience oppression attempt to overcome it by becoming high achievers — a prescription that is appropriate for oppression in a graduated parameter but not in a nominal parameter.

What, then, is the outcome when such conceptual distortion of social organization as that described becomes conventional wisdom? The adaptations of some whites who are poor and of some blacks who are affluent are two good illustrations of the negative consequences of accepting a distorted view of social organization that treats a nominal variable as if it were a graduated variable, and vice versa.

Comparative studies of family life reveal that some poor whites are alienated from society, more alienated than some blacks, and adapt to others in an apathetic and fatalistic way. And some affluent blacks are high-achieving conformists, more conformists than whites, whose adaptation to others is filled

with anxiety as they aggressively pursue the goal of excellence
— trying to be better, trying to be the best. These facts may contribute to the experience of poor whites who tend to score
higher on alienation scales than other groups (Brink and Harris
1961:135), and of blacks who tend to have a higher rate of
hypertension than other groups.

Those who wish to exploit poor whites do not encourage
them to view their station in life as a function of the vertical
dimension of society in which the rich and the poor are func-
tionally interrelated. Believing their poverty to be fully a function of family of birth, which is a nominal variable, poor whites
tend to be fatalistic. They need not feel this way if they realize
that poverty is a graduated variable and that some people are
poor because others are rich, that the affluent are responsible
for the poor and must give an accounting of why their wealth is
not used for the benefit of all.

Some affluent blacks experience adversity because of discrimination between minority and majority populations. They
sometimes mistakenly attribute their difficulty to the fact that
their occupational and educational achievement is unrecognized.
Achievement, of course, is a phenomenon of the vertical dimension of society, a graduated variable. When blacks believe that
they are discriminated against because others do not recognize
that they are just as good as or better than the majority in terms
of capacity and will to achieve, some become obsessed with getting ahead. Thus, some affluent blacks chart a course that is
designed to overcome racial discrimination by attempting to
become the best in whatever they do. They aggressively pursue
the goal of excellence and drive themselves so hard to attain the
highest rank that some become exceedingly anxious. Racial
discrimination, however, is not a function of achievement or the
lack of it. Racial discrimination is not a property of any
graduated parameter. Racial discrimination represents a failure
in relationships between the minority and majority populations
because one or both groups do not recognize that they are interdependent, that they need each other, and that the welfare of
one depends on the other. Whites who wish to exploit blacks
encourage them to model their careers in the image of the ma-

jority as if their low estate were a function of their capacity to achieve.

These examples are sufficient to make the point that whites as well as blacks have a stake in clarifying the association between race and socioeconomic status, or caste and class as I prefer to call it.

REFERENCES

Altshuler, Alan A. 1970. *Community Control.* Indianapolis: Pegasus of Bobbs-Merrill.

Blau, Peter M. 1977. "A Macrosocial Theory of Social Structure," *American Journal of Sociology* 83 (July).

Birmingham, Stephen. 1977. *Certain People: America's Black Elite.* Boston: Little, Brown.

Bowles, Samuel, and Herbert Gintis. 1976. *Schooling in Capitalist America.* New York: Basic Books.

Boggs, James. 1969. "The Influence of Malcolm X on the Political Consciousness of Black Americans." In *Malcolm X: The Man and His Times,* edited by John Henrik Clarke, New York: Collier.

Brink, William, and Louis Harris. 1966. *Black and White.* New York: Simon and Schuster.

Cirilo-Medina, Amelia, and Ross Purdy. 1981. "Corpus Christi, Texas, A Tri-Ethnic Approach." In *Community Politics and Eductional Change,* edited by C.V. Willie and S.L. Greenblatt. New York: Longman.

Fletcher, Joseph. 1966. *Situation Ethics.* Philadelphia: Westminister Press.

Newman, Dorothy K., et al. 1978. *Protest, Politics, and Prosperity.* New York: Pantheon.

Pettigrew, Thomas F. 1971. *Racially Separate or Together?* New York: McGraw-Hill.

Rawls, John. 1971. *A Theory of Justice.* Cambridge: Harvard University Press.

Simkus, Albert. 1978. "Residential Segregation by Occupation and Race in Ten Urbanized Areas, 1950-1970." *American Sociological Review* 43 (February).

Taeuber, Karl E., and Alma F. Taeuber. 1969. *Negroes in Cities.* New York: Atheneum.

Tillich, Paul. 1955. *The Courage to Be.* New Haven: Yale University Press.

Chapter **3** THE CONTINUING
SIGNIFICANCE OF RACE

"'My daddy was a blue-eyed man,' swears black-eyed, white-skinned Susie Guillroy Phipps, a ... southern belle ... from southwest Louisiana ...'"

"[Mrs.] Phipps ... says she was 'raised white' and 'even married white twice....' [F]ive years ago ... she drove 230 miles to the Bureau of Vital Statistics [in New Orleans] to get a copy of her birth certificate for a passport application.... [T]he document listed her parents as ... colored."

"'It took me for a spin,' [Mrs.] Phipps recalled. 'I told the lady it was wrong. My parents were white.... I was sick for two weeks. If I'd had a heart problem, I think I would have had a heart attack.'"

"[S]he hired a lawyer, who filed a suit asking that the record be changed, and that a state law ... defining as black anyone with [a fraction of] 1/32 'Negro blood' be declared unconstitutional...."

"[A] state magistrate upheld the ... law ... and declined to change [Mrs.] Phipps' birth certificate ... [because] she is the great-great-great-great-great grand-daughter of a black slave woman and a white planter...." (Ben Bradley, 1982:2).

Langston Hughes concluded that black blood is real powerful since all it takes is one drop to make you black (quoted in Bradley, 1983: 2).

The president of the Louisiana NAACP (National Association for the Advancement of Colored People) called attention to the Creole ancestry of many people in Louisiana and said that state has the blackest white people and the whitest black people (quoted in Bradley, 1982: 2).

To Mrs. Phipps, these all may be bad jokes. They probably would not be funny to her. Already she has spent several thousands of dollars on this case. In a decisive way, Mrs. Phipps

34

said, "I don't want to be what I'm not; and I'm not black" (quoted in Bradley, 1982: 2).

Race is one of the most sensitive and sure indicators of the presence or absence of justice in our society. To repress the guilt of racial discrimination through denial and other means is to permit injustice to fester and erupt from time to time in race riots and other forms of rebellion.

Our society has not learned how to deal with guilt because it has not learned how to listen to minorities who experience the conditions that should stimulate guilt. Those who are most capable of helping a society to expiate its guilt are those who suffer because of injustice — the minorities. However, our society tends to listen to minorities only when they think and speak like the majority.

Guilt is to the social system what pain is to the organic system — a signal that something is amiss, a warning that something is wrong. By acknowledging pain and dealing with that which caused it, corrective action can be taken in time to prevent permanent harm to the organic system. To suppress pain is to deal with the symptom rather than with the cause. Likewise, if we acknowledge and accept guilt as a signal that something is wrong in the social system and take appropriate corrective actions, we may avoid permanent damage of our society. Both the suppression of pain and the repression of guilt can be fatal.

Reflecting upon the bus boycott in Montgomery, Alabama, that launched the direct-action phase of the modern Civil Rights Movement, Martin Luther King, Jr., said that discrimination "scars the soul and degrades the personality": it creates within some whites a false sense of superiority and among some blacks a false sense of inferiority (King, 1958:37). These false beliefs encourage the dominance of one group over another.

The family life of black people in the United States can be classified as subdominant in the community power structure. Whites control a disproportionate amount of the nation's resources, and the result is that the customs and conventions of whites are inappropriately considered normative for the total society.

In Biblical literature, the scapegoat is an animal upon whose head the sins of the people are symbolically placed. Such an animal is then ceremonially sent out or exiled into the wilderness as a way of expiating the community of its evil deeds. In our contemporary communities, black families bear the blame of others as scapegoats, through the irrational hostility and guilt of whites.

Whites have projected their own fears upon blacks and black families. A more objective analysis of the status of black families is possible when we recognize that the increasing concern about black families represents not so much a new and unique pathological adaptation of blacks as it does a projection upon blacks of the concerns about the pathological adaptations increasingly found among whites and all families. We know, of course, that the practice of scapegoating is harmful and unethical.

Growing affluence is a fact of life within the black population that has been recognized by a range of scholars, including William Wilson (1978) and Reynolds Farley (1984). In income, occupational opportunity, and educational attainment, Farley reports definite improvement among black households. The gap in median school years completed between black and white groups has been substantially reduced; the proportion of blacks in prestigious and higher-paying jobs has increased; and black earnings have improved (Farley, 1984:194-195). E. Franklin Frazier reported in an article published near the midpoint of the twentieth century that only approximately one-eighth of black families were able to maintain a middle-class way of life (Frazier, 1968:207).

Some social scientists such as Wilson have linked "the improving position of the black middle class" to an alleged "worsening condition of the black underclass" (Wilson, 1987:ix, vii). The Wilson analysis, however, is flawed on two counts: it does not demonstrate that poverty among blacks is increasing, and it does not provide a logical explanation of how improvement in one sector of the black population is harmful to another.

We know from an analysis of data published by the U.S. Bureau of the Census over the years that the proportion of black and of white families below the poverty line has been reduced. Three decades ago, approximately 56 percent of all blacks in families were poor. Today, the proportion is about one-third. Three decades ago, one-sixth of all whites in families were poor. Today, the proportion is approximately 10 percent (U.S. Bureau of the Census, 1985:455). The ratio of the poor in these racial populations has remained more or less constant over the years, although the proportion of the poor has diminished. The proportion of black poor was 3.4 times greater than the proportion of white poor three decades ago, and is 3.3 times greater today. These data indicate that although the size of the poor population in both groups has decreased, the condition of the black poor with reference to the white poor has not worsened. Neither has the condition of the black poor with reference to the white poor improved over the years. As stated above, the ratios for the two different time periods have remained more or less the same. Thus, there is no decline in the significance of race as a circumstantial factor in poverty.

Even when the analysis is limited to an examination of indicators for blacks only, Farley states that "it is an oversimplification to claim that the black community is now split into an elite and an underclass" (Farley, 1984:190). With reference to education he found that "lower-class blacks are not falling further behind upper-class blacks" (Farley, 1984:177). Moreover, Farley reports that the distribution of family income within the black population has changed very little over the last 30 years: "the richest five percent of black families have received about 16 percent of all the income obtained by black families, while the poorest 20 percent of black families have received about four percent" (Farley, 1984: 191). These data indicated that racial discrimination is a constant experience in the United States and probably accounts for continuing differentials in status position between blacks and whites, that the proportional size of the poor population has declined among both racial groups, and that improvements among some sectors of the black population have not contributed to a worsened condition among other sectors of the black population.

The analysis thus far confirms the assertion by Martin Luther King, Jr., that "we are caught in a network of inescapable mutuality" (King, 1958:199). An analysis of the Civil Rights Movement reveals linkages between affluent and poor blacks have been helpful rather than harmful. Based on an examination of successful educational reform initiatives among blacks, such as those for school desegregation, it appears that "a subdominant population is likely to intensify its press for affirmative action with reference to equal access and equitable distribution of community resources when it grows in numbers from a small minority to a larger and heterogeneous population. . . . The size of a population and its socioeconomic differentiation are interrelated phenomena that must be examined to determine their joint effect, if the pattern of the press for social action by a subdominant population is to be understood" (Willie, 1983, 197).

If a diversified population is essential in social action efforts among blacks and other subdominant populations, then a one-sided analysis that focuses only on the poor or lower class or underclass among blacks is a perspective that is too limited for the formulation of adequate public policy. A fundamental fact about black contemporary life is the increasing socioeconomic differentiation found among such households in the United States. This is a fact that should be celebrated.

With reference to income, the interracial distribution for black and for white families has manifested only a modest change over the years in a positive direction favorable to blacks. The ratio of black to white median family income was .54 in 1950 before the Brown Supreme Court decision that outlawed segregation, and .56 slightly more than three decades later (in 1983 constant dollars). This ratio represented a slight gain of only two percentage points in median annual income for all black families in comparison with such income for all white families (U.S. Bureau of the Census, 1985:446). During nearly a quarter of a century, beginning in 1959, blacks—whose proportion of poor was three and two-fifths times greater than that for whites in 1959—continued at only a slightly reduced differential of three and one-third times greater in 1982 (U.S. Bureau of the Census, 1985:455).

Despite the more or less constant ratio of the association of black to white annual family income when studied by a central tendency measure like the median, analysis of the income range reveals substantial improvements favorable to blacks. A ratio of the proportion of black families with incomes in the lowest quintile of the range in 1954 was 2.17 times greater than the proportion of whites similarly situated. However, in 1977 (nearly a quarter of a century later), the ratio of the proportions for these two populations was down to 1.98. In the highest quintile of family income, the ratio of the proportion of blacks to whites at this income level was only .27 in 1954. By 1977, the ratio of the proportion of blacks to whites in the highest fifth of the income range had increased to .47. The actual proportion of blacks and other races in the bottom fifth of the family income hierarchy decreased from 43.3 percent in 1954 to 39.6 percent in 1977; in the top fifth of the family income hierarchy, the proportion of blacks and other races increased from 5.3 percent in 1954 to 9.4 percent in 1977. Data were not analyzed for the 1980s but probably reflect the same pattern of the past two decades (U.S. Bureau of the Census, 1980:483).

While black families continue to have a higher proportion of their population in the low-income range and a lower proportion of their population in the high-income range compared with white families, the proportion of blacks in the bottom quintile has decreased while the proportion of blacks in the top quintile has increased. While these findings represent a severe judgment upon our society and its continuing discriminatory practice in the distribution of income among families of different racial groups, they also confirm that poverty among blacks and all families has decreased, and that affluence among blacks and all families has increased. Moreover, this analysis indicates the importance of studying the prevalence rate of families by race for the entire range of income categories rather than focusing only on measures of central tendency such as the mean, median, or mode. This analysis reveals that race has not declined but continues as a significant variable differentiating blacks from whites at all income levels, and that the proportion of poor black families has decreased while the proportion of affluent black families has increased. Thus, the condition of lower-class blacks has not worsened as the condition of middle-class blacks has improved, as claimed by Wilson in his book, *The Truly Disadvantaged* (1987:vii).

With reference to employment, the proportion of white males and black males who work in the most prestigious professional-technical, managerial-administrative jobs had only modest increases during the past decade. White males in these occupational categories varied from 28 percent of the white employed population over 16 years of age in 1972 to 30.5 percent of such workers in the race in 1979—an increase of 2.5 percentage points. Black males and those of other races exhibited a similar rate of change for these occupations; they increased from 13 percent of those employed 16 years of age or older who worked in these most prestigious jobs in 1972 to 17.4 percent in 1979—an increase of 4.4 percentage points (U.S. Bureau of Labor Statistics, 1980:46-48). The ratio of these proportions of blacks and whites at the top of the occupational hierarchy changed slightly in a direction that favored blacks and other races. The increase in the racial ratio ranged from .46 in 1972 to .57, the final year of the decade.

For the bottom of the occupational hierarchy, the decade of the seventies showed slight changes that also favored blacks and other racial minorities. While the proportion of white males 16 or older who worked as laborers, private household workers, and service workers remained constant at 15.9 percent in 1972 and 1979, the proportion of black males and employed males of other races in these least prestigious jobs dropped slightly from 36 percent in 1972 to 31.4 percent in 1979 (U.S. Bureau of Labor Statistics, 1980:46-48). The racial ratio of the proportion of black males to white males at the bottom of the occupational hierarchy moved from 2.26 in 1972 down to 1.95 in 1979.

Again, when racial difference is analyzed, it is shown to continue as a mediating force in inequitable distribution of jobs. At the close of the 1970s, for example, the proportion of professional and managerial workers among white males (30.5 percent) was nearly twice as great as the proportion of such workers employed as laborers and service workers (15.9 percent). The converse was true for black males: their proportion of laborers and service workers (31.4 percent) was nearly twice as great as the proportion of professional and managerial workers (17.4 percent). Nevertheless, there was a change for blacks both at the top and the bottom of the occupational hierarchy. The modest increase in the proportion of blacks who got high-income jobs during the 1970s was accompanied by a modest decrease in black workers in low-income jobs. Apparently help for affluent blacks did not harm poor blacks as claimed by William Wilson (1978, 1987).

The disadvantaged circumstances that black families have experienced as participants in the labor force in the United States is not simply a result of inadequate education, another Wilson contention (1978:104-109). A majority of all adults 25 years of age and over in black and in white racial populations are high school graduates. The median school years completed by blacks and whites differs by only a few months today compared to a difference of 2.5 years in 1950 (U.S. Bureau of the Census, 1985:134). Nevertheless, whites had a median family income that fluctuated from 40 to 45 percent greater than the median for blacks during the first half of the 1980 decade (U.S. Bureau of the Census, 1984:5, 1985:446). But the median education for these two populations as mentioned differed only minimally (U.S. Bureau of the Census, 134).

To test the Wilson hypothesis that low-income black households are locked into the low-wage sector because of their inadequate education, a ratio was computed of the median family income of poorly educated blacks (those with less than a grade school education) and the median family income of poorly educated whites. Poorly educated blacks in 1982 earned 23 percent less than the income received by poorly educated whites. The same pattern persisted for highly educated blacks who are college graduates; they earned 22 percent less than the income received by highly educated whites. The ratios of .77 and .78, respectively, for these pairs of least- and most-educated households among blacks and whites are almost identical (U.S. Bureau of the Census, 1985:447). The diminishing gap in educational achievement between the races has not brought with it equitable employment and earning experiences; inequity that is racially based remains.

Despite their continuing experience of discrimination, black families are upwardly mobile. During the first half of the 1980s, 9.5 percent of blacks twenty-five-years old and over had graduated from college (compared to 18 percent for the total population); 13 percent of blacks 16 years of age and over were employed as managers and professionals (compared to 22 percent of the total population); and 2.6 percent of black households earned $50,000 or more each year (compared to 10.9 percent of the total population) (U.S. Bureau of the Census, 1985:134, 402, 445).

Education may be conceptualized as an input variable, occupation as a process variable, and income as an outcome variable. If these three are interrelated, then what one earns is a function of the kind of work one performs. And the kind of work one performs is based on educational attainment. High-level education as an input variable should beget high-level employment as a process variable, which in turn should result in high-level income. Blacks in families lag behind the population at large as participants in the highest levels of educational and occupational attainment; their participation rate is approximately 40 to 50 percent less than others. This means that the proportion of blacks in the highest income level should also be approximately 40 to 50 percent less than that for the population at large. Actually, blacks lag behind others in the proportion who received highest income by approximately three-quarters. The penalty which blacks experience in reduced numbers who receive the highest income is disproportionate to their participation rate in the highest levels of occupational and educational attainment. This disproportionality is a sign of continuing racial discrimination.

Although the proportion of black families in the first income quintile (the lowest) is twice as great as it should be, and the proportion in the fifth income quintile (the highest) is one-half less than it ought to be—if such families were distributed equally (U.S. Bureau of the Census, 1980:483), blacks nevertheless have made progress as participants in the economy at all income levels. The black population is no longer homogeneously poor.

Some social scientists view with alarm this increasing diversity as having the possibility of polarizing the population. Actually, the opposite is likely to occur. A diversified population is more capable of cooperating and adapting to changing circumstances because of the presence of multiple resources and complementary talents.

From population genetics we learn that "a species [is] polymorphic if it contains a variety of genotypes, each of which is superior in adaptive value to the others ... in the territory occupied...." Moreover, population genetics reveal that "polymorphic populations [are], in general, more efficient in the exploitation of ... opportunities of an environment than genetically uniform ones...." (Dobzhansky, 1951:132-133). Thus, the increasing diversity of black families in the United States is not a liability but a sociological asset.

In *Stride Toward Freedom,* Martin Luther King, Jr. described how a diversified black population worked together and eliminated segregated seating in the city public transportation system of Montgomery, Alabama, in the 1950s. He said the mass meetings associated with this movement cut across class lines. They brought together "working people" and "professionals." He described the Montgomery bus boycott by blacks as bringing together "men and women who had been separated from each other by false standards of class." They cooperated with each other in a "common struggle for freedom and human dignity" (King, 1958:86). The struggle continues for black families at all levels of social organization. *The New York Times* reports that "racial discrimination is a significant contributor to the disproportionate number of blacks in the underclass" (Wilkerson, 1987:26).

There is ample evidence that family income varies by race, on the one hand, and that family stability correlates positively with household disposable income, on the other hand. A plausible explanation of the different rates of family stability found among blacks and whites, therefore, would seem to be the different economic circumstances experienced by the two racial populations. And their different economic circumstances, according to economist Herman Miller, are largely due to racial discrimination. He said "the average [black] earns less than the average white, even when he has the same years of schooling and does the same kind of work" (Miller, 1964:21).

Well into the 1980s, the median income figures for blacks and whites demonstrated the absence of parity. The median for blacks hovered around 55 percent of that received by whites (U.S. Bureau of the Census, 1985:32). Thus, the difference between the proportion of white families (84.7 percent in 1983) and the proportion of black families (53.4 percent in 1983) who lived in married, two-parent units is probably a function of unequal income rather than different cultural norms.

We know, for example, that affluent households have a higher probability of being two-parent families than poor households. More than three-fourths of black as well as white households in the United States with incomes above $25,000 (in 1983) were husband-wife families. While half of the whites were in the top half of the income range and earned more than $25,000, only one-fourth of blacks had such income (Farley and Allen, 1987:174-175). It is reasonable to assume that if more blacks were in the top half of the economic scale, more would live in two-parent households.

Evidence also shows that a majority of poor whites as well as poor blacks with income below the federal poverty line live in single-parent or single-person households (Farley and Allen, 1987:174-175). However, only 10.6 percent of white persons are poor compared to 34.9 percent of black persons (U.S. Bureau of the Census, 1985:455). Since family instability is associated with low-income status, it is reasonable to assume that a higher proportion of white families than is presently seen would be unstable if a higher proportion of white persons were poor.

On the basis of this analysis, one may conclude that racial discrimination and its negative effects upon the economic status of blacks make a substantial contribution to their higher rate of family instability compared to whites, and that cultural differences, if any, are of limited value in explaining differential rates of family instability among racial populations in the United States.

The black family is undergoing profound change in a society in great flux. We must recognize that—as an institution—the black family is under siege from a dominant culture that is alternately indifferent or hostile.

That black families survive is testimony to their strength, endurance, and adaptability. Survival, however, is not a goal, but a means. The challenge to the black community and the nation at large is to build upon survival strengths and continue to lay the groundwork for black achievement and full participation in all aspects of American life.

REFERENCES

Bradley, Ben. 1982. "Louisiana Legal System Grapples with Old Issue of Blood and Race," *Boston Globe* (September 18), p.2.

Dobzhansky, Theodosius. 1951. *Genetics and the Origin of the Species.* New York: Columbia University Press.

Farley, Reynolds, 1984. *Blacks and Whites.* Cambridge: Harvard University Press.

Farley, Reynolds and Walter R. Allen. 1987. *The Color Line and the Quality of Life in America.* New York: Russell Sage Foundation.

Frazier, E. Franklin. 1968. "The Negro Family in America." In *Franklin Frazier on Race Relations,* edited by G. Franklin Edwards. Chicago: University of Chicago Press.

Keniston, Kenneth. 1977. *All Our Children.* New York: Harcourt Brace Jovanovich.

King, Martin Luther, Jr. 1958. *Stride Toward Freedom.* New York: Harper and Row.

Miller, Herman. 1964. *Rich Man, Poor Man.* New York: Crowell.

U.S. Bureau of the Census. 1980. *Social Indicators III.* Washington, D.C.: Government Printing Office.

U.S. Bureau of the Census, 1985. *Statistical Abstract of the United States.* Washington, D.C.: Government Printing Office.

U.S. Bureau of Labor Statistics. 1980. *Handbook of Labor Statistics.* Washington, D.C.: Government Printing Office.

Wilkerson, Isabel. 1987. "Growth of the Very Poor Is Focus of New Studies," *The New York Times* (December 20), p.26.

Willie, Charles Vert. 1983. *Race, Ethnicity, and Socioeconomic Status.* Dix Hills, N.Y.: General Hall.

_____. 1985. *Black and White Families.* Dix Hills, N.Y.: General Hall.

Wilson, William Julius. 1978. *The Declining Significance of Race.* Chicago: University of Chicago Press.

_____. 1987. *The Truly Disadvantaged.* Chicago: University of Chicago Press.

PART II

Case Studies of Black Families: Affluent, Working-Class, and Poor

Chapter **4** AFFLUENT, WORKING-CLASS,
AND POOR BLACK FAMILIES:
AN OVERVIEW

AFFLUENT BLACKS: The Conformists

The affluent, or middle-class, population among blacks is increasing but it is still relatively small in size — about one out of every three or four black families. The influence of the members of these families within the black community and upon the society at large is extensive and therefore merits our attention. Affluent or middle-class status for most black families is a result of dual employment of husband and wife. Black men and women have relied heavily on the public sector for employment at livable wages.

The public school has been an employment haven for black working wives. It has provided steady and continuous work and often has been the first professional occupational role in black households. Because of job-connected requirements, black female teachers in middle-class families may be more highly educated than their male spouses. The length of employment of professional working wives is likely to be as long as that of their husbands, with only brief interruptions for child-bearing. The number of children in black middle-class families tends to be small, ranging from one to three, but more often two or less. Thus, the black woman in a public sector job with prescribed yearly increments and retirement benefits, with only a few interruptions in her labor force status, tends to have significant earnings by the time she reaches middle age.

Continuity in employment also is a characteristic of black men in affluent households. Public sector jobs, especially in the postal service, have been a source of support and security over the years. A few black men, however, occupy financially rewarding business and professional positions in industry, education, and as self-employed private practitioners.

The economic foundation for most affluent black families is a product of the cooperative work of the husband and wife. Their way of life is an illustration of a genuine team effort. Few if any family functions, including cooking, cleaning, and shopping, are considered to be the exclusive prerogative of the husband or the wife. Probably the best example of the liberated woman in American society is found among wives in black middle-class families. They and their husbands have acted as partners out of necessity and thus have carved out an equalitarian pattern of interaction in which neither husband nor wife has ultimate authority. Because of racial discrimination and the income limitations on the kind of jobs available to blacks, joint efforts are needed to achieve a comfortable style of life. Together spouses are able to make it, and this they have done. Affluent black families in our study have earned annual incomes — usually the joint income of husband and wife — at or above the national median.

Such income is lavishly spent on a home and on the education of children. Unless restricted by racial discrimination, affluent black families tend to trade in older homes for newer structures as their earnings and savings increase. The real expense in housing, however, is in the up-to-date furnishings and modern appliances. For most affluent black families, their home is their castle, and it is outfitted as such.

Because work is so consuming for the husband and wife, little time is left for socializing. Most families have nearby relatives — usually the reason for migrating to a particular city. They visit relatives occasionally, may hold membership in one or two social organizations, participate regularly in church activities, and spend the remainder of their free time in household upkeep and maintenance chores.

In most affluent black families, one spouse almost always is a college graduate. Often both are college graduates who struggled and made great sacrifices to complete their formal education. Not infrequently, college and graduate school are completed on a part-time basis after adulthood and while the husband or wife, who also may be a parent, is employed full-time. Parents who have experienced these struggles and hardships know that their middle-class status, which usually is not achieved until middle age, is directly correlated with their increased education. New jobs, especially public school teaching, and salary increments can be traced directly to the added schooling. Other public sector jobs use variations in level of education to determine qualifications. Thus, education has been a major contributor to occupational upward mobility for blacks employed by government.

Because education and consequently economic affluence are so closely tied together for middle-class black households, parents tend to encourage their offspring to complete schooling. Particularly do they wish their children to go to college immediately after graduating from high school so that they will not have to struggle as long as did their parents, whom middle-class status eluded during young-adult years. An ambition of most parents is to give to their children opportunities that they themselves did not have.

As a starter, almost all children in affluent households are given music lessons. Daughters, in particular, are expected to learn to play a musical instrument, usually the piano. In addition to developing musical and recreational skills, most children in affluent black families are expected to work around the house for an allowance. Most affluent blacks try to inculcate in their children positive attitudes toward work and thrift.

Active involvement in community affairs is found among some but is not the way of life for other middle-class, middle-aged blacks. Black adolescents may be deeply involved in various movements but seldom are their parents. It is difficult to determine whether limited community participation by some parents is due to insufficient energy and time because of the extra demands of joint employment of husband and wife.

Middle-class black families in the United States manifest probably better than any other population group the Puritan orientation toward work, success, and self-reliance so characteristic of the basic values of this nation. For them, work is a consuming experience. Little time is left for recreation and other kinds of social activities except perhaps regular involvement in church affairs. Based on his analysis of the correlation between religion and economics, Max Weber authored a major work called *The Protestant Ethic and the Spirit of Capitalism* (Weber 1948). The way of life of affluent black Americans is a scenario patterned after the Weberian theory, except that most blacks have little capital other than the house that they own, which, of course, is their primary symbol of success.

In summary, affluent or middle-class black families identify with the basic goals in American society; family members are achievement-oriented, upwardly mobile, and equalitarian. They immerse themselves in work and few have time for leisure. Personal property, especially residential property, is a major symbol of success. These family members appropriately may be called affluent conformists.

WORKING-CLASS BLACKS: The Innovators

Family life in the black working class is a struggle for survival that requires the cooperative efforts of all — husband, wife, and children. Income of black working-class families in this study ranges from just above the official poverty line to just below the national median. This is hardly enough for luxury living when the family size is considered. Black working-class families tend to be larger than affluent households, sometimes consisting of five or more children.

There is some indication that the size of the family is a source of pride for the parents, especially the father, and maybe the mother too. The bearing and rearing of children is considered to be an important citizenship responsibility, so much so that black working-class parents make great personal sacrifices for their families. They tend to look upon children as their unique contribution to society, a creative contribution they are unable to make through their work roles, which at best are semiskilled. The size of the black working-class family also may be related to age at marriage of the parents — usually before 21 years and often during the late teens for the wife and mother. Husbands tend to assume parenthood responsibilities early too; they tend to be only one or two years older than their spouses.

Cohesion in the black working-class family results not so much from understanding and tenderness shown by one for the other as from the joint and heroic effort to stave off adversity. Without the income of either parent or the contributions of offspring from part-time employment, the family would topple back into poverty.

Parents in black working-class families are literate but have limited education. Most have completed elementary school but may be high school dropouts. Seldom have any gone beyond high school. This is the educational level these parents wish their children to achieve, although some families hope that one or two of the smarter children in their brood will go on to college. The jobs that they wish for their children also are those that require only a high school or junior college education, such as work as a secretary, nurse, or skilled manual worker.

Racial discrimination, on the one hand, and insufficient education, on the other, have teamed up to delimit the employment opportunities for black working-class households, whose mobility from rural to urban areas and from South to North usually has been in search of a better life. Families tend to be attracted to a particular community because of the presence of relatives, who sometimes provide temporary housing and other relocation assistance.

In general, the moves open up new opportunities and modest advancements such as, for example, from gas station attendant to truck driver. The northern migration has resulted in some disappointments, too; a barber, for example, may be unable to pass the licensure examination to practice his trade and, therefore, becomes a janitor. On balance, new employment opportunities have resulted from the move from South to North, particularly for wives, who have found work in institutional settings such as hospitals more profitable than private household work. Nursing aide, cook, and other semiskilled jobs or service work are outlets for women in the black working class and have enabled these women to supplement the family income.

One sacrifice that the members of black working-class families have made so as to pull out of and stay beyond the clutches of poverty is to give up on doing things together as a family. Long working hours and sometimes two jobs leave little time for the father to interact with family members. In some households the husband may work during the daytime, and the wife during the evening hours. In other families, children work up to twenty hours a week after school and on weekends. Such work schedules mean that the family as a unit is not able to share any meals together, except possibly on a Sunday.

Despite the hardships, there is a constancy among the members of black working-class families that tends to pull them through. They tend to be long-term residents of their neighborhoods and stable workers with a long work history with one employer. Though their earnings are modest, the family's continuity in area of residence and in other experiences has had a stabilizing influence and has enabled members to accumulate the makings of a tolerable existence without the losses that come from frequent stops and starts.

Another unifying experience is the home that some black working-class families own. Rather than renting, many are paying out mortgages. Home ownership for some is a major family goal. The owned home may be located in an isolated rural or unsightly urban area, and may be in a poor state of repair exteriorly, but neat and clean on the inside. Home ownership for black working-class families is not so much a symbol of success as an indicator of respectability.

Black working-class parents boast of the fact that their children are good and have not been in trouble with the police. They also have a strong sense of morality that emphasizes clean living. The home that they own is part of their symbol of stability. The owned home is one blessing that can be counted. It is a haven from the harsh and sometimes unfriendly world.

There is little time for participation in community activities by adults in black working-class families. Most spare time is devoted to associating with household members or with nearby relatives. Religion is important; but participation in church affairs is limited to regular or occasional attendance at Sunday worship services. The mother in such families tries to maintain tenuous contacts with at least one community institution, such as the school. She even may be a member of the school-community council or another similar association, but she is not deeply involved as a volunteer.

Black working-class parents do well by their children if no special problems are presented. Their comprehension of psychological maladaptions is limited. These problems, when they appear, are dealt with by a series of intended remedial actions that seem to be of little assistance in solving the real problem and that usually result in frustration both for the parent and the offspring, or between spouses. Black working-class families have learned to endure; and so they bear with the afflictions of their members — those that they do not understand as well as those with obvious sources of causation.

Cooperation for survival is so basic in black working-class families that relationships between the husband and the wife take on an equalitarian character. Each knows that his or her destiny is dependent upon the actions of the other. Within the family, however, husbands and wives tend to have assigned roles, although in time of crisis these roles may change. The husband tends to make decisions about financial expenditures. He also has responsibility for maintenance of the housing structure. The mother tends to be responsible for the cooking and cleaning, although she may delegate these chores to the children. She also maintains a liaison relationship with the school and may be the adult link between the family and the church if the father is not inclined to participate.

Many working-class black families are households moving out of poverty into "respectability"; they are households that emphasize mobility, goal, and purpose; they are committed to making a contribution to society by raising and maintaining a family of good citizens. This, of course, involves a struggle. But the struggle may be a function of the ending of good times rather than the overcoming of adversity. A black working-class family may be a lower-income household on its way up or a middle-class household on its way down. In black families with limited capital there is little margin for error. A middle-class black family beset with illness, for example, can slip into the working-class status because of reduction in income and the attendant requirement for change in style of living. How often this occurs, we do not know. It does occur often enough to keep the working class from becoming a homogeneous lot. For this and other reasons, one should not expect to find a common philosophical orientation within the working-class.

In summary, the black working-class family also is an example of a household that has internalized the basic American values. Not being able to make a creative contribution through their work roles, black working-class parents consider the rearing of respectable and well-behaved children as their major contribution to the community. They therefore emphasize the fact that they are stable, that they can be counted on, and that none in their household has been in trouble with public authorities.

Black working-class families with limited education and occupational opportunities are ingenious in their methods of coping, surviving, and overcoming adversity. From multiple employment of the husband to dual employment of husband and wife that requires tandem parenting, they find a way. The means used to cope are tailor-made for each household and are most innovative. The black working class is a conglomerate group consisting of poor families on their way up and middle-class families on their way down. They probably are the best manifestation of self-reliance in American society. They are sustained by few institutional supports beyond the kinship system. By hook or crook they make it when others say, "it can't be done."

POOR BLACKS: The Rebels

The most important fact about poor black families is their low-income status. They therefore are forced to make a number of necessary, clever, and sometimes foolish arrangements to exist. These arrangements represent their rebellion against common goals and conventional ways of doing things in society. These range from extended households consisting of several generations under one roof to taking in boarders or foster children for pay. "Boyfriend-girlfriend" relationships between adults often assume parental functions when children are involved, while the participants maintain their autonomy unfettered by marital bonds. Because every penny counts, poor households often do whatever they must do to bring the money in. Conventional practices of morality may be set aside for expedient arrangements that offer the hope of a livable existence. The struggle among poor families is a struggle for existence. All else is secondary. Family income is near or less than the official federal poverty line. Some families cannot survive without public welfare.

The struggle is severe and there is no margin for error. Poor black families learn to live with contingency. They hope for little and expect less. Parents love their children but seldom understand them. Men and women become sexually involved but are afraid to entrust their futures to each other. There is much disappointment. The parents in broken families sometimes have broken spirits — too broken to risk serious involvement with another mate and possibly another disappointment. For this reason, black lower-class parents often appear to be uncommitted to anyone or to anything when in actuality they are afraid to trust.

Movement is constant, as if poor blacks were trying to get away from something, as if they would be caught by someone if they settled down. Jobs, houses, and communities are changed, and so are spouses and boyfriends or girlfriends. Unemployment is a constant specter. The womenfolk in the households usually find employment as maids and private household workers or in other service occupations that require few skills. The males are unskilled factory workers or maintenance men between periods of no work at all.

Marriage may occur at an early age, as early as sixteen years for some girls. The first child may be born before the first marriage, or pregnancy may be the reason for marriage. Other children tend to come in rapid succession. Some families have as many as eight or more children, while others are smaller. The size of the family often is a function of the number of years of marriage. First marriages may dissolve after three or four years. Other marriages or arrangements may follow. When the burdens of more children, illness, and unemployment strike at the same time, they often are overwhelming. Drinking, gambling, and other escape behavior may increase. A fragile love and capacity for endurance are shattered and the man in the house moves out or the woman elopes, no longer able to take it. One more failure is experienced.

The parents in poor black families are grade school or high school dropouts. Neither spouse has much more education than the other. Thus, parents in lower-class families sometimes hold themselves up to their children as failures, as negative images of what not to do. There is only limited ability to give guidance concerning what ought to be done. Children are advised not to marry early, not to drop out of school, and not to do this and not to do that. There is admonition but little concrete effort at prevention.

Scapegoating is a common way of explaining deviant behavior in children. Juvenile delinquency may be attributed to a disreputable parent. The mother on location seldom knows what to do. Although little love may exist between parents, there is fierce loyalty between mothers and offspring, and grandmothers, too. The children come first. Mothers will extend every effort to take care of their sons and daughters even into adulthood. Grandparents are excellent babysitters. They are expected to teach their grandchildren good manners and other fundamentals.

Also, a strong custom exists of brothers and sisters helping each other. The problem is that siblings often are struggling too. About the most one can do for the other is share already overcrowded living quarters when a new member comes to town or when a two-parent family breaks down. The move from one city to another often is for the purpose of being near kin. There is strong loyalty among siblings, and a standing obligation to help.

Little participation in any community association is seen. Religion is important for some poor families, but for others, it is no more than a delusion. Those who attend church regularly are engulfed with religion. They affirm its saving grace and reward system after death. Some shy away from the church as one more disappointing promise that has copped out on the poor without helping. Poor blacks are seldom lukewarm about religion. They are either all for it or all against it, although the latter are reluctant to deny their children religious experience, just in case there is more to it than was realized.

It is hard for a poor black family to overcome poverty; so much is lined up against it. If illness or unemployment do not drain away resources, there is a high probability that old age will.

In summary, poor black families are rebellious. They reject the society that has rejected them. Their rejection is often passive but sometimes active to the point of riotous behavior. Failure and disappointment recur regularly as if they were a refrain. Because the black poor have been given so little, they have not learned how to receive — which is to say, they have not learned how to trust. Thus, they appear to be uncommitted to anyone or anything. However, mothers are loyal to their offspring, and brothers and sisters have a standing obligation to help each other. Men sometimes act as fathers even when they are afraid to risk the commitment of marriage. Most poor families hope for a better day. But when the hope of the black poor is taken away, violent rebellion is their method of responding; it is a costly way of changing things, including the institutions of a repressive society.

REFERENCE

Weber, Max. 1948. *The Protestant Ethic and the Spirit of Capitalism.* London: Allen and Unwin.

Chapter 5 AFFLUENT CONFORMISTS

The family patterns of six affluent black households are presented in this chapter. All are two-parent families in which both husband and wife work. The husband and the wife have both finished college in all six families. In two of the six, at least one spouse has earned a doctoral degree; all told, four of the six have one or more spouses who have received graduate education. In the Newsom family, the husband is a physician and the wife, a physical therapist; the father in the Bellows household is a public administrator in city government and the mother, a teacher in a publicly supported college. The Miller children have an engineer in industry and a public school teacher as parents; and the Hines household includes a letter carrier and a public school teacher. Mr. and Mrs. Phillips also share the post office and the schoolroom as occupations, although Mr. Phillips is a postal clerk, not a letter carrier. Both husband and wife are public school teachers in the Emerson family. These reports of family patterns have been prepared by undergraduate and graduate students, with only minor editing. They are fresh in perspective, devoid of cant, and presented with honesty and sympathy.

HEALTHY AND WEALTHY, BUT NOT HAPPY
Dennis Ashby

It was the first time that I had met this family, and the atmosphere surrounding the session was quite pleasant. I left the interview pleased with what had been accomplished. The interview took place in St. Louis, in the home of Dr. and Mrs. Harry Newsom. The father and stepmother are parents of Tami — the middle child in the family who arranged for the interview. The mood of the parents was very receptive and cordial.

We spoke for about an hour and a half about the various problems faced by this family. The head of the household is Dr. Harry Newsom, a dentist. He is self-employed and his office is in a business district of St. Louis. His wife, Sylvia, also works, as a physical therapist in a private hospital in St. Louis. These two jobs contribute to a family income that is quite satisfactory.

Sylvia Newsom is Dr. Newsom's second wife. The children in the family were from the first marriage of Dr. Newsom. It ended in divorce. Richard is the oldest of the Newsom three, then Tami and finally Ruth. Ruth lives with her grandmother. She has lived with her grandmother since the divorce several years ago. Richard was living in an apartment in St. Louis but recently moved back home for financial reasons. Tami is the other daughter, who now resides in Boston, Massachusetts. She is presently a senior at Boston University.

All three offspring have been provided with good educations. Dr. Newsom has been described as being extremely hard with his children concerning their school progress. Grades were very important throughout high school. Richard has completed three years of college, but has now taken a leave of absence. He left school to work for a newspaper and live on his own. Eventually he plans to return to school and finish college. He, too, wishes to go into dentistry, which requires college and graduate school. Richard is excellent in sciences and mathematics. He is majoring in chemistry. His decision to go into dentistry is his

60

own. Dr. Newsom did not try to direct any of his children toward any particular profession.

Tami, as I mentioned, is in her fourth year at Boston University. She transferred there after a year at Western Reserve University. When she first enrolled in Western Reserve her grades fell. She attributed this to being away from home without her father's presence to force her to study. She attended a junior college to pull her grades back up, and was then accepted at Boston University for her sophomore year. She will graduate in June. Tami states that she has no immediate plans for the future, but will probably work during the summer, and then continue her education at Boston University in a graduate counseling program. After that, nothing is definite.

The youngest of the three, Ruth, finished high school last year. She then enrolled in a junior college for only one semester. The second semester there was a teacher's strike. During this period she left school. She has applied to other schools and hopes to continue her education in September wherever she is accepted. Presently, her only plans are to return to school as soon as possible and finish at least her initial four years.

Dr. Newsom attended a junior college before going on to complete his college and graduate work at the University of Missouri. Sylvia Newsom also did graduate work. She attended Washington University and completed three years of graduate school. Both husband and wife are good examples that education does pay off, and apparently this feeling is being transferred to their children.

This present marriage has been in progress for about twelve years. Sylvia Newsom, as stated earlier, is the stepmother of all three Newsom children. The first marriage of Dr. Newsom ended in divorce when Tami, the middle child, was a preschooler. After the divorce, all three children moved in with their grandmother. Richard and Tami rejoined their father after he married Sylvia and established a new household. The first Mrs. Newsom is now deceased.

The relations within the family are strained due to the divorce, the living arrangements after the divorce, the creation of a new household, and the death of the natural mother of the children. As an indication of estrangement, most members of the family eat dinner alone. There is no specific hour for dining when everyone gathers, except perhaps for breakfast. Tami's father has never taken time from his work to visit her at her college. He has promised to visit but has not appeared. She is uncertain whether he will be on hand for her graduation. He sends money to his children when they ask for it. The children feel that material wealth is shared with them by their father rather than love and kindness.

The husband and wife in the Newsom family lead relatively quiet lives, as is indicated by their weekend and weekly schedules. On a normal Sunday, Dr. Newsom describes his schedule as eating three meals a day, reading books and newspapers, and watching television. Mrs. Newsom does the cooking for the household and also does housework, since she works away from home during the week. On weekends, Richard often visits his friends after lunch and Tami visits her friends also or stays home and reads or watches television.

On an ordinary weekday, Dr. Newsom has breakfast early and is off to his office. Following work and dinner that evening, he usually watches television for a while. Mrs. Newsom follows a similar schedule — an early breakfast and then off to work. At night, she cooks dinner and relaxes afterward by enjoying television also. Richard either attends classes or goes to work. When Tami is at home during vacation time, she does very little and relaxes.

Dr. Newsom is originally from Texas and his wife, Sylvia, is from Idaho. Both moved to St. Louis many years ago. Since living in St. Louis, they have done quite well financially. They have a family income well over the national median and live quite comfortably. They live in a racially mixed neighborhood in a rather large house that has ten rooms altogether, including four bedrooms, a kitchen, a living room, a dining room, plus two bathrooms and a library. It is a single-family home that the Newsom household owns. All of today's luxuries are to be found in and around the house.

Dr. Newsom and his family know between ten and twenty people in his neighborhood, and he says he likes the neighborhood because of the friendly people. However, he is think-ing of moving elsewhere in the St. Louis metropolitan area because of the "large amount of noise" in the current neigh-borhood that is disturbing, and also because of recent experiences of thefts and break-ins. The present neighborhood he classifies as "an average area."

Regarding family members' roles in this household, the mother chooses the foods for the family and cooks the meals, decorates the home, and makes decisions about home fur-nishings. The father decides what house and car the family shall buy. Difficulties with children at school were always left to Dr. Newsom. He always spoke to his children's teachers concerning their progress in class. He states that he has a little influence as to what political candidates he and his wife vote for. Otherwise, both parents shared in raising their offspring. When the children are sick, both mother and father take care of them. The teaching of manners is a responsibility assumed by both parents. And when there was work to do, both parents assigned chores to the children.

Many aspects of the children's lives were left entirely up to them. They did their own homework, although their father often made them do it but did not help them with it. The father paid for the education of his children but they chose their own schools. They spent their allowance money as they wished. They chose their own clothes, and what to wear on a specific day. They also were left to decide on any particular religion they wished to try, if any at all.

Although Dr. Newsom's preference is Protestant and Mrs. Newsom's is Catholic, neither go to church on a regular basis. They have not attempted to influence their children regarding religious preferences.

Dr. and Mrs. Newsom are not very much into any types of community organizations. As I mentioned, they lead a rather quiet life; after working hard all day, they do little else but relax. Dr. Newsom is, however, a member of the National Dental Association, which is the black counterpart of the American Dental Association. Otherwise, the Newsoms are not connected with any church or secret societies or civil rights groups or the like.

This family has enough money to afford luxuries and can afford a private family home. This does not necessarily lead to happiness for all the family members, however. In the United States material wealth is all important. It is sad that the gaining of material wealth may leave little time for understanding one's own children. This seems to be a problem in the Newsom household. As the children grow up in this affluent black family, it seems that the family split is widening instead of coming closer together.

It is often assumed, too, that only poor families get divorced or separated. A great majority of black families are thought to be welfare recipients. And, black people are normally associated with run-down communities called ghettoes. Yet, here we find quite an exception. Here is a family in which the mother and father have several years of graduate school work between them, which shows better than average education. Both have fine jobs that are considered highly respectable. And money is not lacking. Yet harmony and togetherness are lacking. This may be the result of the first divorce, which occurred when the children were young and unable to cope with the major change brought about by a divorce. Little was done to remedy this situation and what began then exists today. When the parents divorced, it seemed that they thought only of themselves and not of their children's welfare.

It is quite strange that the goals Americans strive for most, education and money, do not in themselves provide happiness. This family is a prime example. On the outside one sees a large comfortable home. A father with the title of doctor. A mother who is a physical therapist. All of these point to a sufficient income.

Money can buy homes and cars and television sets, but it can never buy a close relationship within a family. From this interview I gained a lot of insight into the minds of people. It was well worth the experience to learn how other black families live.

GRACEFUL LIVING IN GREEN ACRES
Levi Moore

My friend, who was driving me to my point of destination, had high praise for the Green Acres suburban area. He spoke of his own hopes of someday being able to get away from it all. We took the freeway to the Green Acres exit and entered a very modern and beautiful park-terrace shopping area, spacious with trees and flowers planted in every available spot. We continued through the shopping area, turned off the main road and continued for about two miles along a sparsely settled road until we reached Silver Village. The houses were set back from the road and all of the lawns were immaculate. Children in casually well-groomed, expensive clothing rode bikes or strolled along the streets.

We continued deeper into the division and located the house. A two-story ranch style with a long drive leading to a two-car garage connected to the house by a covered walkway. Parking space was provided to the right of the garage with a wide walkway leading to the front door. The house had the contour of the gently sloping hill on which it was built. Behind the house and extended along the rear of several was a very large lake. I rang the bell and a friendly voice from an intercom above the door asked what it could do for me. I explained that I was the man from Harvard and the voice said it would be with me in a minute. I said good-by to my driver friend and went back to the door. Mr. Bellows opened the door welcoming me to come in and I stepped in a large foyer with steps to my left leading to the second floor. Mr. Bellows, a small man, was very cordial, asking about my trip and my work at school. He seemed really glad to be of help. He said that he had been working on his boat and would need to put up a few things and asked if I'd like to go with him. We walked down a long corridor toward the rear of the house through a huge den and outside. We walked along a covered walkway through a drydock a little distance from the lake to where the boat was moored. The boat slept four people, had its own galley, and was air-jet powered. Mr. Bellows said he had been interested in boats since he was a kid. He often took the boat either for the fishing or just to get away, sometimes with the family. We went back to the house and continued our conversation in the den. The wife and two of the children were away. The housekeeper baby-sitter brought coffee and danish rolls to the den at Mr. Bellows's request.

Mr. Bellows is at the beginning of middle age. He was born in Philadelphia and had lived in the vicinity all of his life. Mrs. Elsie Bellows, six years younger than her husband, was born in South Carolina and had come to Philadelphia to study when they met and subsequently became engaged. They were married in South Carolina. They have three children, a son, Spencer Bellows, Jr., 8 years of age; a daughter, Cynthia, 5 year of age; and another son, Michael, only 1 year old. Mr. Bellows had a Doctor of Education degree and Mrs. Bellows had a master's degree in music. The oldest son, Spencer Jr., was in public elementary school, having spent three years in private school. Cynthia, not yet of school age, was in the same private school kindergarten that Spencer Jr. had attended. Mr. and Mrs. Bellows had no previous marriages and had been married ten years.

Mr. Bellows was responsible for much of the building and contract work for the city of Philadelphia. His work had to do with compliance of contractors, their ability to do certain jobs, special work with minority contractors, and needs assessments for certain new construction. He said that his job made it possible to help a lot of minority contractors get work they would not normally have heard of. Mrs. Bellows worked at a local public college. He didn't know exactly what she did but she later told me that she helped the college work on improving the music curriculum especially for the brighter students. They were good at producing high school music teachers she said, but the bright students really had to go on to private school. She had studied at a private school.

Mr. Bellows was Protestant and never attended church except on festive or celebratory occasions that involved the children. Mrs. Bellows was a Catholic and attended services regularly. The children were also Catholic and attended services with the mother. Mrs. Bellows was to tell me later that her family had practically built the church in the South Carolina city where she grew up.

Mr. Bellows described the family as close but said he did not get out with the children as much as the mother. Of children and the police, he said that the security patrol, paid by the community, kept down the pranks, mostly speeding, to a minimum. The kids did well in school especially as far as grades and deportment were concerned, but he'd just have to spend more time with Spencer Jr. to toughen him up a little. The mother did what little disciplining needed to be done, but he thought the children took advantage sometimes. There was no regular time for eating supper and only the mother and children ate breakfast and dinner together regularly. The children were transported to school and other activities by private car. The children normally studied their homework after dinner in the family room. This helps to develop good habits, Mrs. Bellows said. She liked to visit the school whenever she could, and she had had the principal to dinner. The children, she said, would all be professional workers. She would really like one to be a doctor and one to be a lawyer.

Mr. Bellows talked freely about their family income, which he estimated at more than twice the national median. His father, he said, had given him a good start in real estate. The tax shelter helped out also; if the houses don't pay, deduct, he said. Both were completely satisfied with the neighborhood; they enjoyed the sense of neighborliness of all the people living there. They could be depended on to watch your property, check your mail, and see that your lawn was kept when you were away. They also exchanged tools, recipes, and sometimes even kept each other's children.

They wanted to stay in the neighborhood because it seemed to be child oriented and the public schools were very good and they were close to recreation for the entire family. They are members of a local club that is quite expensive but that provides good leisure activities, including a private golf course.

They classify the neighborhood as an upper class, white one because of the few nonwhites living there. Mrs. Bellows does not think that children in the neighborhood are necessarily well behaved, and thinks the whites believe in too much cheap psychology. She felt that both the private and public police did a good job.

The single-family home and grounds on which it was located was quite valuable. The house had a kitchen, three bedrooms with baths, nursery, living room, dining room, breakfast room, family room, recreation room, den, and a hobby room for Mrs. Bellows, music room, and basement. There were several color televisions in the house, several with wall-size projectors. There was an intercom system throughout the house adapted to a stereo-phono-tape set. They subscribed to several magazines, several daily papers, as well as *Better Homes, Changing Times, Jet,* and *Ebony.* They had several telephones with a separate line for the children. The best features of the neighborhood is that it is safe, convenient, and with plenty of space. They would both like to have more blacks in the neighborhood, but said the racial ratio is typical.

Mrs. Bellows knew from five to ten people but Mr. Bellows knew from twenty to thirty. Both would turn to their respective families if they needed help. The wife's family were land owners and bankers. The husband's father was in the retail liquor business and real estate.

They both felt that the community provided equal opportunity, excellent education, cultural opportunities. They felt that recreation and community organizations could be improved but were not too satisfied with the predominantly white government officials.

They both contributed generously to community chest, church, and many other charitable purposes. They both served on boards and had leadership responsibility for civic improvement. They were both declared Democrats and were very active in the past and the present national political campaigns. They were both very vocal on the needs and shortcomings of government and governmental institutions. They were regular voters and voted two to five times in the last four years. They both wrote, spoke, and visited congressmen several times, and were very concerned over the qualifications needed for public office.

Mrs. Bellows' leisure time activity was chiefly around the family which she liked most, and weekly bridge with her club on a regular basis. Mr. Bellows liked to hunt deer and fish in Canada, which he did annually. He also liked camping and had a vacation lodge accessible by boat where he went fairly often with two other friends. Both had traveled extensively in foreign countries.

Mrs. Bellows, a very beautiful woman, had returned home in the early afternoon with the two servants, who commuted to the house daily. They prepared the meals and kept the house. Mrs. Bellows supervised the shopping, and principally ran the home. The decor was obviously Old South.

The conversation automatically turned to her on her arrival. Mr. Bellows took the kids out on the grounds to the playground elaborately equipped with a miniature basketball court, swings, slides, etc.

I remained for a very elaborate dinner which we all ate together, had wine and cigarettes in the den, and waited for my friend to pick me up.

THE LONELY INTEGRATORS
Michael Rettig

The Millers live in a nicely furnished house about ten blocks east of the University. When I came to visit, Mrs. Miller had just returned from the beauty salon and she and her nine-year-old daughter Sandy were listening to records on a beautiful component stereo (Harmon and Kardon, Daul and Fisher). We immediately got to talking about jazz and Mrs. Miller told me how Sandy had once stunned her uncle by asking him if he "dug Dave Brubeck."

Mr. and Mrs. Miller both hail from a suburb of Pittsburgh, Pennsylvania. They both grew up in a racially mixed neighborhood and attended mixed schools. She said, presumably with no degradation intended, that they grew up with a bunch of "honkies" who were their friends, enemies, and classmates. Although her family wasn't well to do, Mrs. Miller told me that they never went hungry. The church played a large part in their growth and development with both Mr. and Mrs. Miller attending Baptist services, as, Mrs. Miller chucklingly put it, "God-fearing people." After he left the home of his parents, Mr. Miller stopped going to church. Graduating from high school, Mrs. Miller attended a small college with a predominantly white student body in Pennsylvania. She was one of the three blacks in a freshman class of 300 students. The majority of her friends were white and during these years she had little social contact with blacks at school. Mr. Miller also attended college and graduated with a degree in electrical engineering. Continuing her studies after graduation, Mrs. Miller took the necessary courses for certification in elementary education. She also joined an honorary black sorority in Pittsburgh. A year after her graduation from college, Mr. and Mrs. Miller were married.

The Millers are an affluent family. Having taught school for ten years, Mrs. Miller earns a good salary from the Rochester school district, while Mr. Miller works as an electrical engineer. Their combined income is about twice the national median. When she saw the highest category of earnings on the interview schedule, Mrs. Miller remarked, "I almost earn that myself." Their life as a family has been characterized by a great deal of movement due to Mr. Miller's job. In fact, at the end of this school year they are moving back to Pittsburgh, this time for a different reason (to be discussed later). Mrs. Miller usually enjoys teaching, but in the interview she stated frustratingly that, "inner city kids are a different breed of kid. They have no motivation and I don't know how to get them going." She is the only black teacher in the school and again all her friends are white (at school).

Although he enjoys his job, Mr. Miller has had to work a great deal lately. He must be on the job at 8:00 a.m. and often he doesn't return until after 8:00 p.m. (In fact, the night I interviewed the family Mr. Miller had not yet returned when I left at 9:30.) Both Mr. and Mrs. Miller seemed very diligent at their work and rarely miss work because of sickness. Their hard work has paid off, at least materially. Besides the new stereo, I observed two cars, a piano for Sandy, and a beautifully furnished house.

The Millers are a close family. This was manifest (to me) in Sandy's hanging all over her mother during parts of the interview. Their closeness could be a function of both the loving state of the family and the great amount of moving the family has done in the last few years. When you don't live in an area for a long time it is difficult to form long-lasting relationships outside of the family. This makes for increased contact among the members of the family.[1] Unable to eat breakfast and lunch together because of different schedules, the Millers try to eat dinner together even though Mr. Miller sometimes works late. (I discovered when I was leaving that Mrs. Miller and Sandy had not yet eaten).

After Sandy and Mrs. Miller return from their respective

---

[1] This could be an erroneous generalization, but it seems true in the Miller family because neither the parents nor Sandy have any strong outside relationships.

schools, Mrs. Miller begins cooking and then spends a lot of the time before dinner talking to Sandy about her school day or just giving general motherly attention. On the weekends much of the free time is spent on individual pursuits. Sandy reads, does homework, watches television, or practices the piano. Mrs. Miller might read, watch TV, or do her lesson plans, while Mr. Miller is often found listening to records and reading in the living room. Mrs. Miller told me that often after a hard day's work, she would find her husband asleep in his chair with a book on his chest.

Although Mrs. Miller makes many everyday decisions, husband and wife join together to make the major family decisions, such as where to live, what car to buy, and the upbringing of their daughter. It should be mentioned that Mrs. Miller is the one who made the decision to have only one child.

The Millers chose to bring Sandy up in a disciplined manner. Thus she must do her homework, practice piano (not excessively), and always obey. Mrs. Miller feels that she is leading her daughter to be an independent person because she has "no time to pamper her." This method of child-rearing could be the cause of Sandy's advanced achievement in school (not to mention the fact that her mother is a teacher). Mrs. Miller seemed very proud of her daughter's performance in the classroom as she told me. Although in the third grade, Sandy was reading on fifth-grade level. Both mother and daughter complained that the kids fooled around too much. Sandy told me that, "One day the teacher gave us a sheet to do and I started right away. Then the girl behind me yelled out, 'Sandy's up to 24 already!' The teacher gave me a new sheet and told me to start over again." Mrs. Miller has met with the teacher at both PTA meetings and the parent-teacher home conference. The above reprimand was typical of what Sandy thought of her teacher and classmates. Another reason for Sandy's low opinion of teacher and classmates could be the contrast between the public school she is attending now and the private schools she has attended in the past. The move from private to public schools was made because Mr. Miller didn't want his daughter to live a sheltered life. As far as her daughter's future was concerned, Mrs. Miller put the emphasis on what Sandy wanted, as long as it was in the professional vein. Having once visited a female doctor's office, Sandy was all excited about the prospect of being a doctor, even though she knew it entailed eight years of schooling after she was finished with high school.

Because the Millers have just been living in the neighborhood a few months, as I said before, they have not had a chance to form any very close relationships outside of the family. When Mrs. Miller was asked how many people she knew in the area she could only cite ten. There was not much said about Sandy's social life, but playing with friends was not mentioned. In case the family ever needed outside help, Mrs. Miller said she would probably first call her minister. Because, she said, "he is a sympathetic and helpful man." Both mother and daughter attend church regularly while Mr. Miller only goes on special holidays, such as Christmas and Easter. Although Mrs. Miller and Sandy do go to church they have been too involved in the settling process to be able to participate in church-organized community activities. Mrs. Miller does have one other friend, a woman she met registering for a graduate course at the University. "She is the only black person who has been in the house since we've moved in," Mrs. Miller told me.

The neighborhood the Millers live in is satisfactory in every way except for the fact that Mrs. Miller wishes there were more black people in the area. She likes the neighborhood because, as she said, "The people are home owners, they take pride in their house and yard." Also she commented that it was a "quiet neighborhood with no buggy kids and no police problems." No member of the family has become active in community affairs mainly because of the short period of their residence.

The Millers are returning to a suburb of Pittsburgh. This move is being made for a combination of reasons headed by their dislike of Rochester. They have met few friendly people in this city. She couldn't describe her bad feelings, but perhaps it is analogous to a mild case of a midwesterner moving to the East. Another motivation for the move is Mrs. Miller's dislike of teaching inner-city children, and the fact that except for church and children in school, "the family is not exposed to enough black people in the course of a day." They seem eager to leave the area.

After finishing the interview schedules, I felt as though we had built up a good enough rapport to talk about her views on present-day race relations. We talked freely about times when racist attitudes might have affected her family. It turned out that she never really had been exposed to such views. Having grown up in a mixed and liberal suburb, Mrs. Miller was never overtly confronted with racial hostility. Even at a predominantly white college there was little tension. She did mention that when Mr. Miller was looking for a house to rent in Rochester, he had encountered some jacked-up prices. Mrs. Miller admitted being unable to identify with the poorer blacks in this country who are struggling for survival within the racist system. She and her family, in the upper echelon of society, have never been hungry and have always had the money to pay their own way.

When talking about radical black movements, Mrs. Miller came out against any type of extreme action. She felt that extremists' militant action would not "change the minds of the whites." Resigned to a slow evolutionary process, Mrs. Miller saw the solution to American's race problems in the actions of good whites and nonviolent blacks who pattern their behavior in the image of the Kennedy brothers and Martin Luther King, Jr.

Her students, Mrs. Miller told me, were a part of the "welfare generation." She based this thought on her experience with free lunch tickets granted by the Welfare Department. It turned out that 15 of the 18 children in her class who stayed for lunch received free lunch tickets. Mrs. Miller felt that the parents of inner-city children didn't care about their children and didn't provide an environment at home conducive to learning in school. Continuing about her students, Mrs. Miller said that many of the white teachers were afraid of repercussions from severe disciplining of black students on race charges, but that she could treat them as they deserved without that fear.

THE POSTMAN AND THE PUBLIC SCHOOL TEACHER
Beryl M. Dakers

Mr. and Mrs. Hines have been married twenty-four years. Both parents are employed full-time. Mr. Hines is a letter carrier for the U.S. Post Office and Mrs. Hines is a high school science teacher, employed by the City School System. The family's income is slightly above the national median. To supplement his stable income, Mr. Hines often seeks extra employment as a yard man. The children are also employed in various part-time jobs to cover their minor personal expenses.

Mr. Hines was born in Atlanta, Georgia. Orphaned at age eight, he was raised by an uncle and aunt who had twelve children of their own and little extra money or love to spare on an additional child. He vividly recalls the trials of this early childhood, particularly the pangs of poverty and hunger. At age seventeen, Mr. Hines came to Raleigh, North Carolina to work his way through college. He did this by securing a number of indiscriminate and often low-paying jobs. Majoring in history, he graduated from college *cum laude* and taught school for two years before being drafted for World War II.

Mrs. Hines was the oldest of five children born to a rather prosperous farmer in rural North Carolina. Her family was extremely close-knit, and education and religion were stressed as the foundations for a good life. Mrs. Hines attended State College, where she met Mr. Hines at a football game. They dated rather infrequently, both as students and later, as young teachers. With the outbreak of the war, Mrs. Hines went to Washington, D.C., where she worked. She continued to correspond with Mr. Hines and accepted the engagement ring he sent her from overseas. Upon his return, they were married, and returned to Raleigh to make their home.

Unable to find steady employment in a well-paying field, Mr. Hines accepted various odd jobs at the Veterans Hospital. To supplement the income, Mrs. Hines became a secretary.

Eventually, Mr. Hines became a postal employee and Mrs. Hines stopped working to await the arrival of their first child. They began making payments on an old, two-story house in a quiet, residential black section of town.

Daughter Jane was born at mid-century; then Mrs. Hines returned to work. The baby was cared for during the day by an elderly couple who lived across the street. At age two, Jane got her first taste of school, when she entered the neighborhood nursery.

During the next eight years, the young couple worked very hard. Meanwhile, Mrs. Hines had secured a Master's degree and was again working as a teacher. The couple had paid off the mortgage on the house and owned all of their dilapidated furniture and second-hand appliances.

At just about this time, one of Mr. Hines' foster brothers died and a seven-year-old son was left homeless. The Hineses decided to adopt the child as their own — and Peter became a full-fledged member of the family. Parents and children seemingly enjoyed the enlarged family set up and soon began clamoring for another sibling. Through a process of "familial consensus," they decided to adopt a little girl who really needed a family. The result was the addition of Beverly, who was then four years old. Both child and family evidently made the transition quite easily, as there is no outward evidence of discrimination on the family's part, or insecurity on the child's part. Beverly is treated as any other "baby of the family."

All of the Hines children were brought up in an upwardly mobile family group. Each child was given music lessons for the instrument of his or her choice, and each was sent to dance school for at least four years. Explains Mrs. Hines, "We wanted to give them as much culture and refinement as we could. Besides, any musical endeavor is worth encouraging."

There is a strong emphasis on education in the Hines family. The bookshelves overflow with five sets of encyclopedias, assorted textbooks, and remnants of numerous Book Club memberships. Interestingly enough, all three children are avid readers. Jane has proved herself to be a very intelligent young lady and is remembered to have "practically read herself blind as a child." The most enthusiastic reader is Peter, often referred to as the family egghead. An aspiring young scientist, he reads just about anything he can get his hands on. Like Jane, he has been an Honor Roll student all through high school. Beverly, on the other hand, has trouble in school. Math is her personal cross — whether old or new. "She just can't seem to buckle down in school," says her father. Nevertheless, Beverly is faithful to her books and brings home at least two books a week from the school library. Last summer she begged for membership in the Children's Book Club and most of her present allowance is spent on books.

Another major influence in this family's life is the church. Mr. Hines is a Baptist deacon and staunch church-goer. His wife was born and bred a Methodist and has remained true to her native denomination. Characteristically, each of the children expressed a preference for "Daddy's church" while they were young. Now, Jane goes to church with her mother, Peter attends a Baptist church (different from his father's) where he plays the organ, and Beverly attends the Lutheran church on the corner. "We don't care where they go to church," remarked Mr. Hines, "just as long as they go."

The character of the Hineses' neighborhood underwent a rapid transition as the older residents died. Their single-family homes were converted into low-rent apartments, and those neighbors who could afford it began to migrate to the suburbs. The Hineses talked it over and decided they, too, should move, for Beverly was picking up traits that Mrs. Hines did not particularly appreciate. Thus they built a home in a previously undeveloped suburb. This section has now developed into one of the more prosperous black sections of the metropolitan area. The Hineses are quite content with this neighborhood and feel that it provides the "proper atmosphere" for rearing children. They do not anticipate moving again. When asked what he liked most about the neighborhood, Mr. Hines replied, "The neighborhood is nice, clean, and secure. It is easily accessible to churches, schools, and shopping centers. It is spread out enough to give you some sense of freedom, and yet, compact enough to ensure a sense of community."

The Hineses are quite active in civic affairs. Mr. Hines is president of the Community Club and works hard to establish solidarity among the neighbors. He takes an active interest in the welfare of the children and, despite his age, coaches a Little League baseball team. He is president of the Parent-Teacher Association at Beverly's school and works actively in several civic and civil rights groups. Mrs. Hines works basically with professional organizations — especially those dedicated to bettering educational opportunities for blacks. She is the voting ward representative for her area and spends much time encouraging others to vote and to participate in citizenship activities. Though their interests are diverse, the Hineses express a mutual respect for each other's independence. They do believe that their activities stem from like concerns and that they are working for the same types of goals.

The Hineses are a rather close-knit family, although individuality is important to them. The family rarely eats together during the week, but seldom does a member eat entirely alone. The varied schedules usually allow for at least two people to sit down at the table together. However, weekends are different. For Saturday breakfasts, Mrs. Hines eats with the children, and everyone waits for Mr. Hines to join them at Saturday's impromptu dinner. Sunday breakfast is the meal the family considers most important, as they all gather around for prayers before eating. Sunday dinner is a major production and everyone is involved, either in its preparation, or in cleaning up afterwards.

The parents do not indulge their children's whims. However, they see to it that the children have everything they need — and more. Thrift and industry are necessary components of each child's upbringing. Each child was encouraged at a very young age (six to nine) to get a weekend or part-time job, and to use his or her earnings to buy some of the things he or she wanted. Each of the Hines children receives an allowance, with a starting weekly rate doled out at age five that increased regularly until age eighteen. Commenting on this somewhat meager allowance, Mr. Hines said, "It lets them know that Mom and Dad are willing to help financially, but it gives them the incentive to get out and do for themselves." Apparently this logic has been effective, as all of the children earn their own spending change, as well as contribute substantial amounts to their savings accounts.

The Hines children are fiercely critical, and yet extremely tolerant and extremely protective of each other. They class themselves as a tough lot to beat, saying, "We are stubborn like Daddy and independent like Mom — and that's quite a combination!" Though they all evaluate themselves as being somewhat shy and reserved, they come across as being very self-confident and quite capable of any task they may undertake. They are competitive among themselves and their peers, but not jealously or covetously so. "Competition," says Jane, "keeps you from stagnation. It lets you know that no matter how good you are, you can always be better."

The Hines children have an enormous respect for their parents and a deep appreciation for the way in which they have been brought up. Commented Jane, "Mom and Dad instilled us with certain basic values and then allowed us to apply these values to our individual personalities. We may express ourselves differently, but I don't think any of us will ever really depart from our upbringing. We know and respect the difference between right and wrong."

When asked if there was a generation gap within the family, Peter replied, "Only when it comes to money. Pops still doesn't realize that things cost more now than they did in the twelfth century when he was growing up. Other than that, he is much more liberal and eager to understand than are the parents of most of my friends." Mrs. Hines' response to inquiries about a generation gap was this: "I want to understand my kids, so I ask and listen to find out what they are thinking and why." She feels that she is able to communicate well with her children as a result of this effort. "If there is a gap in this family, it is more likely to be between me and my husband," she laughs. The children agreed. Beverly summed up the whole question by saying "They are pretty hep for old folks!"

Father — Mr. Hines, over fifty — is a rather easygoing man. He is a big man (200 pounds), with a rather stern countenance, but a quick smile. He is devoted to his family and to fulfilling what he considers to be the "fatherly" role. He respects and admires his wife's independence, commenting that he could not have married a "tie-me-down" type woman.

Recalling his boyhood poverty and deprivation, Mr. Hines is determined that his family have the basics for a good start in life. These basics include: a good home (food, shelter, clothing), and education, good principles and love. He is a concerned father who disciplines his children with a heavy hand and admits that he often listens after he strikes. He takes an active interest in whatever the children are doing, always joining or organizing a corresponding parent group. He shows his affection for both his wife and children mostly in play, admitting that it is hard for him to be affectionate in the conventional ways.

Mr. Hines is undisputedly the man of the house, and the final authority — but not, he insists, the authoritarian. "We are a family," he says, "not a military company."

Mother — Mrs. Hines, middle-aged — is a typical, atypical mother. She is bouncy, yet often fatigued; fussy, but understanding; older in age, but young in actions; quiet spoken, but quick to make her opinions known. She is rather short and about fifteen pounds overweight (a nervous eater she says.). She suffers with every conceivable ache and pain (a typical hypochondriac her husband says), yet lets nothing slow her down.

During the course of the interview, her face changed back and forth from school teacher and disciplinarian to loving, compassionate mother. While acknowledging obstacles and personal limitations, Mrs. Hines firmly believes "you can do anything you put your mind to doing" and hopes she has instilled this feeling in her children.

"My husband and I worked long and hard to give these kids the opportunities we never had. We are not going to force them to take advantage of their chances but if they choose to do so, they will have enough stamina and love behind them to make the best of any opportunity." So said, and apparently, so believed, Mrs. Hines.

Daughter Number One — Jane — is a coed at the University of North Carolina, where she is enrolled in the pre-medical program. She hopes to be a hematologist. An honor student throughout high school, Jane excelled in many things and participated in practically everything. She is a good musician, being an accomplished pianist and a "half-cocked" flutist. She is a member of the Modern Dance Troupe at school and has been (to her parents' dismay) excessively active in the Black Student Movement. She does not consider herself a militant, but she does believe in asserting the rights of the individual.

Jane is easygoing and appears, at first glance, quite reserved. She can, however, get very excited over some idea she is interested in and often finds herself thrust into leadership roles. She says of herself, "I am an incurably romantic, realistic idealist. I know what the world is really like and I accept it. At the same time, I want it to be better, and deep down inside, I believe someday it will be." "I am," she says reflectively, "the product of my parents' love, wisdom, and being."

Son — Peter, a teenager — is a big man on his high school campus. President of his senior class, he is both an athlete and a scholar. Particularly interested in physics ("I get it from Mom," he grins), he hopes to major in bio-physics at Cornell, MIT, or Harvard. He is a very outgoing young man with both an easy smile and a quick temper. He is incredibly honest, hates phonies, and will go to any end for a friend. Very industrious, he works at a gas station and plays with a jazz band on weekends, and is church organist on Sunday morning. When asked which of his parents influenced him most, he replied, "I guess Dad had the most influence on my manliness, while Mom influenced my being the kind of man I am."

Daughter Number Two — Beverly — is a perky, button-nosed Miss. Often called "The Brat" by her brother and sister, she is the most precocious of the Hines children. Although she is active in many groups, she confesses that she often gets very lonely. Unlike her siblings, Beverly has an acute dislike for being alone and often feels compelled to seek out friends for company.

She idolizes her older sister and brother and adores her parents. When asked what her family is like, Beverly said,

"They are like my family — You know, like you wouldn't want to belong to any other family but them." An engaging little girl, Beverly has the amazing ability of switching instantly from "Little Imp" to "Little Angel." Extemely outgoing around adults, she is somewhat timid with new friends her own age. Beverly thinks that, all in all, her family is a real "groove."

Upon visiting the Hines family, I was ushered into the den of a very modern, well-furnished home. The atmosphere was decidedly informal and congenial. The family was most cooperative and I was able to interview each member of the family individually.

In this stable, middle-income family, the influence pattern is obviously equalitarian and the system of family decision-making is democratic. All members of the family concurred that theirs is a stable and happy unit. From observation, this interviewer must agree with their consensus.

THE SCHOOL MARM AND THE POSTAL WORKER
Judy Mesinger

Hillsborough, New York, population 72,000, is a suburb of New York City. For more than fifty years, this four-square-mile city has been bifurcated along black and white racial lines by the railroad tracks. Though economic status and racial identity overlap to a great extent, the wealthy reside in the northern part of the city and the poor reside in the southern part. Elementary and junior high schools are also populated on this basis, while the city's sole high school serves all youth from ninth to twelfth grades.

Driving up the Phillipses' block on Hillsborough's south side at 9:00 a.m., I noticed the neatly kept old houses. Considering the morning hour and the fact that the children were on vacation, the street was very quiet.

Mrs. Phillips had just come back from driving her husband to work and was talking on the telephone when I knocked on her door. She hurriedly excused herself from the phone and ushered me in through the foyer and a well-equipped modern kitchen to their dining room, where she offered me a cup of coffee.

The Phillipses are a black family headed by Andrew and Sara, ages sixty and forty-six respectively. They have been married twenty years and have two daughters, Carol, age eighteen, and Shirley, age sixteen.

While Mr. Phillips was born in Pennsylvania and Mrs. Phillips in South Carolina, both their daughters have been life-long residents of Hillsborough. Before coming to Hillsborough to live, both husband and wife lived in Virginia. Mr. Phillips has been a resident of Hillsborough for thirty years, though Mrs. Phillips has lived there for only twenty years.

Currently a freshman at Wellesley College (Wellesley, Massachusetts), Carol spends about four months out of the year at home. All information concerning Carol is based on vacations spent at home during the academic year. Her younger sister is

83

a junior in Hillsborough high school. Mr. Phillips has completed three years of college and Mrs. Phillips has her Bachelor of Arts degree plus an additional thirty-nine credit hours towards a doctoral degree.

Andrew Phillips is a postal clerk at the local post office, selling stamps and processing mail. Before becoming an employee of the post office, he was an upholsterer. When the couple married, he switched from this trade to his present job because of better salary conditions. He still keeps the latter up as a hobby and has made all the furniture for his house. When he retires, his wife said he intends to return to upholstering on a full-time basis.

Sara Phillips teaches sixth grade in a south side elementary school and has done so for the past five years. She did not work when her daughters were younger because she did not want to be away from home. Before coming to Hillsborough with one of her sisters, she taught elementary school for more than three years in Virginia.

Together, Andrew and Sara Phillips gross a yearly income that is slightly above the national median. Mrs. Phillips has contributed slightly more to the family income than her husband.

Both Mr. and Mrs. Phillips are Presbyterians. When they switched churches several years ago, Mr. and Mrs. Phillips made individual choices. Nevertheless, they chose the same church. Both girls attend the same church regularly each Sunday with their parents. Before services, Mrs. Phillips teaches Sunday school and during the services, Mr. Phillips sings in the choir. In addition to these church activities, the senior Phillipses are members of a play reading group and The Couples Club, and Mrs. Phillips participates in The Women's Society. Meetings of these church-affiliated organizations require Mr. and Mrs. Phillips to be at their church at least one day a week other than Sunday.

Mrs. Phillips classified her family as "close." She felt there should be something more if one were going to label a family "real close."

Carol and Shirley, their daughters, never got into trouble with authorities and did very well in school. Their mother also reported that she and her husband share the responsibility of disciplining the girls. Mrs. Phillips, however, admitted that she played a slightly bigger role in this area because she was home more often.

The Phillipses dine together every night at 6:00 p.m. except on Sundays, when they eat at 5:00 p.m. During the normal school year, the entire family has lunch separately. Carol is the only one to eat lunch at home; the other three family members eat at their places of work. Mr. and Mrs. Phillips have breakfast together and Shirley has hers about half an hour later with her sister, if the latter is home.

Mrs. Phillips characterized Sundays at her home as quiet days. The whole family has breakfast together at 8:00 a.m., or shortly after. Mrs. Phillips then leaves to teach church school while her daughters clean up. Before they go to church, they join their father to read the newspaper. The entire family, as noted before, attends services and Mr. Phillips sings in the choir. They return home for a noon dinner, after which the girls wash the dishes. By approximately 2:00 p.m. the girls are studying. After lunch, Mrs. Phillips naps or sometimes corrects papers. Mr. Phillips spends his afternoon constructing furniture or making repairs about the house. After a 5:00 p.m. supper for the whole family, the parents frequently visit friends or relatives. Meanwhile, Carol studies and Shirley goes to a youth group meeting until 9:00 p.m. Upon returning, the latter studies until 11:00 and both sisters retire a half hour later. Despite the fact that both children have desks in their rooms, Shirley studies at the dining room table, usually along with her sister. Mr. and Mrs. Phillips also return home at 9:00 and go to sleep an hour later.

On weekdays, such as Tuesday, Mr. and Mrs. Phillips have breakfast at 7:00 a.m. By that time Carol and Shirley are getting up. While the girls are eating breakfast, Mrs. Phillips leaves to drive to her elementary school, which she does not normally leave until 3:30 p.m., or later. Mr. Phillips, on the other hand, works until 5:00 p.m. Shirley is at school by 8:45 a.m. and is finished with her classes by 2:45 p.m. From then on until 5:30 she usually attends meetings of various school organizations.

Carol, on the other hand, spends most of her morning studying until lunch time. In the afternoon she visits friends or travels to New York City. When Mrs. Phillips does not have her 4:00 to 6:00 p.m. university course (it usually meets on Wednesdays), she picks her husband up from work, after an hour and a half of making lesson plans. Mrs. Phillips then spends the next hour preparing dinner. Usually, the girls will wash the dishes. Carol and Shirley spend the rest of the night studying, going to sleep about 11:00 or 11:30. The elder Phillipses are generally in bed an hour before the girls.

The Phillipses are active in school affairs. They attend PTA meetings regularly and go to parent-teacher conferences. No teacher or school official has ever visited their household, although Shirley's math teacher called Mrs. Phillips once because of poor performance on her daughter's part.

Until recently, Mrs. Phillips has been satisfied with the education of her daughters in Hillsborough schools. Now, with the elimination of counselors in the elementary schools, where they are needed most urgently, Mrs. Phillips believes more youth will "turn bad" and never complete high school. Furthermore, she thinks classes are too large and floating classes are not a good idea for elementary-school-aged children. In elementary schools more help is needed so that the children don't fall behind in their work to the point where they can't ever catch up, Mrs. Phillips believes. Moreover, she would have supervisors and longer planning periods, so that teachers would not have to take too much work home with them.

Mrs. Phillips described herself and her husband as being very interested in their daughters' futures. Having attended Metropolitan School of Music for five years on Saturdays, Carol entered Wellesley College as a piano major this past fall. She is doing very well, according to her mother, but does not find it challenging enough. Carol has a new interest in psychology and her mother has encouraged her to pursue it. However, she would like Carol to continue with music, which could serve as a hobby. Mrs. Phillips said she'd be delighted if her older daughter decides to become a school psychologist. Considering Shirley's talent with her hands, as well as her artistic and sewing ability, the Phillipses could see their younger daughter becoming a decorator. Furthermore, it is expected that some day both girls will marry.

Mrs. Phillips has mixed feelings about her neighborhood, which is comprised of a majority of middle-class and many working-class people. She is dissatisfied with the neighborhood, and the nearby school in which she teaches because of some juvenile behavior problems. She stresses the need for more parental supervision. Otherwise, any amount of cohesiveness in a neighborhood will be insufficient when it is a problem of coping with occasional juvenile misbehavior. Though she is most troubled by these discipline problems, and would like to change them, she thinks the people are the best thing about her neighborhood and knows 150 to 175 of them. The Phillipses' immediate neighborhood of two blocks has formed a block association, which has increased this family's satisfaction. Within this association, caring about one's neighbors has greatly increased, and its members can talk about common problems of the area. Police law enforcement is considered just by Mrs. Phillips. She would like to see, however, more police protection. Generally, Mrs. Phillips sees the area as average, tending to safe.

The Phillipses have never considered moving away from their neighborhood, but Mrs. Phillips would like a larger house within this section. They have been living in their present seven-room house for about ten years. The Phillipses own their single-family home. Both daughters have their own bedrooms and the parents occupy the third one. There is also one kitchen, living room, dining room, and basement. They own a radio, television, and two telephones. They also have a stereo and a piano.

If she ever needed help, Mrs. Phillips would turn to her two sisters and their husbands or her neighbor across the street. (Her sisters were the deciding factor in her move to Hillsborough). She sees their families several times during the course of a week. Though she has known her sisters all her life, she has known the neighbor only thirteen years.

The decision-making pattern in this household is largely equalitarian. Non-crisis decisions are shared equally by mother and father, with two major exceptions. First of all, Mrs. Phillips makes all the decisions traditionally connected with her role as mother and wife. She plans the meals and cooks them and has decided on the number of children to have. Now that her daughters are older, she will no longer take care of them all of the time when they are sick because they are more capable now of doing it themselves. Since she works, both parents can share responsibility. Parent-teacher conferences are no longer her sole responsibility; she shares them with her husband. With older daughters, her duty to help them decide what to wear has been replaced by the girls consulting each other. Mr. Phillips' has sole power to choose his occupation.

This family actively participates in numerous and varied organizations. Mr. Phillips is in a play-reading group; he is a PTA and block association member and belongs to church groups. Mrs. Phillips participates in a church-connected organization too. In addition, she belongs to the PTA, Nursery Association for the Education of Young Children, Foreign Student Exchange Committee, and the County Chapter of the Association of the Study of Black Life and History. During her freshman year at college, Carol has become a member of the choir and the Black Students Organization. Shirley belongs to the Girl Scouts, Foreign Student Exchange Committee, a youth group at the YWCA, and Future Teachers of America.

Consequently, it appears from the above discussion that the Phillipses are a stable, middle-class, black family living in a combined middle-class, working-class black neighborhood. The stability of their family is increased by regular church attendance and dinner-time activities. More important, perhaps, familial stability is enhanced by the respect accorded each member, especially in making decisions. For example, when a daughter must make a decision regarding her future, she discusses the matter with her parents and vice versa; when a church had to be selected, Mr. and Mrs. Phillips chose independently. As Mrs. Phillips has stated, she could have never forced her husband to compromise on a matter of deep personal concern to him.

Mr. Phillips' position as a postal worker seems to indicate that his education has not fully paid off. Mrs. Phillips' decision to go back to work after her children were older seems to represent a desire to increase the family's socioeconomic status within society's main stratification system and thereby obtain the additional material benefits which accompany financial well-being.

It appears, moreover, that Mr. and Mrs. Phillips have been very effective in socializing their children. This socialization, when added to the factors of an increasingly open society for mobility, available familial resources, and the children's ability, indicates that Carol and Shirley should be able to achieve their goals.

Though the Phillipses are not an extended family as commonly defined, they maintain a very close relationship with Mrs. Phillips' two sisters and their families.

DOING WHAT COMES NATURALLY
Karin Caruso

Mr. and Mrs. Emerson have been happily married fifteen years. Samuel is thirty-seven and his wife, June, is thirty-five. They live with their two children in a middle-class residential area. Samuel, Jr. is thirteen and in the eighth grade. His ten-year-old sister, Sarah, is in the fifth grade. Mr. and Mrs. Emerson are originally from New England but they have lived in the upstate New York area since their marriage.

Both Mr. and Mrs. Emerson graduated from college. Mrs. Emerson is an elementary school teacher and her husband, who has obtained a MS degree, is the head of the science department in a public high school. Mr. and Mrs. Emerson are employed by the same public school system and have excellent performance records.

Mrs. Emerson was happy that family illnesses were minimal this past year. Her husband suffered no illness that was serious enough to confine him to bed. She, however, spent about one week in bed while recovering from a minor operation. Since the children have been inoculated or have had all of the usual childhood diseases, their only illnesses were minor viruses and the common cold. Mrs. Emerson considered this fortunate since she is more likely to stay home from work and care for the children if illness strikes.

The family's religious preference is Methodist. They do not regularly attend church, but are somewhat "holiday goers." However, they feel that this is no measure of their belief. Their children attend Sunday School moderately during the winter, but never on a beautiful summer day. And, the parents are members of the Church Couples Club.

The family is very close, with both parents sharing disciplinary responsibilities. The children are assigned few chores beyond keeping their bedrooms picked up. Spring cleaning and any outside work is usually done by the family as a whole. The children are responsible enough to decide when they should do their own homework. This is done at their respective desks in their bedrooms while sometimes listening to a radio in the background. The parents offer assistance equally. Mrs. Emerson helps with English, while her husband's assistance is concentrated in science and mathematics. She said laughingly, that if it was a foreign language, neither of them would be of much help.

A typical day would start with the mother and father waking at six-thirty. The children are awakened at seven a.m. Mrs. Emerson helps her daughter decide what to wear; but Samuel, Jr. makes his own decisions. By seven-thirty, the family is ready to sit down to a big breakfast. Mr. Emerson is off to work by eight o'clock, and the children catch separate school buses at about eight-thirty. The mother leaves for school at eight-forty since she takes a more direct route, which gives her plenty of time to see everyone off safely.

The family members eat lunch at their designated times while in their respective schools. Since the children ride home by bus, Mrs. Emerson arrives home before them at about three-fifteen. Samuel, Jr. and Sarah bid their friends on their buses good-bye between three-thirty and three-forty, as their mother awaits them with an afternoon snack.

The children may watch television, or if there is dissent over the program, Samuel, Jr. usually wanders to the set in the recreation room. If it's nice outside, the children may go and play with their friends in the neighborhood. But if the weather is bad, their friends are invited into the playroom in the basement — possibly for a game of ping-pong. Once a week Sarah has her Girl Scout meeting and biweekly Samuel, Jr. meets with his Boy Scout troop.

Mr. Emerson rarely arrives home before four-fifteen. His first move is towards his favorite chair with the *New York Times* in one hand. He may put on the stereo to create a relaxing background. Since he and his wife both work, it is not unusual for him to lend a hand to his wife in picking up the house. He and his wife are capable of discussing the headlines, but afternoon conversation is generally more related to the events of the day and issues which they are immediately affected by or responsible for.

The children may or may not come in before dinner to start their homework. Dinner is usually served around "sixish," but changes in time for convenience-sake are easily made. Mrs. Emerson does most of the cooking and Sarah often likes to help. The meal is planned by mother with welcomed suggestions from her husband and her children alike. The dinner conversation attempts to include everyone and may range from a movie, to a family member's new bicycle, to plans for the weekend or summer vacation. After dinner, Sarah clears the table and Samuel, Jr. disposes of the left-overs while Mrs. Emerson stacks the dishwasher.

By seven o'clock, one may find the Emerson family gathered around the television or each member about his or her own activity. Mr. and Mrs. Emerson may correct papers and draw up lesson plans. The children may do their homework or they may play a game such as Monopoly. School activities are usually attended by the family.

So pass the hours between seven and ten, and then it is the children's bed time. Time for bed is not unalterable but may vary with the evening's activities. Therefore, the children rarely contest their time for sleep. Mr. and Mrs. Emerson enjoy being alone together. They usually watch the eleven o'clock news. They may watch a movie, listen to records, or converse. The lights in the Emerson home are extinguished by twelve.

Both Saturdays and Sundays are family days. The family sleeps until nine and Mr. Emerson often makes the breakfast to give his wife a rest. On occasion, the children may be up and out playing before the parents awake, leaving a note to say where they can be found. The children may attend Sunday School at ten or the family may go to church at eleven. Sunday is a day for relaxing. Activity is rarely predictable for any hour of the day. In the winter, the family frequently goes skiing for the day or sledding around the neighborhood. Summer may find members working in the yard. The children may play with friends or go swimming at the club pool to which the family belongs.

The family may go to visit friends or relatives. If they remain home, a big meal is served at three o'clock. And the evening snack is often accompanied by friends or relatives invited for coffee and a chat.

Mr. and Mrs. Emerson each chose their professions before marriage. Mrs. Emerson does not work during the summer. She spends her summer months taking care of her children and relaxing. She catches up on some of the reading she wanted to pursue during the school year. Her husband, as the head of the science department, makes about one and one-half times what she earns. He remains employed by the school board during the months of June and July, when he helps organize the high school curriculum for the coming year. This summer job adds about 20 percent more to his yearly income. The combined family income contributes to comfortable but not luxury living. The Emersons anticipate that their children will attend college. Parents have not attempted to influence their children's choice of adult occupation, at such an early age. Samuel, Jr. is presently enthralled with science and would like to go into research, while Sarah wants to become just like her mother and be an elementary school teacher.

If a parent-teacher conference was called, Mrs. Emerson would try to schedule it at a time when she and her husband could attend. Teachers frequent the Emerson home for meetings and social occasions, but not to discuss Samuel's or Sarah's school problems. The children are quite bright; and they have no problems either academic or social in school.

Unlike household decisions made on an equal basis, the parents make political decisions on an individual basis. As school teachers, the parents are members of the PTA and a teacher's union. Mrs. Emerson belongs to the Women's League and her husband is a member of a local men's club.

The Emersons are close to seven families in their neighborhood. However, when they entertain, more than seven neighborhood names will appear on their guest list, as friends. It is a racially mixed neighborhood, with a solid middle-class status. Because of compatible incomes and interests, there is no noticeable racial segragation. The Emersons entertain and are invited in the homes of neighbors. The Emersons enjoy their home environment and have no desire to move.

Their eight-room house, which they own, is a four-bedroom semi-colonial. It has all the conveniences of any other middle-class home. What Mrs. Emerson enjoys most about her neighborhood is the opportunity for privacy as a family unit, complemented by healthy and friendly surroundings. The Emersons are self-sufficient, but could easily turn to their next-door neighbors for assistance. They are close friends with the engineer and his family who moved next door five years ago. And, if Mrs. Emerson had any power to change her neighborhood, her request would be to stop building more houses and to put an embargo on developers who cut down all of "my trees."

Mr. and Mrs. Emerson are not exactly racial-integrators. They were not the first black family to move into the neighborhood. Mrs. Emerson said that the neighborhood had no "noticeable" racism. However, she feels some of the same patronizing attitudes — "Did the school principal remember my name, among all those people at the PTA meeting ... because of what we are?" — that many black suburban families experience. The Emerson family also leans toward social, fraternal, and professional clubs, and does not ally itself with social action organizations.

The equalitarian locus of family power in child-rearing, recreation, and other roles is probably due to the fact that both parents work, although Mrs. Emerson seems to have slightly more influence on the children's plans than does the father. This may be partially attributed to the fact that she spends more time with the children during the summer.

The Emerson family is stable, is apparently a more well-adjusted family than most. Mr. and Mrs. Emerson both came from stable middle-class families; and they look forward with optimism for a satisfactory future for their children.

Because of their backgrounds, Mr. and Mrs. Emerson both had the opportunity to attend college. Both parents chose the teaching profession because they realized that it was the one most accessible to them as blacks at that time. Mr. Emerson attained a higher level of education than his wife.

Samuel and June Emerson were married at ages twenty-two and twenty respectively. Mrs. Emerson had both of her children before the age of twenty-five. Her "null" fertility from age twenty-five on supports the finding that college-educated black women have a low fertility rate. This is especially true of black teachers.

Mr. and Mrs. Emerson have gained more than a middle-class socioeconomic status. They have also gained and maintained a happy and healthy family.

Chapter **6** WORKING–CLASS
INNOVATORS

The family patterns of six working-class black kinship units are presented in this chapter. Five of the six families are two-parent; one intact family has a very sick father who is not expected to live. Spouses in two families are in second marriages; death or divorce contributed to the disintegration of the first marriages. The wife is a high school graduate in two of the families, and probably a high-school dropout in the other four cases, although education is not mentioned in two cases. The husband is a high school dropout, having completed only the tenth or eleventh grades, in three cases, and an elementary school dropout in one case. Mention of the husband's education was omitted in two cases but is believed to be at the high school level or less. Four of the families live in inner-city black ghettoes and two live outside cities — one in a suburb and the other in an isolated rural area.

The Chandler household consists of husband, wife, and four children, together with the mother's sister and the wife of one of the sons. The father is a self-employed junkyard dealer and the mother, a part-time receptionist. Ms. Eaton has four children derived from two marriages. Mr. Eaton, a sandblaster, died from a disease connected with his occupation. His widow works as a case aide for the school system. The Brown family is a six-child family. The wife and mother is a nurse's aide and the husband's occupation is not given. The Farmers have two children; the father is hospitalized and not expected to live much longer. When employed, he was a semiskilled worker; the mother is a cook. The Wilson household is a two-parent family that includes seven children and one grandchild. The father is a janitor and the mother, a nurse's aide. The Henderson family lives in public housing and has two children, one an adult offspring of a first marriage that was dissolved because of the death

96

of the wife, and the other a young child from the present marriage. The mother does not work outside the home.

In five of the six working-class households, the mother is in the labor force. In all households where there is a father present, he is employed, or was employed in the case of the hospitalized man. The wages of the offspring also are significant in family finances in five of the six households. These families exist on annual incomes that range from slightly above the official poverty line up to the national median.

POOLING EARNINGS FOR FAMILY SURVIVAL
Alan Haymon

The Chandler family lives in a two-family home in Chicago, Illinois. The Chandlers are in the process of paying off the mortgage on their modest house. The exterior of the 13-room house (which includes a finished attic) is in need of painting and minor repair. The home is equipped with attractive but old furniture. Several televisions and a pair of stereo systems are present, as well as many modern appliances. The interior of the home is immaculate. The driveway is laced with cars (the Chandler family owns three of varying vintage, including a 5-year old Buick, the newest of the collection). Mrs. Chandler was quite cooperative and anxious to show and discuss the home and several "special" pieces of furniture. The dining room table received particular mention as the first piece of furniture purchased for the house about 20 years ago. Mrs. Chandler, a rather soft-spoken small woman in her early fifties, exhibits obvious pride and happiness when speaking of her home. The cleanliness of the household is a result of her personal efforts.

When asked, Mrs. Chandler described the members of the household as being very close to each other and seldom at odds with one another. Although rather quiet, Mrs. Chandler obviously commands the respect of the children as evidenced by how readily they respond to her commands. The youngest son, James, was asked to empty the garbage while I was present and he heeded this request immediately. When asked about obedience, Mrs. Chandler said, "I've raised four boys and none of them have ever talked back to me, not even once."

Mr. Chandler's only participation in the conversation was to greet me with a resounding "hello and make yourself at home" upon my arrival. A rather muscular man in his mid-fifties, Mr. Chandler has an imposing voice which also commands respect. He clearly is *the* "man of the house."

Mr. and Mrs. Chandler have been married for 34 years. They have had what Mrs. Chandler described as "many lean years." Now, however, Mr. Chandler owns and operates a junk and scrap yard which provides the family with a livable income but not much for luxury living. Mrs. Chandler works part-time as a receptionist in an office and earns about half as much as her husband. The family would experience great difficulty if it had to exist on the single income of the mother or the father. Even their combined income is less than the national median.

The Chandlers have four sons ranging in age from 17 to 33. They all live at home. Also living in the household are the oldest son's wife and Mrs. Chandler's younger sister. Mrs. Chandler's sister has been living with the Chandlers for almost 10 years, ever since the death of her husband.

All of the Chandler offspring, except the youngest who attends high school, work full-time. The oldest son has been married for six years and is an auto mechanic for a local car dealer. His earnings are about the same as his father's. The wife of the oldest son works part-time as a secretary in a physician's office and earns about as much as her mother-in-law. The second son works for his father at the junk yard and performs a variety of odd tasks, including driving the tow truck to pick up scrap autos. The third son is employed full-time as a maintenance man for the Public School System.

When asked about the family's combined earnings, Mrs. Chandler's quick reply was this: "My sons work and earn their own money, they live with me and pay no rent because we ask for none. More often than not on their own they offer money for the weekly groceries and the mortgage payments. I usually take it and occasionally I don't. But if we were in trouble, we would simply all pool our earnings to survive." She said that her sister gets a check from the government, and "if it's not enough we don't worry." Thus the Chandler household is comprised of eight members. All of the sons were born and raised in Chicago, except the oldest, who was born in Alabama as were Mr. and Mrs. Chandler. The family has lived in Chicago for about 31 years. They report that they came to Chicago because they had been told work could be found there.

Mr. and Mrs. Chandler met in Alabama and married over 30 years ago. They both came from rather poor families, although Mrs. Chandler states that her family owned the house and land they lived on. Mr. Chandler's family was less fortunate and survived primarily by farming. Neither set of parents received much education. However, Mrs. Chandler was the third of 11 children. She said, "My parents were much quicker to discipline our kids." She described them as the kind who believe in kids behaving and knowing right from wrong.

Clearly Mrs. Chandler was the undisputed spokesperson for her contemporary family. But contrary to what one might expect, Mrs. Chandler said that her husband administers all punishments and acts as household disciplinarian. Mrs. Chandler's role in the discipline process is to single out who has to be punished and to indicate why. When asked if she and her husband usually concur about such matters, she said, "yes."

All of the Chandler boys, except the second, completed (or are in the process of completing) high school. Mrs. Chandler said that the second child "has been mentally deficient since birth and wasn't able to finish school." He attended the local public school and took classes for slower students, but did not receive any special education services. When asked why he never attended a special school, Mrs. Chandler stated that "We didn't think he needed any special school. He can learn like anyone else; it just takes him a while longer. Right now he's learned how to help my husband run the scrap yard." The only individual in the household who attended college is the wife of the oldest son; she quit after two years. The oldest son went to mechanics school upon graduating from high school.

Mrs. Chandler states that all of her sons "had done fair in school," and that the last child now in high school is "doing O.K." For this reason she never had to stipulate a specific time for him or others to do homework. She tries to attend local Parent-Teacher Association meetings and has always done so in the past. Mrs. Chandler believes that you cannot force education on anyone. She said, "I have always insisted that my kids graduate from high school and go on if they so desire. I wanted very much for one or more of my sons to go on to college and thought that my oldest son would, because he is so smart, but he didn't want to. Now, the youngest is the only child left in school, and he's just not cut out for college. I'd be satisfied seeing him become a foreman or something."

Mrs. Chandler was quick to say that none of her boys had ever been in any trouble with the law. But later in the interview she revealed that the third son had once gotten into a bit of trouble. He had been driving a friend home when he was in high school; the friend pulled out a gun and shot at someone they passed on the street. No one was injured and charges against her son were dropped before the case ever got to court. Mrs. Chandler more or less dismissed the incident as being very "unintentional" on her son's part.

Mrs. Chandler said that she and her husband's main goal in raising their children was to "teach them right from wrong" and instill in them a belief in God. She went on to say that they believed no matter what a person did for a living, as long as he did it well, then he was successful. Thus, they were very proud of their sons, whom they considered to be hard workers.

The members of the family belong to the Baptist Church. One son, however, joined the Methodist Church. Mrs. Chandler and her sister attend church weekly and often are accompanied by her oldest son and his wife. None of the other boys attends church very much, but, according to Mrs. Chandler, "they all have faith." She further mentioned that the entire family had attended church earlier in the year when Mr. Chandler suffered a mild stroke. Other than a stroke which immobilized Mr. Chandler for a month earlier in the year, none of the family members has been very sick. Mrs. Chandler's sister has what was described as "a nervous condition."

The influence of religion on Mrs. Chandler's life was quite apparent. There was a large Bible on display in the living room and a large painting of Jesus Christ in the room. Mrs. Chandler states that attendance in Sunday school or church services was mandatory for all her sons when they were quite young, but that she could not and would not force them to attend as adults.

The Chandler family receives morning and evening daily newspapers as well as a couple of magazines such as *Essence* and *Jet*. The family receives most news by watching television and reading the newspapers. Mrs. Chandler spends four to five hours a day watching television and talking on the telephone to friends. She watches the news daily, several soap operas, and an occasional detective story. Often, she views the television with her husband, who misses the news on weekdays because of his work. He watches late evening programs when he is not out on the street with the "fellas."

Televison is very much a part of the Chandler household. Mrs. Chandler and her sister watch several hours daily; the oldest son and his wife watch television together with family members two or three hours in the evening. The other three sons spend more of their evening hours "out in the streets." On Sundays the men in the household watch football, baseball, or whatever sport is on while Mrs. Chandler and her sister attend morning and evening church services. Sunday is the only time that all in the household eat dinner together. Except on Sundays, the family hardly ever eats together because of the work schedules. For example, the father and son who work in the junk yard often work until 7:00 p.m. and therefore miss the 5:00 p.m. dinner eaten by five members of the household. The oldest son works until after 6:00 p.m. and misses the 5:00 o'clock dinner hour also. Thus Sunday is the only day they have a "family dinner," as Mrs. Chandler puts it. Though Mrs. Chandler insists that the family is quite close, seldom do they do anything together. She did make reference to trips the entire family used to make to Alabama 10 or more years ago to see their parents and grandparents. They do not take these together anymore.

Mrs. Chandler's sister helps her on weekends and she usually cooks the weekday meals since Mrs. Chandler works part-time. Her sister watches television often and occasionally sews.

Mrs. Chandler had mixed emotions about the neighborhood they live in. In general she seems moderately satisfied with it. She expresses a favorable opinion of her neighbors but said that she fears the rising crime rate. The neighborhood itself is predominantly black and best described as working class with a few lower-class residents. When asked about children in the community, she responded, "I can only talk about my own sons, and I know they are good. All I am sure of is that crime is rising fast in this area and I don't think the police really care that much one way or another about it." For this reason she describes the neighborhood as being of "average safety." Mrs. Chandler knows about a dozen or so other families in her neighborhood. She feels that in time of trouble she could depend on her neighbor two doors away whom she has known for 20 years. She also expresses great faith in her first cousin, whom she has known all her life, as well as another cousin who also lives in Chicago.

Mrs. Chandler said: "Now that we're almost finished paying for the house, the neighborhood has begun to go down. But we've worked hard to get this house and we're going to stay here. Besides, all the boys are grown up now, we don't need to move."

PERSEVERANCE AND SELF–HELP
Susan Kluver

Ms. Eaton has been a Providence, Rhode Island resident all of her life. One year after her second marriage, she and her husband bought a modest two-family home in the oldest, most stable section of the black community in Providence. Ms. Eaton was 25 at the time of her second marriage. She has been married before at the age of 18 and was divorced within two years. A son was born of this marriage. He now is 35 years old. Ms. Eaton referred only briefly to this former marriage and the problems of her oldest son, who had, as a teenager, been arrested for theft and who later as an adult was in and out of jail on weekends for nonsupport of his own wife and family.

Her memory, as well as her present emotional life, were invested in the family from her second marriage — a marriage which lasted for a decade and which ended 18 years ago due to the death of her husband. Mr. Eaton's death was related to his occupation. He had been a sand-blaster; when he developed a lung condition he changed his occupation to take up barbering. However, his lung condition was to lead to his death two years later.

Although Ms. Eaton had spoken acceptingly and affectionately of her eldest son, she described in greater detail her three children of the second marriage. Yvonne, her oldest daughter, had left home two years previously to join the Navy. Ms. Eaton spoke of Yvonne as a good student but without a strong interest, "still floundering." Ms. Eaton feels that Yvonne may be tiring of the service already after only a year. She had joined the service in order to travel and obtain different experiences. After completing the local high school, Yvonne had gone away for two years to Knoxville College in Tennessee and then had finished her college work closer to home at Rhode Island State. For a while after completing college, Yvonne worked in a boutique and lived in the downstairs apartment of

104

Ms. Eaton's home. Ms. Eaton thought that someday Yvonne might really be most fulfilled by opening up her own small boutique. She allowed as how Yvonne would need to conserve her money made in the service.

A son, Samuel, age 23, was born two years after the birth of Yvonne. Samuel, as all of her children, "loved school and didn't want to miss a day." Samuel, who had initially had aspirations to become a schoolteacher, was counseled away from this field by his mother at the time of his graduation from high school. Ms. Eaton, at that time, was concerned about the surplus of teachers. Samuel had attended two years of college at Oberlin College and had returned to complete his junior and senior years at the University of Rhode Island. Samuel was a strong support to his mother. He resided downstairs in the apartment that Yvonne had formerly used, worked part time to help earn money, and did the marketing during the week for the meals that he and his mother shared together. Samuel always had a part-time job during high school as well.

The youngest daughter, Ruth, was born two years after Samuel. She, like the other children, was "well behaved" but showed a "normal amount of adolescent rebelliousness." She was an excellent student in grammar school and wished to study medicine. By the time she completed high school, Ms. Eaton humorously noted, she didn't wish to continue with any schooling. "I had to think quickly," Ms. Eaton said, to help her daughter make a sound career decision. She recommended to her daughter that she enroll in a 16-month course in laboratory technician's work given at a nearby university because of her daughter's earlier interest in science and medicine. To Ms. Eaton's great relief, her daughter accepted her advice and has now graduated and is working as a lab technician in a Hartford area hospital. Ruth has recently married a fellow lab technician and the young couple have established themselves in a new apartment in Hartford, which is close to the site of their work.

Ms. Eaton characterized her marriage to Mr. Eaton as an extremely happy and companionable one, in which all decisions were mutually arrived at. Although she herself had come from a family of four children, and her own father had died when she was 4, she never considered that this marriage, which was such a strong one, would be terminated by her husband's death. She spoke at length of her husband's passing as a devastating time in her life. At the same moment that she recognized the honesty of these feelings, she stated that it was impossible to dwell on such feelings. It was an important concern to her to demonstrate to her children, and especially to her son, Samuel, who had expressed terrible feelings of loss and insecurity, that she, as well as his older brother from the first marriage, would look after Samuel and see to his well-being.

There were many examples cited by Ms. Eaton which demonstrated the sense of well-being and solidarity her second family had created. It was customary for her and her husband to take the children on Sunday outings to the zoo or to see the foliage in autumn. She and Mr. Eaton would often stop with the children for dinner out on weekends. They had begun to redo the upstairs apartment. They had made a den for themselves that was off-limits to the children. Ms. Eaton proudly showed me the room with a small bar. As she moved about the room one could sense that she moved easily in her mind back to those shared moments; and they were a consolation and support to her. Mr. Eaton was able around the house; not only could he do minor repairs, but he was a good craftsman and had paneled the living room with pine. The wood paneling and the leather furniture and wall-to-wall carpeting created an air of warmth and tastefulness in the small, main living room of that apartment.

The family life-style was altered substantially by Mr. Eaton's death; where before all decisions and disciplining of the children had been shared and both had assisted the children with their homework, looked after them when they were sick, or cooked when needed, she now assumed responsibility for all aspects of the children's development. Ms. Eaton commented that she often felt like her mother, and it seemed most probable that she derived her strength to go on in part because of the experience of loss of her own father as a child. She had seen her mother make a life for her and her brothers and sister, so that internally she had a prior model and sense of survival through an earlier family ordeal.

Ms. Eaton had worked during the early years of her marriage and had had the assistance of a cousin to care for the children; during the years following Mr. Eaton's death the financial circumstances of the family worsened. Ms. Eaton's job as a computer operator and then as a case aide in a federally funded school department program provided an annual salary slightly above the official poverty line. This salary was augmented by veteran's and social security payments for each of the children until they reached the age of 21.

Although the apartment downstairs had been renovated approximately four years previously and could bring in a monthly income of a few hundred dollars, Ms. Eaton had not yet earned that income from the apartment because of her concern for assisting her immediate family members. Prior to her own children living in the apartment and paying modest rental, a cousin rented it for minimal rent but also assisted in the care of the children. At considerable cost to her own sense of financial security, Ms. Eaton has supported the needs of her extended family. Indeed, she is looked to by her brothers and sister as the main source of strength in their family. Interestingly, when asked to whom she would turn in case of emergencies, she said, "My own children, they have more sense than any of my other relatives."

Ms. Eaton realized after her husband's death that she would need to encourage both closeness and independence among her children. As they grew up she stressed the need for working together to help and look out for each other. There continued to be regular meal times for communication when the children could "let it all hang out." Ms. Eaton instituted a time for herself, when she first came home from work extremely tired. Although at first, she recalled, the children came clamoring around her with news and questions, soon they came to respect her need for repose. She had helped the children with their homework before her husband's death; now this responsibility, along with all the new burdens of life, seemed too much. She recalled how she had told the children directly, "that's your responsibility now, to work out your homework." She observed that she had made the children less dependent upon her, more self-reliant, and that it was in the children's best interest that she did this. They seemed to accept her new rules.

Ms. Eaton characterized the family as a close one in which humor and mutual caring and support of each other had carried them through difficult years. One example of closeness, which demonstrates to this day her children's ability to ask for and receive nurturing from their mother, is their half-humorous, half-serious expectation that she will bring them treats from parties or functions she might attend. Since she and her husband would regularly visit with friends and attend weekend parties, they would regularly bring back treats for the children, and Ms. Eaton, by continuing this practice, was strengthening memory of the father at the same moment that she was demonstrating her ability to carry on alone. She said, emphatically, that she never forgot to bring them something.

Ms. Eaton described her own relationship to "causes" and the community in which she lived as basically a nonjoiner of groups or political movements. Although both she and her husband were Protestant, she ceased attending church after her hospitalization nearly two decades ago for the removal of a kidney. She has resided in this same community, in the same house, for 26 years. She is satisfied with the neighborhood, knows her neighbors on either side of her, an Italian and an Armenian family. She stated half in jest, half seriously, "familiarity breeds contempt." She characterized the neighborhood as a mixed working-class community. She felt that police services were relatively unused since the neighborhood was safe and quiet.

Much of Ms. Eaton's leisure time, when she can find some in the summer and during school holidays, is spent reading and attending good movies. She rarely looks at television unless there is an interesting movie or programs about different cultures. She regularly reads the paper, and with the resumption of her own schooling this year at Rhode Island State, much of this spare time may be given over to reading or preparing for schoolwork. The family's Sunday routine does not vary much from that during the week. Mother and son Samuel have breakfast together and then Samuel goes off to his part-time job. They have Sunday dinner together; both read the paper and perhaps watch a few television programs if there is something of interest on. Ms. Eaton stressed that when the children were younger she discouraged them from watching television and urged them to use their imaginations. The children had been active in sports. Her own activities had become more constrained after her husband's death; whereas before she had attended house parties and dances on weekends, she rarely did any of these things as a widow.

When asked to sum up the goals of their family life, Ms. Eaton said she was working towards the independence and security of her children but could never guarantee such a state. For herself, she would like to grow old gracefully. When we talked about her life moving into a different phase, when all of her children would have completed their schooling or training and were "out in the world," Ms. Eaton recognized the forthcoming loneliness in store for her, but seemed to ward it off by turning to her son nearby and laughingly suggesting that he "stick around for a while." Still, her decision to return to school, which she said she should have begun 10 years ago, is a recognition on her part of the need to improve her financial status and broaden her associations. Certainly her student status will provide her with a new source of institutional support in her development.

ONE FOR ALL AND ALL FOR ONE
Kathleen Dickinson Rockwood

The Browns' house is well kept but in need of a new coat of paint. The rooms were dimly lit but there seemed to be a great deal of chatter and noise emerging from various rooms. All six children were home, including Mr. and Mrs. Brown and a guest. Jimmy, twenty, was asked to "entertain" me while Mrs. Brown finished up some chores. I could hear her rapidly speaking voice in the background, directing her children to finish the dinner and other tasks. She finally came in, followed by her husband.

The conversation began with questions about their roles as parents within this family; Mrs. Brown did most of the talking, being more gregarious than her husband, a tall, slender, good-looking man of forty-six, who sat back with a pleasant smile on his face most of the time. However, she constantly looked to her husband for recognition and asked for his verbal reassurance. They both came to the consensus that there existed an equal balance of influence between them in family decision-making, with a few exceptions. Mrs. Brown thought that it was her domain to prepare the meals and see that the children were dressed properly. Her husband controlled the domain of the financial and purchasing aspect of the household. Upon saying that, Mrs. Brown pointed to the sofa, chairs, and other major items which her husband had bought years ago without her help. "He just came home with it all!" But she didn't seem to mind his dominance in this area. She also added with a chuckle, "Honey, you decide on how many children we have, don't you?"

Every so often in the midst of a conversation, Mrs. Brown would correlate what was being said with religion. It became rapidly obvious that politics and other outside forces had little influence on this family. None of the family members was involved in any association in the community, except Jehovah's Witnesses. "The family unit is the most important thing to us; everyone in government and politics is so corrupt. How can they

110

help us achieve a better life in the next world when all their concerns are so worldly? We are not anxious about this life, but are awaiting the times of eternal peace when Armageddon comes." Even though Mrs. Brown expressed these views, it was obvious the beliefs were those of the whole family. Just from observing the family, the close-knit ties became evident, permeating the household with a sense of contentment. Perhaps much of this could be attributed to their secure allegiance to the Jehovah's Witnesses and their accompanying hopes of future attainment.

Being a Jehovah's Witness calls for living a strict religious life. "If I didn't know that you were morally clean I wouldn't be speaking to you." Because of this and other similar notions the Browns stick to themselves; they restrict their friendships basically to the brothers and sisters of the Kingdom Hall. Mrs. Brown added:

Actually, I feel kind of bad about it, since we've lived here nearly twenty years, but I really don't know any of the neighbors well personally. I know them all by sight and say "hi" but that's it. As a whole the people here are very nice, I just don't have time between my Bible studies, work, and the family. Do you know that I have one neighbor who gives us a turkey every year? That's such a kind thing to do. There's one neighbor who really annoys me though ... the lady next door. She and her sister sit at the windows every day and just put their nose into everyone's business. One day this woman accused my son of stealing something from her car. Well, I found out who did it and told her. Do you think she'd say she was sorry about accusing my son? No, not at all, instead she continually screams at my kids. My children are so good I even can't believe it. I honestly think the neighbors are jealous that they obey me so well. You just can't let your kids go running off into anyone's house. Lord knows there are so many horrible things today with the drug problem and all. I'm scared of that, so I control my children pretty much. The little ones play right outside. If they want to go across the street to ask a friend to come out to play they must ask me first. They do that very thing most of the time. They know that the one thing my husband and I can't tolerate is downright lying and disobeying. They get punished good if that happens. But you see they're good kids, maybe that's because of the way we have brought them up. I've learned that the only way to raise children is to tell them the truth at all times. We tell them everything they might question — from drugs, petting, to other concerns they might have. We don't want our kids learning these things incorrectly on the streets.

Mr. and Mrs. Brown are bringing up their family with values and ideas which both contradict and comply with the parents' past. "First of all," said Mrs. Brown, "I was raised as a Baptist. My mother made us all go to church; she never told us why. Matter of fact, she never answered many of our questions. We don't do that with our kids; we tell them everything. When I was a Baptist we had no hope. Then I took up studying the Bible. We teach our children what the Bible says. This is the right way."

Mrs. Brown confirmed, though, that she really had a nice childhood and family life. Her father was a barber and managed to do pretty well. "My father loved my mother so much he wouldn't let her work. Isn't that nice?" The one thing that really stood out among her many recollections was her education. She said rather proudly that she did excellently in school when she was young. Now, she confided, she didn't feel half as smart as she used to:

When I was in the first grade I was so smart I was promoted to fourth grade. I believe I finished elementary school at 10 years of age. My father made me stay home for a year because he didn't like to see me going through school so fast. I went back to school but my father was still concerned. You see I was just as mature educationally as my grade but didn't act that way. Come senior year my parents took me out of school. Actually, I guess I could have stayed in school but we couldn't even afford food. I was really upset about this and almost had a nervous breakdown. It still bothers me that my parents didn't motivate me to complete school. We lived on a farm, and there were other things for me to do. I used to wonder why my father didn't push me on. When I was younger I thought it was because of lack of love. It's funny, I'm not as smart now, but I still hold the same high hopes. Do you know that I have had the biggest urge to go to the university and be an English teacher? That's what I always wanted to do. But since I can't be a teacher I'm satisfied being a Nurse's Aide. Do you realize I go to work to relax? I have so much to do at home with the kids and all that I actually look forward to going to the hospital. It's such a fulfilling job. You see, people need a little understanding and love; unfortunately they don't get enough.

She went on to speak about Mr. Brown, in reference to his background. "He was brought up as a Baptist too, but he didn't have to go to church as much. His father and mother were real farmers; we just lived on one. They were all very satisfied with what they had, and this is the way that Mr. Brown acts today. He's never been the aggressive type. What I mean is he's always been happy with the same old job; he doesn't like changes.

Whereas I could pack up and move tomorrow!" Mr. Brown completed his education up to the fifth grade level only.

Mrs. Brown was very happy to speak about her children. With the exception of the two middle children, the rest are doing about average work in school. She expressed great concern about their educational achievement. Diane, the oldest, is in the twelfth grade and is seventeen years old. She's involved in the Nurse's Aide program in her spare time. In addition, Mrs. Brown commented that she was a tremendous dancer. As far as her future plans go, Diane wants to be a business secretary. Therefore, her mother would be satisfied with her just completing high school. Edward is fifteen and is presently in the tenth grade. In his spare time he plays basketball and goes to the library to read. His greatest interest, though, is to be a mechanic. Mrs. Brown foresees that this might call for mechanic school after high school. She was very worried about the performance of both Cathy, age thirteen, who "thinks she's hot stuff," and James, age eleven; they are barely getting through school. Outside of school Cathy loves to sew or knit, while James spends most of his time catching bugs. Neither of them has expressed interests beyond that. Even though Mrs. Brown didn't want to admit it, Susan, the next to the youngest child, is her "most favorite". This little nine-year old is the carbon copy of Mrs. Brown when she was younger. She does well in school and always reads. According to her mother, the child wants to be a teacher, which means a college education. Howard, age six, is the youngest of the family. His most enjoyed pastime is playing outside. He never can have enough of it. He loves trucks and keeps talking about being a truck driver when he grows up. Mrs. Brown stressed that neither she nor her busband were pushing their children towards any specific vocation. There are apparent variations of aspirations within the family. However, she did say: "My children have to go to high school — they can't be dropouts!"

As a family they spend some time together on weekends by going for rides or going to parks. However, they all have hobbies and have to allocate individual time for these. The time when they're all together is dinner and breakfast, with the exception of the father, who has to leave early in the morning. During the night the children are usually at home. At 11:00 p.m. Mrs. Brown goes to work at the hospital while her husband stays home with the family. They both work hard for their children, averaging a sum in combined salaries just below the national median. The house has enough space for the whole family; there's a kitchen, five bedrooms, a living room, dining room, den, and two bathroooms. Mrs. Brown mentioned that they were eventually going to own the house but had to continue monthly payments for approximately five more years. "I don't know if I can wait that long because I want to move back down to South Carolina." Supposedly she and her husband moved to Centerline because of her health, but she's been dying to go back home. The family roots are firmly laid down in this particular neighborhood; therefore, it is doubtful the great move will ever occur.

Mrs. Brown made it a point to show off some of her prize possessions and furniture her husband bought, even if they were many years old. She appeared to be very proud of the household and other possessions. She rattled off all the items they owned: two televisions, four radios, one record player, and a large, white station wagon.

The problem the two middle children present to their parents is a good example of the concern and care of the Browns, on the one hand, and their lack of understanding of some child-rearing problems, on the other. Mrs. Brown stated that she first thought the two children were so apathetic because they weren't getting enough attention and love. Thus she went out and bought them extra toys and special gifts. This didn't bring about any changes so she and her husband tried talking to the children individually and to their teachers. No real headway has been made to satisfy either parent. At this point the parents are frustrated.

IN SICKNESS AND IN HEALTH
Carol Blanck Tannenhauser and Jill Kirschner Katz

Mrs. Farmer is a middle-aged, attractive, black woman. She was born in a small Pennsylvania town where she lived until her marriage to Mr. Farmer. Mr. Farmer, also a Pennsylvanian by birth, came to Rochester, New York in search of a job and finally settled into operating a screw machine for a local factory.

The Farmers live in the suburbs of Rochester. Their neighborhood is primarily a white one, in which only two black families reside. The Farmers have two sons, John, nineteen, and Seth, seventeen ("going on eighteen soon," he insists!). John graduated from high school and is now employed as a messenger at a bank. Seth is presently in his last year in high school.

The Farmers' home is a modest, green ranch house, consisting of six rooms, including three bedrooms. We were particularly impressed with the orderliness of the grounds as we approached the house with a sizeable plot of land and a well-kept rock garden to one side of the entrance. The lawn was carefully trimmed and edged. "That's Seth's job," said Mrs. Farmer. The exterior of the house was bright and cleanly painted with small white shutters brightening the pale green shingles. On the lawn, a group of high school boys, all white except for one later identified as Seth, were tossing a ball between them in a rather lazy game of touch football.

Mr. and Mrs. Farmer had been high school sweethearts, "madly in love since they were sixteen." They had married immediately following Mrs. Farmer's high school graduation, while Mr. Farmer, two years her senior and having completed only ten years of school, was employed at a Pennsylvania can factory. With the added responsibility of a wife and hearing of industrial job opportunities elsewhere, the couple moved to Rochester, where Mr. Farmer was accepted into a training program to operate a screw machine. Three years later, the Farmers had their first son, John, and moved into their present home. Previously, they had occupied a small two-room apartment. With Mr. Farmer doing well at his job, employment for Mrs. Farmer was unnecessary. Seth was born and the family was doing etremely well both financially and emotionally.

Sixteen years later, "the roof caved in" on the Farmers. Mr. Farmer had been feeling poorly for months, suffering from headaches and sharp pains in his lower back. An examination by the family physician revealed that Mr. Farmer was suffering from a terminal kidney disease that would gradually worsen and intensify, leaving him bedridden and unable to work. What was worse, the disease was revealed to be genetically transmitted, and the early signs were detected in the then nine-year-old John. As the year progressed, the disease weakened Mr. Farmer, causing him first to leave his job, and confining him to his bed, and finally making it necessary for him to be admitted to the hospital. The Farmer family, previously so secure and promising, faced a crisis in its stability, placing most of the burden for survival upon Mrs. Farmer.

Determined to instill in her young sons a sense of security and well-being, she found a job as a maid in a university fraternity house, and worked evenings in a supermarket. Convinced that a strong parent's presence was imperative to their emotional stability, she managed to confine her working hours to the times at which they were in school, or involved with their homework and was always home by 8:00 p.m., so that the three of them could go together to the hospital to visit their father. This routine kept up until John was old enough and able to get a job washing windows after school, thus allowing Mrs. Farmer to give up her own evening job.

So the Farmers held together, despite the unfortunate odds of a sick father unable to leave the hospital. Mrs. Farmer's income added to the payment of medical bills; however, the majority of them were handled by compensation and state funds. The family, according to Mrs. Farmer, became closer as a result of Mr. Farmer's illness and began eating meals together whereas they previously had "just grabbed whatever was around." "I guess we sort of had a combined guilty conscience — what with

Hal so sick," commented Mrs. Farmer. The family developed a closeness and consideration for each other, learning to sub-stitute family decisions and responsibility for the previous authority of the now absent Mr. Farmer.

The Farmer boys did average work in high school and pro-ceeded with the knowledge that "no matter what, they would finish." When Seth was old enough, he too got a job with the janitorial company where John was employed, and thus, the family income was again supplemented. Mrs. Farmer became the cook for the fraternity at which she was previously a maid, again raising family income and adding security to their existence.

Presently the Farmer family appears stable, close, and pro-mising. Mrs. Farmer enjoys cooking for the fraternity brothers, and loves the closeness she has developed with them. Her week-day routine, followed six days out of seven, consists of rising at 6:30 a.m. to cook breakfast for her sons, shopping, and head-ing to the university in time to prepare lunch for forty hungry brothers. She works until 6:00 p.m. and is home by 6:15 p.m. in time to prepare and serve dinner to her own sons at 7:00, which is the family's regular dinnertime. The three eat together and then Mrs. Farmer does the dishes while John and Seth retire to their "makeshift basketball court to shoot the hoops," for about a half hour following dinner. Then at 8:00, Seth pulls the family's old car from the garage and the family heads for the hospital to spend an hour with their father. They each spend fif-teen minutes alone with Mr. Farmer relating personal needs and events, and then conclude the visit with the four of them together, concentrating on cheering up and encouraging Mr. Farmer. They are home by 9:00 p.m., at which time John heads for his girlfriend's house and Seth to his homework, leaving a tired Mrs. Farmer to collapse in her "favorite" soft chair in front of a TV.

Out of necessity Mrs. Farmer has become the everyday head of the family. However, Mr. Farmer is still consulted on important decisions and plans. Even when Mr. Farmer was still living at home, Mrs. Farmer took an active part in raising the children. Having completed more education than her husband, she always helped the boys with their homework and in addition, took care of them when they were ill, decided what to serve for meals, cooked, helped them decide upon their clothing, went to school to talk with their teachers, decided upon the house they would live in, helped the boys find part-time work against Mr. Farmer's wishes, and decided upon what furniture to buy — "since I have to clean it," she joked. Mr. Farmer always handled the financial aspects of the family such as the children's allowances and what the family could afford to spend money on. Other important decisions were made as a group in an open-minded and fair manner.

"With their father gone I try especially hard to be open-minded with the boys. They even know what bills are coming in and how and when I pay them. If I refuse them something, you can be sure they know why. I encourage their independence and disagreement because I have to with Hal gone. But I'm not one of these old people who can't be wrong — I do apologize to them."

Even discipline is discussed in the Farmer household, with the offender present. "But my boys don't need much — they feel a responsibility to behave because of Hal's condition, I guess — neither of them has ever been in any serious trouble either at school or with the police."

As far as ideals and goals for her children, Mrs. Farmer leaves the final decision to her sons. She is a Protestant by birth and has seen to the baptism of her sons. However, they are aware that they are free to choose their own religion if they desire to change. This policy carries through to their employment futures as well. "John is a steady, family man — he has always been — I wish him only a wife whom he loves and who can give him children. Seth has always wanted to be a baseball player — I hope he makes it." Mrs. Farmer holds no stock in the idea that everyone should go on to college. According to her, John was never a student, so she insisted only that he finish high school. Seth is different, he wishes to go on to college; so his desire becomes a family decision, as college for Seth would mean sacrifices by everyone. Therefore, everyone has a say in the ultimate decision. As far as Mrs. Farmer is concerned , her goals for her sons are that they grow into "good, healthy, honest, clean men," and anything more is asking too much.

Mrs. Farmer is an energetic woman completely satisfied and involved in the affairs of her neighborhood. The area is classified as a white, working-class one, "filled with children who are well-behaved to the point that we never see the police at all!" Most of the couples belong to both the church clubs, and a neighborhood service organization. The latter runs charity drives and picnics. In addition, Mrs. Farmer is active in the PTA and attends all the school athletic events in which her son Seth participates.

As far as social action and civil rights, Mrs. Farmer remains passive. In fact, she considers herself an "outcast" from the current black freedom movement as a result of her location in a white neighborhood. She describes herself and for the most part her sons, as "not politically-minded at all," and seemed to have no commitment whatsoever to black protest. Her attitude seems to suggest that she has enough trouble keeping her own family going. She is a hard-working sincere woman, co-existing happily with her neighbors. She called hers a safe neighborhood, filled with people she knows (20-30), "who aren't rich and who don't live on top of each other, without racial prejudice, where you can always count on people, but where everyone minds their own business 'cause they're busy trying to make a living." Her only complaint was the absence of sidewalks and bus lines which cause minor inconvenience but no real problem. As far as Mrs. Farmer was concerned, she "wouldn't move even if she could afford to."

John, age nineteen, the older of the Farmer sons, is a serious-minded boy, perhaps as a result of his father's illness, or perhaps because of his own condition. He was never an outstanding student, but was always well liked by his peers and active in high school sports. However, in his junior year his own kidney condition worsened and he was forced to resign from the football team of which he was once captain. He was never a college-oriented student and always intended to only finish high school; that he did with a blaze of glory, for in his senior year he was presented the "Most Well Liked Senior Award" by the town civic association.

After high school John, who continues to live at home, secured a position at a bank where he now works as a messenger with a chance of promotion after one year's employment. In addition, he attends night school financed by the bank, but views it with extreme distaste. "I never was one for school," he smiled apologetically. But John is happy, except when he thinks of his father. He has a "great job, and an out-of-sight girl" he hopes to marry some day and with whom he hopes to raise a family. In the meantime, he loves his family and contributes heavily to its sustenance — "It's the least I can do for Mom!"

Seth, age seventeen, a senior in high school, loves being a student and is intricately involved in the athletic program. He spends his days in classes and his afternoons working out with the different teams of which he is a vital part. He plays basketball, baseball, and was named an all-state wrestling champion last winter. Seth is a personable, bright youth, seemingly endowed with his mother's sense of humor. At school he is a part of a high school fraternity, and in addition works from 4:30 to 7:00 p.m. for a janitorial firm, washing windows. This is Seth's contribution to the financial state of his family.

Seth plans to go on to college with the hope of becoming either a professional baseball player, or a recreational director. He recently received an offer from a major league baseball organization to go on to school, financed by it, and then enter into a training program perhaps someday to play major league ball. As of now his future is uncertain, but his athletic prowess seems to indicate that he will probably receive financial aid and thus be able to attain a college education.

Sundays are a day for togetherness at the Farmer home. Mrs. Farmer rises at 7:00 a.m. and "after two cups of coffee and six cigarettes!" manages to get going. The family eats breakfast together and then drives to church for the 10:00 a.m. service. They're home by noon, at which time Mrs. Farmer prepares lunch. After that, "the records go on — the TV is blaring — John and his girl listen to music and Seth is shushing everyone because one game or another is on!" Mrs. Farmer gathers the wash and does the week's laundry. Then she gives the dog a bath, cleans the house and is back to the kitchen to cook again! After dinner it's ironing time and the nightly routine begins. "I cook — they eat — I clean — they mess up. John gets on the phone — Seth does his homework — Seth yells at John to get off the phone, John gets off the phone — Seth gets on the phone — I yell at Seth to get off the phone — and we go to bed."

The Farmers, despite Mr. Farmer's progressive disease, are stable. Mrs. Farmer is a hard-working, sensible, and loving mother and these qualities are reflected in her sons, who are diligent, intelligent young men. Mrs. Farmer seems to have injected a sense of stability in the boys, and both look forward to the day that they will have their own families. Both agree upon one point regarding their future families and that is, "my wife won't have to work like Mom!" The boys have a strong sense of financial conditions and through their mother's guidance have learned to expect only what is within their grasp, or else to go out and work for anything more they desire. As Seth puts it, "Decisions for us are not taken for granted like they are with the other kids around here. I can't just naturally go on to school, 'cause my mother doesn't have thousands of dollars to throw around — and I have to really want it and then we all have to work for it."

Mrs. Farmer is nearing the end of her term as a full-time mother, as her sons are rapidly approaching manhood, soon to have other homes and families of their own. John is deeply in love with a seventeen-year old girl, but feels that they must wait until he is established before getting married. Again, the sense of responsibility of the mother has been passed on to the son. Seth, when asked if he was considering marriage at all, simply laughed.

SEVEN CHILDREN STRONG
Daniel G. Lowengard

I arrived at Mr. Wilson's house at 6:50 p.m. Unfortunately it was dark and I couldn't see much of his house or property. The Wilsons own the dirt road leading to their house. The area was mostly rocks and junk with a few trees, but with the potential to be very beautiful. "Someday, I'll get a chance to clean the place up," Mr. Wilson told me. There was a little stream on the property which separated the house and the dirt road, a foot-thick slab of concrete provided a bridge. The house was obviously isolated, but other houses were in sight and walking distance.

The Wilson living room is small but cozy; it had a broken couch, two wooden chairs, and an old piano. The kitchen is bigger than the living room. A few of the cupboards were broken but it was in much better shape than the rest of the house. Mr. Wilson had redone the whole kitchen himself a few years ago.

Mrs. Wilson is tall and attractive but her face showed the years of work and she looked easily her thirty-six years. Mrs. Wilson didn't sit in the kitchen, but rather chose the adjoining living room. She didn't say much except to supply dates and ages, which her husband usually didn't know.

Mr. Wilson is tall and muscular, had sideburns which met his mustache. He, like his wife, had the rugged look and his thirty-seven years were equally apparent. His hands told the story; they were huge and heavily calloused. His right thumb was abnormally large from an accident in a woodshop where it was smashed. Nevertheless, his life revolved around the use of his hands. We started the interview with talk of his family.

Mr. and Mrs. Wilson have seven children from the ages of nine to nineteen, all living at home. The first five were born in the South: Cynthia, nineteen; Charles, eighteen; Nelson, seventeen; Leda, fourteen; and Norton, twelve. They were born in

122

Georgia. Eleven years ago the Wilsons moved North to York, Pennsylvania. In York they lived with three other families: Mr. Wilson's parents, Mr. Wilson's sister's family, and his brother's family. Andrea, ten, and Alex, nine, joined the family; then the house was severely overcrowded — four to six in a room. The contrast between the Wilsons' old home and new one is immense. Now, they have almost an abundance of room. The family is exceptionally pleased with the change. This change has had an effect on their interaction, or lack of, with the community; but this will be discussed later.

Cynthia's child (six months old, whose father is white and did not marry Cynthia), has provided "no real added burden" Mr. Wilson said. "Everyone realizes they must do a little more and they do." He thinks it has brought the family a little closer together. He explained that Mrs. Wilson was pregnant at about the same time, so the experience did not shatter him or his wife as it might have in a different setting.

Cynthia's life has changed more than the family's from this experience. She was forced to leave the State College to go to the local Community College in order to raise her child. Mr. Wilson said she does not resent the child, but she does resent the father of the child. Her hatred for whites is an outgrowth of this. Mr. Wilson said, "fortunately the other children have not adopted similar views." He is glad that Cynthia did stay in school. "Nowadays you can't do anything without an education."

Mr. and Mrs. Wilson quit school in the eleventh grade to get married; both went to work immediately to raise a family. Mr. Wilson realizes the difficulty in earning enough to raise a family, if one's education is inadequate. He is trying to encourage Charles to "get going;" Charles is the only one having any trouble in school and it is only minimal. Nelson is in an accelerated program and will go to college next year. Leda, Norton, Andrea, and Alex are all in public school doing "average or better work," said a proud father.

We discussed in detail the differences in Northern and Southern schools. He preferred the South because, as he described it, "There, you got an education. You came out of high school with a trade and knowin' what you wanted to do. In the North you graduate and you are still lost." Time and time again he would emphasize college as "a must."

In the Wilson household everyone who can work does just that. Mr. Wilson works over sixty-two hours per week. When he came north he was qualified to be a barber, but without money to start his own business, and due to discrimination in barber unions, he had to look for something else. For the past eleven years he has been the janitor at a temple in York. At night he does similar work for many "important people" in York. He took great pride in his associations with these people and the members of the temple. Mr. Wilson says he know every member of the temple and can even say how many kids each member has and what they are doing. This is quite a feat considering the temple is the largest temple in the city for Conservative Jews. Mr. Wilson considers himself "close to the Jewish people." If Mr. Wilson has any left-over time he spends it fixing the house, though he admits there is little time for that. He has hopes of setting up a wood shop in the garage and pursuing that work while dropping the other extra jobs.

Mrs. Wilson is a nurse's aide at the municipal hospital and has been working there since they moved north. She has never been able to take time from work to raise the kids. None of the children has ever been in trouble with the police, and all but one are doing well in school. Mr. Wilson does wish that his wife did not have to work but realizes at the present time that it is impossible.

Charles works for the *News,* where he runs errands and does odd jobs. Nelson works at a chain restaurant; both put in fifteen to twenty hours per week. Norton is a paper boy for the *News*, and Alex helps, of course. If there is a basic theme to this family it is helping each other. Everyone realizes that financially they aren't well off, so everyone pitches in (Norton shares his money with the little ones). Everyone knows the baby must be taken care of, so they all help Cynthia. These seemingly adverse conditions are transposed into a unifying force.

Mr. Wilson was very proud that he and his family make do on what they make. The combined family income is less than the national median but above the poverty line. Out of their limited funds the family meets household expenses and pays money on the mortgage. Mrs. Wilson contributes a little less than half of the total income. The Wilsons are not on welfare, and they are quite proud that they are not — "that's why I work sixty-five hours a week."

Although Baptists, the Wilsons rarely attend church. Mr. Wilson said, "religion is not that important. The church does not do anything for people, especially black people." Mr. Wilson went on to say that black people don't have enough time for the church. For him Sunday is the only day he can rest. Furthermore, the church speaks of things that aren't close to the reality of his everyday life.

He sends Leda, Andrea, and Alex to church because he feels "it's good for the young ones to hear about God somewhere besides in the home." Charles, Nelson, and Norton all work on Sunday, so they can "get out of it."

Although the Wilson family has a modest income, the mother works, and the family is large; this family should be classified as stable. One possible explanation is the tendency for the "tough to get going, when the going gets tough."

Mr. Wilson said there is little reason for strict discipline in his home because the kids are all "pretty good, and have been taught to work things out among themselves." If there is need for discipline, both parents do it, and it is usually in the form of a "talk" which is "better than a spanking." He wants his children to be independent, though he thinks it is the parents' responsibility to know where the children are at night.

The Wilson family has three groups. Cynthia is usually the loner, and solves problems herself or else goes to her mother. Charles and Nelson form a second group, and can usually work things out themselves, though Mr. Wilson helps. The final group of Leda, Norton, Andrea, and Alex tend to get into more "trouble" than the others. But as Mr. Wilson explains, "kids are kids and you can't expect them to be perfect." Norton is pretty much the leader of this last group; he "likes meeting people, and is by far the most outgoing one in the family."

Things like homework, spending money, and clothing are pretty much left up to the individual. Mr. and Mrs. Wilson will help with such decisions but they like to see the kids "do it on their own." There is, however, a clear indication that the boys seek out their father for help, whereas the girls go to their mother.

BLEST BE THE CHILD THAT BINDS
Nancy Martin

The "man of the house" was very pleasant and friendly, and it was with him that this interview was conducted. Mr. Harold Henderson is the head of a small, black family of three — husband, wife, and three-year-old daughter. The family resides in a publicly assisted housing development in Boston, Massachusetts.

Mr. Henderson, born in Texas 55 years ago, grew up in a family that consisted of his mother and three other children. Apparently his father left home soon after he was born because Mr. Henderson has no recollection of him at all. He said that his mother had taken good care of them; they never starved, but were quite poor. Mr. Henderson attended public school and completed the tenth grade. Then he dropped out because he needed money and felt that he should not depend on his mother any longer. He spoke quite highly of her, and said that she taught him all "the good things" he knows. His brothers and sisters he sees only occasionally because they are scattered widely through the states; and one sister lives in another country.

When he was twenty-three he decided to migrate north. He came to Boston. There, he got married; a son, Jesse, was born. He is an adult and now lives in Los Angeles.

At age thirty-two, Mr. Henderson began working for a large company in Boston, as a custodian, where he is still employed.

Mr. Henderson's first wife died. He lived as a widower for several years. Five years ago, he married again and now has a second child, a three-year-old daughter.

Before moving into the housing development, Mr. and Mrs. Henderson lived in a smaller apartment in the south end of the city. It was an old apartment, difficult to keep clean, he said. Mr. and Mrs. Henderson are satisfied with their present home of almost one year. It is new, clean, and they feel has wonderful

127

facilities for what they are paying. There is a garbage disposal in the kitchen, which Mrs. Henderson "just loves," a parking area below the apartments, laundry facilities in each building, and a play area for children. Mr. Henderson said that they would stay in this housing development indefinitely, if they were permitted to do so. The apartment has two bedrooms, a kitchen, living and dining area, bathroom, and storage closet — much more than they ever had, and for a better price too. They were well pleased with their new housing.

Aside from his regular job, Mr. Henderson also worked as custodian and rent collector for his landlord before moving into the development. He really disliked that because, he said, it made him "the bad man" of the area. He was the one who had to make reports, receive the complaints on behalf of the landlord, and collect the rent. Few people in his old apartment building were fond of him. Also, the Henderson family described the area surrounding his former dwelling as crowded and dangerous. Thus, they were happy to move.

Mr. Henderson has been working in his present job for seventeen years. He likes the work and said that he is going to stay with this company until he retires. He know the people well with whom he works. Moreover, he believes that staying with the same company is good security for him. He is a custodian and also does some pick-up and delivery work when he is asked to. A steady worker, Mr. Henderson hasn't missed a day from work in five years. He is extremely proud of this record.

Mrs. Henderson doesn't work outside the home. He feels that she is a good wife and mother, and that he has been a good husband and father. He says that he has tried his best to provide well for his family, and feels that he has been quite successful. He has arranged so that every week, a certain amount of his check is taken out by a credit union, and held for his rent and future savings. This practice is followed, Mr. Henderson said, because he learned the hard way that it was difficult to get home Friday afternoons with a whole check. It is much safer for the credit union to deduct the rent and savings from his pay before he gets it.

Mr. Henderson is very active in the church, which is the center of most of his activities. He is an usher and never misses a Sunday unless it cannot be avoided. He goes on trips with church groups and participates in most of the church social functions. His wife goes with him at times, but not as often as he would like her to. Mr. Henderson also said that he is a member of the Masons.

Mr. Henderson admitted that he loves parties and really enjoys drinking, but usually confines his "boozing" to the nights out with the boys because his wife feels differently about it.

Cooking is one among several things in the home Mr. Henderson likes to do. When he was younger, he worked as a short-order cook. Now he doesn't have much opportunity to cook.

Mr. Henderson is very proud of and loves his daughter a great deal. He said that whenever he is not with her (if he goes on a trip, or his wife and daughter go away) he misses her very much. He said that he and his wife hope that their daughter will finish school and become either a school teacher or a secretary, which they feel are respectable and worthwhile positions for a woman.

The family's weekdays are fairly consistent. Mr. Henderson wakes up first, eats breakfast alone, and leaves for work. He is gone all day from 7:30 a.m. until about 5:00 p.m. Mrs. Henderson and their daughter get up after he leaves and have their breakfast. Mrs. Henderson does her housework, may go to visit some friends in the morning or have visitors in for coffee while Betty, their daughter, amuses herself or plays with the children of her mother's friends. The Hendersons have only one car which Mr. Henderson must drive to work; so Mrs. Henderson tends to visit neighbors in the area who are within walking distance.

At lunch time Mrs. Henderson and Betty eat together, and since Mr. Henderson is at work, he eats with his friends. After lunch Betty takes a short nap, during which time her mother either relaxes, watching television, or does some laundry or general housework. Later in the afternoon, if she needs groceries, she and her daughter, and sometimes some friends, walk to the store and shop.

Mr. Henderson comes home about 5:00 p.m. and the family has dinner at about 5:30. He said that he always comes home right after work. If he is planning to go out, then he leaves from home, but never goes elsewhere directly from work. At night, after dinner, Mr. Henderson plays with their daughter while Mrs. Henderson cleans up. In the evening he reads the paper and watches television unless he has a church meeting or some other activity to go to. He usually heads for bed around midnight — sometimes Mrs. Henderson goes earlier, or later, depending on what she is doing.

On weekends, a Sunday for instance, Mr. and Mrs. Henderson get up about 8:00 a.m. Mr. Henderson notes that rising time depends somewhat on what he has done the night before. The family has breakfast, usually together, then he leaves for church at 10:50 a.m. Sometimes they all go together but most often he goes alone. (Mr. Henderson really enjoys church and stays there usually until about 2:00 p.m. Mr. Henderson is well-known, liked, and respected at his church). In the afternoon he reads the paper, plays with Betty. The family eats dinner at 4:00 p.m. Sometimes they all go for a walk or drive, and sometimes they stay at home. Time for them on Sunday is not structured — they do what they feel like doing, sometimes individually, sometimes together.

Mr. Henderson is young-looking and acting, for his age, and says strongly, "I really love living." One might classify him a conservative and a very practical person in the matters that involve his family and finances. He has learned from his mistakes and looks at them as good teaching experiences. He is warm and friendly.

Mrs. Henderson appears to be a completely different type of person, compared with her husband. She is younger than he, but does not seem to possess the energy, and ambition that he exhibits. She has a quiet and suspecting manner. She has a few activities outside the home, but does not enjoy the same activities that her husband enjoys.

The one and important sharing that this couple experiences is their daughter. Betty is the target of Mr. Henderson's love. She is a happy child and relates well to her father and mother.

At times Mr. Henderson seems rather lonely, and somewhat dissatisfied with his marriage. He loves being involved in activities and with other people, but his wife does not seem to share his interests. Outside the home, they do little together. Mr. Henderson's love for their daughter seems to be the tie that binds him to his wife and their home.

The family structure seems to be equalitarian in a general sense. Mrs. Henderson takes care of most things within the home. Mr. Henderson takes care of matters outside the home. They both share in the responsibility of caring for their daughter.

Chapter 7 POOR REBELS

All six of the poor black families are city dwellers who live in apartments in the inner city. Four of the six households are single-parent and two consist of husband and wife. The four single-parent households are headed by mothers. In two of these households, a boyfriend visits often and relates to the children as a father would. Three of the single-parent households are that way because of divorce; the fourth single parent never married. Only two of the households had adult parents who were gainfully employed. In all other households, including the two two-parent units, the fathers and mothers were unemployed; however, the family received some income in one two-parent home by taking in foster children.

Education for all was limited. Only one parent was a high school graduate. All other parents in these households were either high school dropouts — the experience of three mothers and one father — or received less than a grade school education.

The Helen Jones family is a one-child family in which the mother is unemployed and receives public welfare; she had never married. The Simmons household consists of four offspring and one grandchild, although only three offspring and a grandchild live at home. The mother is unemployed, divorced, and receives welfare. The Harris home is the residence for two children and a divorced mother who works with a federally funded community development program. The Fishers, a two-parent kinship unit, have eight children, who have all grown up and left home. The father worked in a bakery but recently lost his job and cannot find work; he and his wife take in foster children for pay and babysit their grandchildren. The other Jones family is headed by Coreen Jones. It is a single-parent household because of divorce and consists of the mother, who is a cleaning woman, four children, and a grandmother. The Butler family consists of husband and wife and one child. The husband was a stockroom attendant but is out of work. This is

132

a second marriage; the two decided that the mother should be a homemaker.

DOWN BUT NOT OUT
Kristen Haggman Mitchell

Helen Jones cannot decipher her mother's first name on her birth certificate or adoption papers; it is either Helene or Thelma of whom she has neither recollection nor information. Helen Jones was born in Chicago 27 years ago. Sometime during the first two years of her life, she moved from Chicago to Philadelphia and was placed for adoption when she was 2 years old. She was adopted by a childless black couple. She can remember only fragments of the first eight years of her life, such as the names of the various streets on which she lived. Her most vivid memory was spending days with her father ("me and him alone"). Also, she remembers getting measles and staying home when she was in the second grade; about that time, her cousin came to live with the family when her child was born. Helen attended first, second, and third grades in an inner-city public school and was enrolled in a private church-sponsored school for the fourth grade.

Helen feels that her life changed dramatically at that time. She attributes this to a particular incident that she recalls with indignation. One afternoon, her mother picked her up from school and as they walked home, her mother said to her, "Don't tell anyone you're adopted." Two days later, her mother handed Helen a book about adoption. Helen said that she never understood the meaning of adoption before and that her mother never sat down and explained anything. "Boom! That was that. I felt like I belonged to no one and no where."

Helen Jones went on a stealing binge; she took books, staples, notebooks, and pencils from local stores and school. She says that she would walk into a store and walk out with as much as she could hide. She began to lie about her activities to her mother, who apparently had become suspicious about the new items appearing in the house. For the next two years, Helen continued to lie and steal. When her mother eventually dis-

134

covered that Helen was stealing, she beat her over the head with a hairbrush. Helen says that she eventually stopped stealing because her mother "just beat it out of me." She said that her father never touched her. Meanwhile, she stole pencils, note-books, and paper at the private school and was caught. The priest at the school "tried to find out why, but it didn't help much." Helen says that she couldn't tell him why she had stolen the things because she "honestly didn't know." His response and solution was to ask her to get down on her knees with him and pray. Helen said that she did so because she was "willing to please anyone to get them to shut up and get off my back."

The next year, Helen returned to the public school pre-sumably because her parents couldn't afford the private school. This was the explanation given but Helen doubts it; she feels that she was thrown out. In the fifth grade, her teacher told her that she was a "brilliant child and had to slow down with the other kids in the class." Helen describes this experience as "the beginning of my downfall; a lot of creativity was destroyed in me." The following year, at the age of eleven, she was sent to boarding school. She remembers writing letters home telling her parents how much she hated the place. Her parents then moved to a suburban community in the same metropolitan area; she returned home and enrolled in a local suburban public school.

Concerning her suburban school experience, she says, "Do you know what it's like to be in a crowded room and feel lonely?" Her mother, whom Helen calls "a middle-class, materialistic snob," "inspected" friends "like a piece of meat." Everyone Helen brought home had to be "examined" by her mother. Helen felt that her father never intervened on her behalf. Life became unbearable between mother and daughter. Helen's mother began to drink heavily. After the age of 14, an argument with her inebriated mother, Helen ran away. She stayed away from home for ten days and lived in Philadelphia in a commune crash-pad. Helen returned home but ran away again a year later, "because of mother's drinking, fantastic restric-tions, and noncompromising attitude." She stayed away longer this time, but returned. She and her mother had "nightly rows." It was during one of these rows that her father had a heart attack.

Shortly thereafter, at the age of 16, she ran away from home a third time.

She took the bus to Boston and "hung out" with the street people. She met a young man and together they hitched around the country. They ended up in California; there they ended their relationship. Soon afterward, Helen was "busted" for vagrancy and loitering and was sent to a detention center. After a week there, she was flown home to Philadelphia and was placed in a detention facility for a month. In detention, she said, she "flipped, freaked, and got hysterical; people flew away from me in all directions and I threw around chairs and smashed windows. The matron stopped me, after a lot of struggling, at the point when I was about to smash my hand into some grating." Helen said that she was "tense and nervous" afterwards and was transferred to a state-run school for girls. She stayed there for nine months and "freaked out" again and told a nun "where she could go and where she could stick it." On her seventeenth birthday, just a few months short of her scheduled return home, she told her mother that unless she got her out of there, she would run. Helen and her mother went into court and made a "deal" with the judge whereby Helen could go to summer school and return to high school as a senior in the fall. For the entire summer, Helen says that she was a "good girl." For the first time, Helen felt that "it looked like things were going to work out."

Helen returned to the suburban public high school that fall. For a reason she can't understand and does not know, she went on a "sleeping binge." She would get up in the morning, go to school, come home, and go immediately to sleep. Three days later, her parents called a doctor who, according to Helen, told the parents to wake her up and not let her sleep. When her parents tried to awaken her, she "flipped out again. There was no calming me down." The parents, "not knowing what to do," called the police, who took Helen to the hospital. She reports that the police then returned her to her home, reassured her that it was all right to sleep, and told her parents to let her alone.

By November of her senior year, Helen was cutting school and fighting constantly with her mother. In December, she ran away from home and stayed on the streets. From January until the following summer, Helen hitch-hiked across the country alone, spending a few months "here and there." She returned home for two weeks, and then left. That summer she began to deal in "junk" and "hustle." She met Tim, "the most unreliable man she has ever met." The following December, she decided to "kick" heroin. She stayed with Tim while she was "kicking the habit." She remembers having intercourse with Tim once. When the winter came, she left Philadelphia and hitched again across the country alone. It was the best hitching expedition she had ever had, she said. People took her into their homes readily. She recalls having Christmas dinner with a family in Illinois who took her a week later to Arizona. It was there that she discovered that she was pregnant. Helen called her mother, who insisted that she come home.

When Helen returned home, her mother "tried to talk her into an abortion." Helen "thought and thought about it" until one day, she woke up and decided that she was going to keep the baby. Her mother told her that "she wasn't going to have a grown woman in the house with a kid without a man." She kicked Helen out.

Helen Jones lived in rooming houses and went on welfare for the next few months. She knew many people on the streets, but had no one with whom she was intimately involved and who could support her in a minimal way. After her baby was born, there was a time lag between receipt of general relief and aid for dependent children. Helen did not get the increased allotment for several months. She "hustled" to earn money for "formula, diapers, and rent." For one month, October, she placed her son in a foster home in order to "get her shit together," as she put it. She took him back, stayed another month in the rooming house, and returned home ("my mother took me back"). Three-quarters of her welfare check was demanded by her mother "for rent." Around Christmas time, Helen Jones was talking to her friend on the telephone. They were discussing their New Year's Eve plans and Helen says she was apparently "daydreaming." Her mother came into the room and accused Helen of looking like she was on "junk" again. She attacked Helen with a pair of scissors. For the next two weeks the tension was so bad that Helen couldn't stay in the same room with her mother.

In January, Helen's mother was admitted into the hospital for internal blockage. For two weeks Helen did not visit her mother. One day Helen received a call from the hospital. She found her father, who had gone out for breakfast. They rushed to the hospital; her mother had died of a blood clot in the lung. The entire family blamed her, Helen said, for not visiting her mother while she was hospitalized. In March, Helen moved away from home and found an apartment, in which she is presently living with her son. She started taking courses at Temple University. Finding school, "on top of everything else," more than she could handle, she flunked out. Her central goal, she says, is to return to school and to get off welfare.

RESIDENCE AND COMMUNITY

Helen Jones and her child live in a rented flat with a kitchen, bedroom, living room, and bathroom. She has a radio, television, and telephone but no clock. Her income is minimal and is supplemented by food stamps. She describes the neighborhood as black working class. She doesn't like where she lives because, although the area has a reputation for being "safe," the street lighting at night is poor and she fears robbery. To avoid this, she always takes her child with her wherever she goes after dark because she feels that "no one would bother a mother with a child." Generally, "things are quiet," and there is "no trouble." She thinks that she is getting a "good deal" on her apartment rent. She knows about five other people who live near her, but not well enough to ask for assistance. She doesn't feel that she is in a "community, because in a community, people speak to one another on the streets and the children play together." When she needs help, she turns to her father, her aunt, and her cousin, in that order.

DAILY ACTIVITIES

On the day preceding the day of this interview, which was typical in her life, Helen got up at 8:30 a.m., fixed breakfast for her child and for herself, bathed, and got dressed. She had a ten o'clock doctor's appointment and was out of the house by 9:30. She tells time by the radio and the telephone time service. For appointments, she allows forty-five minutes to an hour from the time she leaves home and arrives at the appointed place. She is always punctual. She and her child stayed at the doctor's office for about an hour and arrived home around noontime. ("The kids had gone in from the playground.") She and her child "hung outside in front of the house and went in around 2:00." Helen then fixed lunch. For the rest of the afternoon, her child ran around the house and Helen read. She cooked dinner earlier than usual (at 6:00 p.m.), read until 8:00, put her child to bed, and cleaned up three rooms. She watched television and went to bed at 11:30. Helen recalled the events of the day easily, although she says that she is usually not aware of how the days pass. On other typical days there is food shopping, appointments (doctor, welfare), more television watching, and housekeeping duties (cleaning and laundry). On some nights, she goes out with a friend to "clubs" and socializes in the bars or after-hour places.

DECISION-MAKING AND PLANNING MODES

When Helen Jones has a particular problem which demands a decision, she will sit down and think about it for a while. Then she will ignore it. She says that it takes a while for her to make up her mind, that she has to feel "really sure and secure." Oftentimes, she will go around in "circles, examining the pros and cons, leave it alone, go back to it, and then it comes to her." Concerning her child, she says that "being a parent requires security," and that she is aware of her control over her son's life. For that reason, she really has to "feel good about whatever it is." Her most recent big decision concerns the possibility of sending her son down south with his aunt for the summer. Such an arrangement, she felt, would allow her to organize her life, make specific plans to return to school and to put her child into daycare, and generally give herself "breathing space." She feels that this took serious thought, particularly because she says that she feels terrible when her child goes away even for a night. She talked to her aunt and cousin about it all and received reassurance from them that summer care of her son wouldn't be "too much of a burden." Generally, Helen feels good about the decisions that she has made in the past, although she says that sometimes she gets into them and finds that she's gone over her head. She cites returning to school two years ago as an example of this.

As far as future planning is concerned, Helen does not look far ahead. She says that she can plan in "terms of a year, but gets frustrated by that." She feels that "it is hard to say that you want to do something, because something will come along and destroy it. ... You just don't know what's going to catch you. I can say that I want to and try it and go ahead and make the effort, but ..." She can't "picture" herself in five years. She thinks that she is "the kind of person who dies young," by forty, and that it's hard enough for her to plan for the month. She deals with her child as he grows "day by day," and thinks that it will be easier to plan ahead "once he gets into school." Being a single parent, she believes, one has "to plan and be sure and feel secure." She doesn't feel secure and thinks that she has "a lot to deal with," so she does things "day by day."

IDEALS AND CHILD

Helen Jones states that her son "surprises" her all the time. He has an "outgoing personality," an extroverted style, and "says 'hi' to everyone." She thinks that he has a "really good personality." She wants to "let him go as he is doing." Concerning morals, Helen says, "Everyone has an attitude about right and wrong and it is hard to say, you know, what to do sometimes. All I can do for my son is to try to be as understanding as possible...

to sit down and listen to what he has to say. I don't want to make the same mistakes. In my family, there was not much listening." She feels that she is opening good lines of communication that will "really stay together," that he is learning right from wrong now, "by knowing what he can get into and can't." Helen emphatically feels one thing: she is grateful that "he's not spoiled."

DISCIPLINE AND CHILD

Helen Jones feels that she has a problem being a single parent. She can become easily frustrated and angry and believes that her child can very easily "become the victim" of her frustration. She claims, nevertheless, that she rarely spanks him and that "discipline is not a heavy thing" in her house. Her son, she thinks, "has a lot of freedom to a point," and that they have a good understanding of what he can or cannot do. Under "extreme circumstances" — such as danger — and/or after she has told him three times, she will spank him. Thereafter, he usually won't do it again and, ordinarily, she never has to tell him anything more than once. Also, Helen has definite ideas about anger. She thinks that "if you hold it inside you, it can destroy you." She, therefore, encourages her son to "get angry." He usually gets mad when his mother tells him not to do something. She responds by telling him "to go ahead and be angry, but what I'm telling you is law."

CHILD AND EDUCATION

Helen Jones wants her son "to have a quality education," which means to her "having people, teachers, look at him beyond his race." ("They classify you by race in Philadelphia.") She wishes for his abilities and "talents to come through so a teacher will develop it." She wants someone "to sit down with him and teach him the basic essentials," but basically these essentials should be "reasons to draw upon life experience." She feels that talents "come out of life experience."

Helen is "seriously thinking about daycare and will in-
vestigate possibilities." She feels that she is "qualification conscious" and "wants to make sure she knows what they're doing;
such as, who and what and how they're dealing with kids." She
doesn't want anyone to "just sit him in front of a television all
day." She feels that "people contact is important for a child's
development and that daycare helps a child begin outside world
development." In general, she believes, daycare "has a lot of advantages for working mothers and school mothers, that it gives
a kid a father, that it gives the mother an opportunity to lead her
own life as a child leads his." She thinks that daycare "went
through a fad; everyone wanted their child in daycare." Since
then, it has "turned down and people are seeing good things
about daycare. It's just a matter of the parent feeling good about
the right care." In addition, Helen prefers that the center be as
"close to home as possible." Finally, as far as future schooling is
concerned, Helen wants her son to finish high school.

FUTURE RELATIONSHIPS

Helen Jones feels that she is "doing good on my own." She
further says that she is "not going to deny that I wish sometimes
that there were a man around to let me fall to pieces
sometimes." She is cautious about men. She thinks that there are
a "lot of men around who are a lot of bullshit." She is "tired of
lines," and wants "security." Nevertheless, she doesn't want a
"permanent re-involvement." She is "not ready for that." She
would really like to be with men, but the men she's been with
she's glad she's without. Generally, men, she feels just "want to
get into bed." She "needs more than that." She thinks that she'll
become re-involved sometime ("It'll happen one day") but she's
cautious about who and why. ("People get involved for the
wrong reasons.") She says that a man once told her that she was
his property. She replied that she was not a "piece of furniture
that you move here and there." She wants respect and feels a lot
of men are not willing to do that. ("There are not many men

liberated out there.") She says, she "teases a little, but leaves men alone." She is particularly not concerned about getting involved with a man so that her son can have a male model. She doesn't think that the absence of a father will take away from her son's masculinity. Furthmore, Helen feels that she can turn to her son's godfather for support.

CONCEPTIONS OF IDEAL FAMILY LIFE

Helen Jones says that she has never sat down and thought of the "ideal" family life for herself. She has fantasized about "having a good man around who could share both of us, love both of us." She wishes for an "emotionally strong man." ("We all have to fall apart sometimes; I need someone around to put me back together again.") However, she has "no conception of perfectness" ("Perfect for me?") and certainly does not see herself in an "ideal family situation." After much concentration, she added that what would be nice for her would be to "live with a man in an apartment or house and be together while we still are ourselves." She doesn't think a man should be the "sole supporter," and doesn't want to stay home herself and be "stagnated like those women who wait 'till their kids go to college and they have nothing." She feels that two people can "stay together as a family unit and be together and still be independent while supporting each other."

RACISM

Helen Jones feels that she has "never really encountered racism." She calls herself laughingly a "half breed" because her biological mother was white and her father black. She feels that she has been and "will always be considered as black." Helen says that "color is a secondary thing" to her; she has "learned to look away from a person's color" and doesn't "associate with people who look at color." She thinks that all people are basically the same physically and that it is a waste of time to look for differences. She does not like black militants. She thinks that they should just "be themselves" and not "condemn" her. A black militant once told her that she was "too black for the whites and too white for the blacks. When the revolution comes, no one is going to want you." Helen replied that "when it's all over, I'll be able to get foreign aid better than you."

Helen is raising her son, she says, "without a color attitude." She feels that he has "two cultures open to him and that the final decision is up to him." ("If he wants to take a Black Studies course, I'll encourage him.") Helen finds it "easier to relate to both sides." She says that she has an "understanding of the white man and his warped mind and an understanding of the black." Concerning her own upbringing, Helen felt that she was "always a person — neither black nor white — but when I was in school, people treated me like a black person." There were no handicaps in being black per se; she says that in her community, it was not a racial thing, but a money thing; who had money made a difference. On the streets, as an adolescent, Helen felt that she was treated "just like a kid on the street. We saw each other as people." She has never felt any discrimination "except when travelling through the South where bigotry is obvious." She says that most of her friends today are white because "people I choose as friends think like I do. We can communicate."

ATTITUDES TOWARD BEING A SINGLE PARENT

A primary asset of single parenthood, says Helen Jones, is that she used to think about being a mother and father to her son, "but not anymore." There is "no real role playing." She does not worry about "the mother-father image." She is the "chief authority figure to her son and treats him like a little human being. We are real close and have a good relationship. A parent, I am. My son calls me 'mamma.' It's just a label." Being a single parent, says Helen, allows one to get away from roles.

A primary liability of single parenthood, she insists, is that "it has its moments when I wish I could push him off." But there are "good moments when he comes at me with his arms outstretched and we hug." She feels she has control over her son's life but is more "like a guide to him." She likes the idea of teaching him "morals, impressing him on how he can live his life when he becomes a man." She does not consider herself a "strict mother," and doesn't feel an "obligation about raising him, teaching him." She feels great pleasure in single parenthood because "it's a learning experience."

SINGLE-PARENT FAMILY NEEDS

The strongest need for single parents, Helen Jones feels, is a supportive group "to see us through dealing with crisis, to relate to each other. We are not free of our anger and frustration." She thinks that single parents are a "highly segregated group" that is stigmatized: "When I go into the hospital with my son they want to know my marital status. I say I'm single. They have a way of looking at you to try to put you down. I look right back and say, 'IS THERE SOMETHING WRONG?' " Helen does not know of any group or organizations for single parents. She thinks that "single parents are a group of loners who need each other's support," particularly around "basic common problems like discipline, child rearing, school. I get confused about what I'm going to do next." She thinks that single parents "find themselves with a lot of restrictions — most are on welfare — and it's important to support one another concerning these restrictions."

Helen says that "when I announced to the world that I was going to have a child, people turned away. I felt a sense of abandonment." She told herself that if she was "not going to get accepted by family, then she needed friends." She feels, in a way, "stigmatized and weird." She wants a "true sense of acceptance among peers;" but family and friends "say one thing and feel another." She feels that "tradition and society have always impressed on people that a woman with a child alone has fallen off the line." She gets the feeling that people look at her son as just another illegitimate child. She responds by looking straight into their eyes and saying, "I am a single woman with a child. I don't really give a good holy fuck what you think. You can shove it up your ass and sit down on it." She adds, "I can look down my nose as good as anyone else. I'm just as good as the next person." She says that most black single parents she knows are "not married and most whites are widowed or divorced or separated." She thinks that there is much more acceptance by society of a single parent who has been married. But Helen feels that she's seen "too many fucked-up marriages and I say that I don't want that for my child. It messes kids' heads. If I believed in the institution of marriage, I'd be married. I believe firmly in being a single parent. I don't think that I should go out and get married because society says so."

HARD TIMES AND HOPE
William A. Mason

The Simmons family: Mother Alice; Cheryl Jackson, 23, and her 2-month-old daughter; Debra Marshall, 28, divorced; Sara Berwell, 24, separated and out of the household; Denise, 20.

Except for Sara, the Simmons family shares a five-bedroom apartment in Roxbury, Massachusetts. Mr. Simmons moved out eight years ago and has since remarried, has a 4-year-old son, and now lives in Dorchester. The Simmons family is a unit with the older siblings providing income through odd jobs and money offered every now and then by their husbands. Alice, the mother, receives welfare. They seemed to be "chummy" with their neighbors, and frequent the neighborhood bars and watch television for entertainment.

Mrs. Simmons has a ninth-grade education and Mr. Simmons attended school through the seventh grade. He worked in numerous low-paying jobs — dock hand, janitor, etc. Mrs. Simmons didn't offer information about the separation other than to say it never seemed to work out easily. I suspect ongoing frictions initiated by Mrs. Simmons' liking to go out led to the divorce. Mrs. Simmons had high hopes for "her girls" but stated, "I let them lead their own lives. As long as I have a home they do too!"

The family was referred to the mental health unit because Denise, 20, had been arrested five times for "boosting" (shoplifting). Mrs. Simmons suggested that she didn't support or condone Denise's activities because since Denise was the baby "she never wanted for anything."

Because Denise was the focus for the family's being at the Mental Health Center, the family is described in terms of her problems and aspirations. She is of average height and weight, fairly attractive with long hair and slightly crooked teeth. She is a senior at a local high school and has completed all the required nursing courses, and expects to graduate in June. Denise wants to go on to college and become a registered nurse. She has a high interest in interpretive dance and even took tapdancing lessons. Mrs. Simmons has encouraged her goals. Denise says that she "boosted" only because "she likes pretty things." Her sisters all had similar goals of finishing school but early marriages and pregnancies thwarted these goals.

Mrs. Simmons suggested that she has always promoted independence for her girls; that way, "if anything happens to me they can survive." She laments that Denise's behavior problems might be caused by spoiling her and is banking on Denise as the one "to make something of herself."

Information sources for the family include bar talk, chats with neighbors, *Jet*, the evening news. Because of limited funds, television viewing is entertainment and in many cases is the real family gathering time. Meals are taken at different times except for Sundays and holidays. Community activities and involvement are limited, although Mrs. Simmons has visited the high school, courts, and the mental health unit because of Denise's run-in with the law. There seems to be no ongoing practice of religion except for observance of holidays — Easter and Christmas. All members have voted in elections when friends and neighborhood workers encourage them to do so through voter registration campaigns, and when black candidates are in the race.

HERE TODAY, GONE TOMORROW
Nanalee Raphael

Mrs. Eleanor Harris' family lived on the top floor of a four-story building. The apartment was clean and had a comfortable, "lived-in" appearance. Stacks of records lined the top of the floor-standing stereo. The living-dining area was tastefully decorated and had a gilt-edged mirror and two inexpensive ceramic flower decorations hung on the wall. Mrs. Harris and I sat down to talk in a small room off the living room, a bedroom which was furnished as a sitting room with a second television (there was another in the living room), a heavy mock leather couch, and a couple of end tables.

As we talked, Mrs. Harris often interrupted the interview to speak with her daughters. Among the many requests, she asked them to start the dinner, turn over the rug, take a dress to the cleaners, or go out and purchase a recently released record. Peggy, the younger daughter, who had not quite lost all of her "baby fat," prepared a cup of coffee for her mother. Mrs. Harris then reminded Patricia, the older daughter, that she was not to go anyplace that evening because she told a lie the day before.

Mrs. Harris was born in Georgia. She was the oldest of four siblings. Of her childhood and youth, she said, "I didn't have to work my way through school. I didn't do babysitting or jobs like that. My parents gave me the money I needed, even after I left school." She said that her parents were above the poverty level and that she and the other family members had good clothes and a decent home. Mrs. Harris' family moved north to New York state when she was less than one year old.

Her father had a grade-school education only, but her mother enrolled in several courses at the college level. Mrs. Harris remembers her mother as the person who checked her homework and encouraged her to get good grades. Despite such encouragement, Mrs. Harris dropped out of high school after the ninth grade. Since then, she has taken some night-school

149

courses but has not received a high school diploma. Her enrollment in such courses is not continuous, although she states that
she eventually hopes to obtain the equivalent of a high school
diploma.

In Albany, Mrs. Harris met her husband and married when
she was 16 years old. Within a period of three years, she gave
birth to two daughters. Shortly after the birth of the second
child, Mr. and Mrs. Harris were separated. Three years later
they were divorced and Mrs. Harris has provided for her
children alone for several years. After the divorce, Mrs. Harris
moved to the apartment in which she now lives.

Mrs. Harris works for a federally funded community action program as assistant coordinator. Before affiliating with
the community action program, she worked for an electrical
firm but was laid off because of absenteeism due to a bout with
bronchitis. Her work with the community action program
began on a part-time basis as a community aide. In that role, she
arranged community meetings for discussion of problems and
conducted door-to-door casework surveys. After about a
month of part-time work, Mrs. Harris decided to apply for the
assistant coordinator position. "I got it," she said, "because they
liked the way I acted and the way I presented myself." Now her
work includes helping people find jobs appropriate to their
skills, helping poor families settle rent and welfare problems,
referring people for job training, and helping families relocate
when their living units are condemned.

Concerning her personal life, Mrs. Harris said, "I like to
travel. When the girls were younger, I lived in California for a
year. They stayed with my parents and I moved all over — Los
Angeles, San Francisco, all around California. I went to Greece
for three weeks for a vacation once. That was real nice." Mrs.
Harris noted that she still would be young when her 11-year old
and 13-year old finished school. Then, she said, "I'll go back to
traveling. I like being independent."

Regarding her children's education, Mrs. Harris said, "If
they want to go to college, I'll give them money to pay for their
first year but after that they're on their own. If they want to
travel, I'll give them money for that after they graduate. I don't

push schooling on them. I think it's a waste of money. But I tell them if they want to do more than their mother, they need better training."

Mrs. Harris reflected on her role as a disciplinarian and offered this opinion of herself: "I'd say I'm stricter with my girls than my parents were with me. I don't think I was spanked enough. When I say 'no' I mean 'no'! Oh, yes, I spank the girls when they're bad. I'm in favor of punishment when it's needed. I don't mind them being punished in school, either, if they deserve it."

Mrs. Harris is not pleased with her housing. She explained that there are a number of people in her building who receive public welfare and that she does not like this because, as she sees it, "They let the place run down and don't take care of their kids very good. I guess I shouldn't talk, really. I was on welfare once, but I'm off now. There are a lot of working mothers in this housing development."

Mrs. Harris thinks the neighborhood in which she lives is "pretty good," but she is not quite sure. She said, "There are a lot of Jews, and it's racially mixed; but there isn't any recreation for the children." She is more favorably impressed by the neighborhoods elsewhere. "They are really nice and well off," she observed.

The girls attend different schools. Patricia walks to the junior high school each morning and Peggy takes the bus to her elementary school. Peggy is in the sixth grade and Patricia is in the seventh. Patricia started school a year late.

This is the household afternoon and evening routine. The girls have to do their homework before they watch TV or play. "I don't check their homework, but I can tell if they've been working by their report card marks. If they have a lot of work to do, they let me know and then they don't have to help with chores. I have never gotten any bad reports from school about their work." When the girls have school work to do, they sit at the dining room table or in the sitting room. Peggy usually finishes her work in school; she has few homework assignments. Patricia was able to do school work beyond her class level and could have skipped a grade but Mrs. Harris decided that it was better that she continued in a class with kids her own age.

Mrs. Harris described her household of three as "real close." No one has ever been in trouble with the police, and the children are getting along very well in school.

Although Mrs. Harris was raised a Baptist, she seldom attends church and hasn't brought her girls up with any religious preference. "Sometimes the girls go to the Episcopal church near here," Mrs. Harris said. "I go when I feel like it, I guess. If I don't go during the rest of the year, I certainly don't go on Christmas or Easter."

Mrs. Harris has a boyfriend, Bob, whose son Wayne (age fourteen) stays with the Harris family when Bob has to go out of town on sales trips. "The girls get along with Wayne real well, like brother and sisters. Sometimes when we have a date, the girls babysit with Wayne but not all the time."

Mrs. Harris usually disciplines Patricia and Peggy, although Bob and Mrs. Harris' parents often help in this respect. "Their grandparents are always teaching them manners. But they spoiled them for awhile. They were the only grandchildren for a long time."

The family has dinner around 5:30 or 6:00 each evening. "I cook for two days usually, so we have leftovers every other day. The girls fix after-school snacks themselves when they get home if they're hungry," said Mrs. Harris. Breakfast is an individual affair. Each family member prepares her own. On weekends the family members eat lunch together.

During the week Mrs. Harris awakens first at 7:00 a.m. Peggy gets up in time to catch her bus for school at 8:00 a.m. Patricia's school day ends at 2:45 p.m. She comes home and plays inside until Mrs. Harris returns from work at 5:30 p.m. Peggy gets home from school around 3:30 and plays with friends until dinnertime. Evenings are spent doing homework and watching TV, except on Tuesdays, which is the evening on which the family bowls.

Mrs. Harris sleeps in until 11:00 a.m. on weekends. But the girls get up around 9:30 a.m. and shop or visit with their grandparents. In the afternoon, on weekends, Mrs. Harris shops or cleans, Peggy goes to the movies, and Patricia plays inside. Dinner is a little earlier, around 4:30 or 5:00. After-dinner activities include TV, visiting, or finishing the cleaning of the apartment.

"I live above my means, I know," Mrs. Harris said when asked if she had problems making ends meet. Her monthly rent on the apartment takes about half of her monthly income. Bob, her boyfriend, helps pay the rent.

The apartment is relatively large. It has a kitchen, three bedrooms, a living room and dining room, two bathrooms, and an outside balcony. The family has three televisions, several radios, and a phone with an extension in the sitting room. "This is a convenient location," said Mrs. Harris. "There is a shopping center and the bus line runs right past us."

Mrs. Harris returned to a theme discussed earlier, that the neighborhood is "going down." "No upkeep," she said. "All these welfare people don't try to get better. There's alot of litter and destruction. And all the large families: I don't think there should be more than three kids to a family. Oh yes, I thought about moving. It's not worth what I'm paying in rent. I'd like to move elsewhere." When Mrs. Harris referred to her neighborhood she was thinking in terms of the five apartment buildings in her housing complex.

She knows about five families in the housing complex. She believes the police do a fine job of enforcing the law, since there are no real problems in the area. "This isn't a real dangerous area, but it isn't a real safe one either. I guess it's about average. If I could I'd have a place for kids here, to keep them off the streets. A recreation center instead of all the grass, a playhouse."

If she encountered problems, Mrs. Harris would turn to her parents or to Bob for help. "I'm closest to them," she explained. "It would have to be money problems, because I can handle all the others."

"Pat, what kinds of chores do you and Peggy have to do for your mother?" the interviewer asked one of the children. "Oh, we mostly have to clean and straighten up; then on Sunday we switch off. We don't need a reason for it, but it helps us if we do. If we don't finish our chores, we have to stay in. One day last week I couldn't go out 'cuz I said I finished and Mama found out that I didn't.

"Peggy and I get along O.K. We argue alot ... mostly over clothes.

"I like school once in a while. If I had another choice, I'd like to travel. Math is my best subject, then English and then gym. I don't like social studies. I don't like to flatter my teacher and she likes to be flattered. There are only two black kids in my class — me and another girl. Other kids can flatter the teacher but I won't. I hurt her once when I read a poem I wrote at an assembly. I didn't mean to and I told her later. It was about who I really respect and I respect Lincoln, not her, but that's the way I feel.

"I want to be a singer or a math teacher. I guess I'll need about four years of college to be a teacher. I'm a real good singer; I've been in a lot of talent shows, sometimes with a band and sometimes just singing to records. I love to sing. Oh no, I don't want to act, that's just ... yecch." Patricia shriveled up her shoulders, stuck out her tongue, and made a face clearly expressing her distaste for the idea.

She got up and moved around quickly as she continued talking. "I don't want to be a singer all my life. I want something to fall back on, that's why I'd like to be a teacher. I s'pose I could sing until I was about thirty and then teach. I want respect for myself and partly for my race. I want friends who respect me for being myself."

Patricia thought for a while but couldn't find an answer to the question, "What kinds of things are good to have?" In the negative sense she answered that envy was bad. "When people are jealous of you it makes it bad for you. The best thing that ever happened to me? ... well, winning awards like in the talent contests."

Patricia enjoys traveling and under a summer program sponsored by a local organization went to Canada. "I got to dance onstage with a popular rock band. A bunch of girls were dancing on the side and they pulled me onstage and I danced for about three songs up there. They wanted me to stay to talk with them after, but I got a little scared (giggles here) and we all got out of there. I have been to New York three times. I don't like it, except for clothes. Other than clothes, it hasn't got anything. Don't see how people can live there. Nothing bad ever happened to me, just good things. I guess I've been pretty lucky."

Patricia's interests reflected the fact that she is still 13, barely a teenager. She likes to sing most of all and can accompany herself on the piano. When she's with friends she likes to talk, play cards or Monopoly, or watch TV. She's scared of dogs but likes puppies. And if she had three wishes she'd wish for clothes, a car, and to be a singer, in that order. "I don't want to wish for money. I don't want everything. If you get everything, then what's the use of living?

"I'm not going to get married until I'm thirty-nine, and have one child. I hope it'd be a little girl. I like to comb their hair. If I have it before I'm married, I hope it's while I'm young, like Mama. She's only twenty-eight you know. She had me when she was fifteen and her parents took care of us until she got married when she was sixteen. I like little kids. During the summer I worked as a babysitter. It was a real good job; I got paid real well. I kept half and gave half to Mama before she asked for it. She gives me money all the time, so I figured I could give her some. I didn't need all that. Yep, I like to hold children and play with them."

Mrs. Harris felt her mother influenced the girls most in finding part-time work (which Mrs. Harris preferred the girls not do) and helping the girls with homework. Everyone, including grandparents and aunts and uncles, had some form of influence in teaching the girls manners. "I let the girls decide what they want to do when they grow up, though. We talk about different jobs, but they're the ones who are going to decide. I don't decide where they go to school; the Board of Education does that. They make their own choice of church, although their grandmother wants them to stay Baptist. If I buy a car, I know what kind I want even though everyone else tells me what kind I should have. Number of children? That's up to me, if I make a mistake, then it's up to nature."

Mrs. Harris does not belong to any organizations, although she has been a member of a church choir, has helped with girls' club activities. Informally she socializes with her co-workers. Her daughters belong to a young people's group at the Episcopal Church, a school-connected girls' club, and the track team. She was vague and did not have specific knowledge about her girls' activities.

Mrs. Harris was unable to describe her family's attitude about the civil rights movement. None of the family has even participated in a demonstration, or has been discriminated against in the way of employment. "I really don't know much about it. Whichever way these college students want it is all right with me. It really doesn't faze me."

Besides bowling together, the family sometimes attends concerts and plays. The girls enjoy going to concerts, whether they're classical or jazz. And as Mrs. Harris' younger brother and sister are all in Albany with their families, there is much family interaction. "We have reunions or get together on special holidays or just get together at my parents'."

Patricia and Peggy don't see their father often, but they do know who he is. Mrs. Harris feels that the girls are very fond of Bob, her boyfriend, and are more apt to respect him than their father. Not only does Bob help support the girls by helping to pay the rent, but also "treats" them by buying presents and taking them out. As Mrs. Harris sees Bob three or four times a week, the girls are also in contact with him often.

Mrs. Harris finds her present job exciting and at the moment is not interested in moving on to something else. "But if I get tired of it, I'll just quit and go somewhere else," she finished laughingly.

FAITH AND ENDURANCE
Donna Willey Schum

It was a somewhat rundown neighborhood and I was very nervous. The first door I went to was opened by a shy, well-dressed little girl with her fingers in her mouth. I asked if I could possibly speak to her mother and she led me up some stairs and into a large apartment with what seemed like a whole living room full of clean, neatly-dressed children. I repeated my question and stood awkwardly for a moment until an older child asked me to sit down and left the room, returning with an older, rather weathered-looking woman.

At first Mrs. Fisher and I had trouble understanding each other. The first few questions had to be explained and repeated; finally the conversation became so confused that the oldest child (the children were all lined up on an enormous sofa gaping at me) began to do a bit of interpreting until we were genuinely communicating ideas. It was difficult to entirely fill out the interview forms because Mrs. Fisher did not want to discuss some things. Consequently, I did not press her to strictly adhere to the interview sheets. I was learning a great deal about the family by just letting her talk.

Mr. Richard Fisher and his wife, Mrs. Gladys Fisher, have been married for twenty-eight years and have had eight children of their own, one of whom is still living at home. The others are all married and have families of their own. One son works for Ford Motors, two are roofing specialists, two are ministers of their own churches, and the youngest son is currently unemployed; and as Mrs. Fisher told me, he is the only one who was ever a discipline problem and had slight trouble with police. Of the two daughters, the oldest one is now working her way through college to become a physical therapist, and the younger, who is still at home, works at a neighborhood health center as a dental hygienist. Almost all of the offspring live in the same neighborhood with their families and Mrs. Fisher babysits for eight grandchildren every weekday while the parents work, and sometimes nights and weekends also. These grandchildren range in age from two to teenage and appear to be thriving. Also, a short time ago, Mr. and Mrs. Fisher took two foster children into their home to raise: Thomas, who is six, and Henry, who is fifteen. In spite of their ages, which Mrs. Fisher refused to tell me, Mr. and Mrs. Fisher are still active parents and loving every moment of it.

Mr. Fisher is from Alabama and Mrs. Fisher is from Georgia, where they met and raised their family, until twelve years ago when they moved directly to Rochester to join their older daughter, who had already lived there six years. One son lives in Florida and is the only one of their children that the Fishers do not see every day.

The family income is below the poverty line. Mr. Fisher has been unemployed for four months. Mrs. Fisher probably did not include in the family income the allowances that she probably receives for the two foster children and funds she gets for babysitting the grandchildren. She did not respond readily to these questions. and she was not at all specific. Mr. Fisher was formerly employed in a bakery for some time. Mrs. Fisher would not tell me how much education she and her husband had, because she said it was too little to mean anything. She seemed to be ashamed of the level of schooling which she had completed. Shirley, their twenty-four-year-old daughter who still lives with her parents, completed high school and attended a training program of some kind for her work as a dental hygienist. Six-year-old Thomas has completed first grade and fifteen-year-old Henry has completed eighth grade, and has a tutor in addition to school.

This family is obviously very close, and has very strong family ties. Mrs. Fisher says that the children never had trouble with the police and all are doing or did very well in school. She does most of the disciplining herself mainly because Mr. Fisher usually works long hours when he is employed. They make all important decisions together. Both help with homework and with teaching and training the children to be "decent people," considered by the couple to be very important functions of child-raising, which they are tremendously devoted to.

Regular meals are planned and prepared by Mrs. Fisher. She gives her family and grandchildren breakfast at 7:00 (their mothers leave early for work), lunch at noon, and dinner for her family at 6:00. All members of the family usually eat together, except when Mr. Fisher is absent for lunch because of his working or looking for work. Mrs. Fisher would not even begin to tell me schedules of her family for certain days. She said the older ones mainly work and go to church and the children play, help out around the apartment, and go to school.

The children do not have any specific time set aside for homework, but Mr. and Mrs. Fisher make sure that it gets done. She feels that the children will form a bad attitude towards school if they are forced to do schoolwork when they would rather do something else. They are learning independence by organizing their own free time. Homework is usually done in the children's room. No one in the household has visited the school this past school year because Mrs. Fisher babysits all the time and Mr. Fisher is usually working. Teachers and school officials do not visit, Mrs. Fisher thinks, because the children behave so well in school.

The foster children have a case worker who visits regularly, and Henry has a special tutor who visits — a white student from a local college who works with emotionally disturbed children. Mrs. Fisher told me that Henry came from a depraved and wretched environment, and that this "home life" had left its mark on the fifteen-year-old's sensitive mind. He needs special care and Mrs. Fisher is confident she can give Henry the love and attention he needs. He already seems to be responding positively to Mr. and Mrs. Fisher and the other children. He's very creative and he does very well in most schoolwork, but he has social problems. His sister also visits him once a week. Six-year-old Thomas also had a difficult home life, but he has not been affected as much by it and he has almost completely accepted his new loving family in the two months he has been there.

Mrs. Fisher says the children have many ideas of what they would like to be. The oldest grandchild, the teenager Carol, told me she would like to work with children in some way — probably with retarded children. She handled the small children all the time I was there. Mrs. Fisher would like the children to do service work and have professional jobs, but she will let them decide as she did with her grown children. She had no idea how much education was needed for this type of work.

Mrs. Fisher is dissatisfied with her neighborhood only in the sense that she has a dream of living away from the city on a farm with her whole family and a lot of animals really "close to nature." She wants to enjoy God's creation as he created it. Her only thoughts of moving are in this context. She classified the neighborhood as white working-class. She feels the police do a fine job of enforcing the law in this area and it is quiet. She likes the idea of living in a white neighborhood because it is quieter and she enjoys the white students in the area, but she is uncertain of the reputation that the neighborhood has and she knows few people outside of her family. There is nothing she would like to change about her neighborhood.

The rented apartment occupied by the Fisher family has six rooms and a bath. What I saw of it was very attractive, nicely furnished, and neat. The front rooms were especially warm and cheerful. The family has three TVs in working order, several radios, and a telephone which Mrs. Fisher feels she would be lost without. When in need of any help, Mr. and Mrs. Fisher contact members of their own close-knit family. They all depend on each other in tight situations, and most family members live in or near the same neighborhood — some even in the same apartment house.

Central and most important in the lives of the Fisher family is religion. Mrs. Fisher told me that they all try to go to church as often as possible, and that they also try to live their religion. "I got no education, but I know Jesus and that's all I need." Mrs. Fisher explained this by saying that she and her husband had been happily married for twenty-eight years and had raised many children with very little difficulty because they followed the "way of the Lord" and had felt the spiritual presence of Jesus, which kept them strong. She said their faith, and especially her faith (because others may be moved in different ways), gave her the insight and understanding needed to raise children, "for one surely needs more than physical comforts to fully develop youthful minds and hearts." The social life that Mr. and Mrs. Fisher have is centered around the church and they leave no time to be members of any other kind of organization or club. Their religion is a major binding force in the family and it is not the only, but the primary and most important tradition and activity that they share together as a family. It gives them strength to overcome difficulties. Of course, the children are involved in groups like Boy Scouts, sports teams, and clubs at school, but they are still actively involved in the church also. I do not believe the children resent this strict church attendance and involvement because it is so much a part of their family life.

Mrs. Fisher talked for quite some time about how she and her husband feel about raising children. She feels fulfilled in seeing them become decent people, strong in spirit and happy. She said that teaching and giving all the wisdom that Jesus gives her to her children fulfills her as a person. She believes that the young generation of today should listen and attempt to learn from their elders, for with age comes experience and intuitive wisdom. Also, she said that the older people should stop complaining about the behavior of the young, and instead show that they have something to give and offer it. "In order for a child to develop in a family, one, as a parent, has to learn to communicate with that particular child and realize that he is a person and not just something to discipline. You must respond to his sensitivities and discipline him accordingly, handling each child in a different way." She said that a child knows if you recognize him as an individual and a person; and the way he develops is a result of the extent to which you allow him to grow and learn and be disciplined as the individual he is. "Parents who react to each child in the same way, see them as objects to be made into people in their own image, with their own standards. But children will not take to this and soon there is trouble."

Her foster child, Henry, who is mentally disturbed, needs very special care, she told me, but not so much that the other children think him more important than they. She and Mr. Fisher are slowly getting to know Henry and have already discovered certain areas which are extremely sensitive in his personality. They feel they are just beginning to reach him and are thrilled by it. Mrs. Fisher appeared to be a strict disciplinarian while I was there, but she made me realize that much more than strictness goes into raising children.

This family certainly has adjusted to the problems and opportunities it has had to face in life. The atmosphere of the setting of the interview was warm, and this warmth seemed to come from the love and companionship this family experienced in their life together. The fact that Mr. Fisher had recently lost his dependable job, seemed to have little effect on their happiness, even though it probably upset family finances a great deal. Raising children is the most important thing in Mrs. Fisher's life, and though she does enjoy what physical comforts she has and misses those she does not have, I feel that even without this sort of economic security she is really happy and contented just being with her family and being able to aid in the development of her children. I also feel that the whole family has probably seen much worse times and yet they are strong and close and have probably been so in their most difficult times. The lack of any family planning is not an accident, for Mr. and Mrs. Fisher do not believe in it; but their large number of children has not caused a lack of attention to any one of them. Also she seems to know how to handle a disturbed child intuitively and from experience. Her and Mr. Fisher's lack of opportunity for more education has perhaps limited them to a lower-class status and a working-class neighborhood, but they have adjusted to this situation and have created strong binding family ties and warm happiness in their lives. I think their religion and their resulting spiritual strength have played a great part in this adjustment. Also, the individual strength in the personalities of both Mr. and Mrs. Fisher has played a great part.

It does sound as though Mrs. Fisher has the more dominant personality, but I did not get the impression from my interview that she dominated her husband or family. She constantly spoke of the strength and help she received from Mr. Fisher and what a good man she had. She said there is none better, and his relatively quiet manner did not fool the children. They knew he could be stern if need be, and she felt that they looked to him for support the same as she did. She insisted that any success she had raising her children was due to the love and encouragement he gave to her. They make all the important decisions together and very seldom quarrel. The spiritual strength and binding family ties of this family have enabled it to face difficulties and the lack of opportunity in their lives. Hardships and good times have been shared, and knowing there is always someone to help out and depend on gives the Fisher family security and strength needed to meet any situation. In making their children "well-mannered, decent people," Mr. and Mrs. Fisher have given them strength of character and family values, preparing them to face difficulties and hardships in life as well as people in any socioeconomic status could be prepared.

LIKE MOTHER, LIKE DAUGHTER
Marshall T. Young

This black one-parent extended family consists of six members living in a five-room apartment house in the city of Watertown, New York. Mrs. Coreen Jones, thirty-one, is the mother of four children and is employed by a boarding school as a cleaning woman. Also living in the household is Mrs. Porter, fifty, who is Mrs. Jones' mother and grandmother to the children.

Mrs. Porter, the grandmother, was born in Alabama. She lived with her aunt and uncle and eight brothers and sisters. The family later moved to Gerogia, where at nineteen she met and married Mr. Porter. Soon afterward, Coreen was born. The Porter family moved to Watertown, where Mr. Porter found work in a local factory. Mrs. Porter stayed at home. During the next six years she gave birth to five children. Mr. Porter remained with the family off and on for ten years. The family moved about five different times within the Watertown area, each time moving because of rent difficulties. The family was once close but Mr. Porter had difficulty finding employment; therefore he left the family. Mrs. Porter got some assistance from the Department of Public Welfare and later went to work as a seamstress.

The children attended the local schools for a while. Coreen quit high school in the tenth grade and went to work in a dairy. At age nineteen, she met Mr. Jones at a party and married him. Mrs. Porter was against the marriage, mainly because of her own experiences as a young bride.

Mr. and Mrs. Jones moved to Cleveland, Ohio, where Mr. Jones was from originally. The marriage experienced many ups and downs. Mr. Jones was an unskilled laborer and at first found it hard to find employment. Mrs. Jones felt the family was "real close" for the first few years of marriage.

164

Despite the financial problems after their first child Michael was born, the family did manage to go out once a week. Mr. Jones' brother often gave the family small gifts to help relieve the burden. In four years, Mrs. Jones had three children: a daughter and twins.

Mrs. Jones said that around the time her daughter was born her husband started gambling and often got himself into trouble. The family then experienced great emotional distress. Mrs. Jones became ill and was forced to remain in bed for a period of two months.

Mrs. Jones tried but was unable to cope with the situation. Mr. and Mrs. Jones got a divorce and Mrs. Jones moved back to Watertown with her four children. She first tried to get an apartment but later moved in with her mother, Mrs. Porter. Mrs. Jones' brothers and sisters were either married or in the armed service; so Mrs. Porter welcomed her daughter and the children gladly.

This extended family has remained together for four years. They have moved only once. The four children attend the local public schools; Mrs. Jones works for a boarding school and Mrs. Porter works as a part-time maid in a private home.

Because Mrs. Jones works all week, the grandmother takes care of the children during the afternoons. Mrs. Jones tries to spend the evenings with the children, but she says she often just doesn't have the time. Mrs. Jones describes her family as close but because of her work schedule she is not able to be with the children enough.

Mrs. Jones has been dating a department store worker that she met three years ago through a mutual friend. She said that she didn't want to marry again but always smiles as if she really doesn't mean it.

Mrs. Jones likes her work; she says it isn't too hard. She quit once for a couple of weeks but decided to go back. She gave no explanation why.

The older child, her nine-year-old son Michael, often gets into trouble with the police and the school authorities. Mrs. Jones feels that he takes after his father. Mrs. Jones does not seem to respect Michael. She states that he will never hold a good job. She has no real idea of child-rearing methods that may help him to grow up without getting into trouble. Michael is part of what she refers to as "the gang."

Mrs. Jones has high aspirations for the rest of the children. She hopes the twins will become businessmen, but there is inadequate information about requirements for these vocations. She hopes the seven-year-old daughter will marry well and will not have to work.

The children are close except for Michael. He appears to resent the females in the family, especially his sister who does well in school. The twins who are six years of age are too young to really be expected to work hard, according to Mrs. Jones. She states that she tries to teach them social manners.

Mrs. Jones has a boyfriend whom she calls Roy. He visits and plays with the children often. Mrs. Jones says that he teaches them games and that he also helps to discipline them. The children seem to like Roy very much. Michael is never around, however, when Roy visits, because of the amount of time he spends with his friends. Roy feels that with time he can help Michael.

The family has few connections with community organizations, except the church, which the family attends regularly on Sunday. Going to church is a family affair; even Michael attends Sunday school with the rest of the children. The family does not actively participate in any civic groups or service groups. They have had contact with case work services because of Michael.

Mrs. Jones has called this black neighborhood an average area and insists that all the children are well-behaved. She has no idea about the police activities or their competence. I sense a hint of resentment with reference to the police. This is probably a result of the problems that have arisen with Michael. She exhibits an apathetic feeling about social change and improvement. She would like to see a better playground area for her children and a cleaner neighborhood; yet she repeats that she has no time to get involved.

A very influential person in the family is the grandmother. She usually cares for the children, does the laundry, housework, and prepares meals. She teaches the children manners, etc. She helps supplement the family income. The family lives with an annual income right at the poverty line. This is sometimes aided by gifts from Roy.

When I asked Mrs. Jones if she had heard from Mr. Jones she only shrugged her shoulder and didn't answer. I am interpreting this as a positive reply yet I assume that it is only an occasional thing. Mrs. Jones has held many things to herself and cared not to disclose them. Although we were on very friendly terms, a few topics were awkward when mentioned.

I feel that this basically describes the Jones family. It is an extended family that, as of now, is not headed in any real direction. The mother and grandmother are not greatly involved with the community. Mrs. Porter has her own set of friends whom she often visits. Mrs. Porter and Mrs. Jones have created their own world, and have produced a relatively stable situation. The family operates as a unit, except for Michael. At nine years of age, he is not a full participant and the family functions without him and does not know how to help him. This family has accepted Roy as if he were a member. The children and their grandmother hope that Mrs. Jones will marry Roy. The children often call him "father" and everyone seems to enjoy this, even Mrs. Porter. Mrs. Porter has mellowed over the years, according to Mrs. Jones. She no longer resents the institution of marriage and the indignities she has suffered.

YOUNG LOVERS AND STORM WARNINGS
Edward Sloan

The interview started at about seven o'clock in the evening and lasted to about ten o'clock. I happened upon the Butler home by chance, just by knocking on doors trying to get an interview. I was depressed and discouraged as I received rejections from several families that I had previously tried to interview. When I arrived at the Butler apartment, I was invited in. George Butler stopped watching television and Elizabeth Butler stopped washing the dishes and talked with me for three hours. Mr. Butler greeted me at the door. When I told him the reason for my visit, he called his wife and asked her to come to the door so that I could explain the class assignment to her. The generosity of the Butlers with their time greatly picked up my spirits. Mr. Butler assured me that he enjoyed the interview after it had ended. He and his wife invited me to visit them socially some time.

At first Mr. and Mrs. Butler were a little apprehensive; but after about twenty minutes, they became much more relaxed. Then, there was a very relaxed atmosphere. They made me feel comfortable and welcome. During the course of the interview Mrs. Butler served us coffee and home-made cookies. I must admit that her cookies were delicious.

While Mr. Butler appeared to be the dominant decision-maker for the family, one got the feeling that usually he consulted with his wife, as he did before I was granted the interview.

Mr. and Mrs. Butler had been married five years. Both were employed before marriage. She worked in an insurance company and he was employed in the stock room of a department store. Neither was explicit about the nature of his or her work. Mrs. Butler said, "When George Jr. was born I had to leave work to take care of the baby." Her mother and mother-in-law offered to take care of the baby so that she could continue working, but Mrs. Butler felt it was more important for a

168

mother to stay home with her child and care for him properly. Mr. Butler agreed with his wife. However, he acknowledged, that it was more difficult, financially, to maintain an adequate standard of living after Mrs. Butler left her job.

Mr. Butler did not finish high school and he believes that this is one reason he has not been able to get a good job. So, the extra income of Mrs. Butler greatly helped the family.

Reduction in household income when Mrs. Butler stopped working was just the beginning of a series of overwhelming problems. George, Jr. was a premature baby and was not very healthy. Mr. Butler explained that the baby was in and out of the hospital for about four months during the first year. The specific illness of their first child was not labeled by the parents. Mrs. Butler simply described his problem this way: "the baby would just stop breathing sometimes."

Mr. Butler said that the constant care of the sick child made things very difficult for them. He missed work often to take the baby to the hospital. His boss became disturbed about the time away from work. As a result, "bad relations" developed between Mr. Butler and his supervisor. At the end of winter, after the Christmas rush, business was slow and Mr. Butler was discharged from his job. He believes that the bad relations had something to do with the fact that he was laid off rather than others who had worked for the company a shorter period of time. Mr. Butler had been employed for almost three years, compared with others who had worked for the company less than a year. At first Mr. Butler had "hard feelings" about losing a job. He has been looking for work but has found it difficult to obtain another job because business is slow and his education is limited. Mr. Butler is a member of the National Guard. He said it has a program which will enable him to get a high school equivalency diploma. He believes that he will be able to obtain a job and one better than the job he had before, after he gets a high school diploma. Mrs. Butler also believes that a high school equivalency diploma would greatly help her husband get a job. She is a high school graduate; but her husband quit because he had to help his parents support his family of orientation. He was the oldest son and had two younger sisters and one younger brother.

Mr. Butler has not worked since he was laid off from his stock room job. His family receives public welfare assistance which, according to Mr. Butler "is the only way we can survive until I can get a good job." Doctor bills for George, Jr., now almost two years old, and care for the newest arrival, a girl about two weeks old, were cited by Mr. Butler as pressing obligations, requiring public assistance, since he was out of work.

Both Mr. and Mrs. Butler are very proud of their children and look forward to raising them and providing a good home. In fact, their children appeared to be most important. Mrs. Butler asked me if I would like to see their children, and then she and her husband took me into the bedroom where they were. I was allowed to hold the baby. It was obvious that the parents were very proud of their little daughter. Meanwhile, Mr. Butler picked up their son to show me what a big boy he was. Clearly, these children meant more to Mr. and Mrs. Butler than anyone else in the world.

We went back to the living room and the story of the Butler household continued to unfold. Mr. Butler said he did not feel right about being on welfare but that it was necessary for the time being in order to take care of his family. Even while working, it was difficult, he said, for the family to get by on his low wages. For this reason, Mr. Butler had pinned all hope on getting a high school diploma as a possible way of improving his earning capacity.

When I asked the Butlers how many children they were planning to have, both responded, saying, "Our family is large enough." They have a boy and a girl and think that this is sufficient. They indicated that with a small family they can provide better things, a better home and a better life — perhaps the kind of life that neither Mr. nor Mrs. Butler had known.

The father in this household sees his life as one in which the odds have been against him; but he would like to send his children to college "so that they would have a better chance of being successful than I had." When asked what type of jobs they would like their children to have when they grow up, both parents felt that the final decision should be up to their children; but Mr. Butler added that he would like to see his son grow up to be a doctor or an engineer. In other words, he would like to see his son in a position with a good future, one that would enable him to earn a good living. The parents would like their daughter to attend college also. They think that it is important for a girl to have an education and to be able to get a good job if ever the need should arise. Mrs. Butler added that she would like to see her daughter become a teacher. She believes that teaching is a good profession for a woman and is also a satisfying occupation. In terms of future plans for herself, Mrs. Butler said that when the children get older and go to school, she would like to go back to work.

The Butlers have a clean and neat apartment. It consists of a large bedroom and kitchen, a medium-sized living room and a bathroom. The furniture was a few years old but the Butlers had kept it in very good shape. Mrs. Butler said that since her husband is not working, he gives her a hand with the care of the babies and the housework.

The Butlers are not fond of the neighborhood in which they live or of the superintendent of the apartment building. "The undisciplined children who run around without parental guidance" was offered by the husband as a reason for not liking the neighborhood. "These children," he said, "are distrustful and have no regard for other people's property." He gave as an example the tires on his car that were slashed and the broken antenna. He assumed that these deeds were done by neighborhood children. Mr. Butler describes the neighborhood as one made up of working-class people with fairly large families. There are regular police patrols; but Mr. Butler feels that they really don't care too much about enforcing the law.

The family would like to move to a larger place. Mrs. Butler cites the need for more space now that they have the new baby. Mr. Butler would like to move outside of the city, where the children would have more room in which to grow up. He thinks it is good for children to grow up where they have room to play. There is a small yard where the Butlers presently live. Mr. Butler dreams of the time when he can be a home-owner. In his words, "I would like to have a place that is really mine." Despite these yearnings, both parents in the family agreed that they probably would miss the neighborhood in which they now live, if they moved. They like the location because it is close to everything, has a little grocery store a half block away. Also, they have some close friends who live in the neighborhood. They said that if they did move they still would get together with their friends, although they guessed that such gatherings might be less frequent than they now are.

Mr. and Mrs. Butler said they read the newspaper every day, read magazines, and watch the news on television. They think it very important to stay informed about the happenings in the world and community. They believe it would be even more important to be informed about the news when their children are older and start school so that they can talk with them about events and circumstances in which they are involved. Mrs. Butler is concerned about earning respect and trust from their children. She believes that this will come from talking intelligently with them and helping them with homework. She said, "It is very important for children to trust and respect their parents and not be afraid to ask for help when it is needed." The Butlers hope that their children will be as proud of them as they are of their offspring. They sincerely hope that they can be good parents and provide well for their children. One gets the feeling that their present circumstances have generated uncertainty as to whether these child-rearing goals can be accomplished.

After this phase of the conversation was over, I asked Mr. and Mrs. Butler if they were close to their families. They replied, "yes." Mrs. Butler said that they tried to see their parents at least once a week and visit them more often when possible. Mr. Butler said that his two sisters were married and lived in the area and that they get together with them and their families from time to time. Mr. Butler's brother and Mrs. Butler's brother used to live nearby but have moved out of the area. They don't see them often now. Mr. Butler said that he especially enjoyed going fishing with his father. He said that this was very relaxing for him and he enjoys talking with his father. He explained that the relationship with their family was very close and that his father, on many occasions, had said that the family should turn to him if it ever needed any help. Mr. Butler did not indicate whether his father's family had been called on during this period of distress because of unemployment.

Although the Butlers would like to move into the country, they would prefer to stay in the region in which they now live. They have lived in this locality all their lives and "just liked it here." One reason may be that most of their friends and family are nearby. If they moved away, they would miss them greatly. Personal friends and family apparently are their greatest source of support, emotionally if not financially.

The Butlers are in their middle twenties but have done quite a bit of living and appear to be older than they are. An outstanding characteristic of this family is, the children come first and are the most important. It is fair to say that the primary goal in life of the husband and wife in this family is to provide a good home and be good parents to their children. All else is secondary. Whether or not this family can achieve its goal is problematical and depends on adaptations of the parents and on many circumstances beyond the control of the Butler household, such as educational requirements, employment possibilities, and welfare public policy. These are contingencies that must be considered in dealing with present problems and in planning future possibilities.

Part III

Black Families
And
The Social System

8 GIFTS TO AMERICA FROM
THE BLACK EXPERIENCE:
THE EQUALITARIAN FAMILY
AND OTHER SOCIAL CUSTOMS

The black family suffers as an object of research because it is difficult to get scholars to study this social institution on its own terms. White social scientists such as Jerold Heiss and Daniel Moynihan have presented the case against the black family. Moynihan's assertion that the family structure among blacks has seriously retarded their progress "because it is so out of line with the rest of American society" has been widely publicized (Moynihan, 1965:29). Less well known is the "indictment . . . handed down against the black family" by Heiss. The key count of the accusation claims that blacks would be "better off if the differences in family form did not exist" (Heiss, 1975:3). His study, entitled *The Case of the Black Family,* sought to determine if "the characteristics of black families . . . differ from those of white families" (Heiss, 1975:5). In summary, states Robert Staples, social scientists who study the black family "have been concerned primarily with its deviance from . . . middle-class white family behavior" (Staples, 1978:vii). Needed, in his opinion, are studies that "concentrate on the unique structure of the Black family and its evolution in meeting its own unique functional prerequisites" (Staples, 1978:v).

The Moynihan Report, although criticized by most knowledgeable family sociologists, nevertheless influenced the development of stereotypic notions about black families that are widespread today. The prevailing stereotype is that most black families are single-parent, matriarchal structures. Actually most blacks who ever marry continue to live with a spouse and two-parent black families are more equalitarian than patriarchal or matriarchal.

Middleton and Putney (1960) studied 40 families—10 white middle-class families, 10 black middle-class families, 10 white

175

working-class families, and 10 black working-class families. Unlike many researchers, and to their credit, Middleton and Putney controlled for social class in their study. The families studied were matched on mean years of marriage and mean age of each spouse. A 15-item questionnaire was filled out separately by each spouse in a family. The questions had to do with child care, purchases and living standard, recreation, and attitudes. In the area of purchasing, for example, the spouses were asked: "If you were buying a house, would you prefer to buy a small new house or a larger but older house costing the same amount?" After spouses had answered the questions separately, they compared their answers and then filled out the same questionnaires jointly. If their separate answers were different, the spouses in each family changed them on the family questionnaire that was filled out jointly.

If the husband won two-thirds or more of the "joint decisions" when joint decisions were different from those of one spouse— that is, if the wife changed her responses to those which the husband had given initially on his separate questionnaire—then the dominance pattern for that family was classified as patriarchal. If the wife won two-thirds or more of the "joint decisions," then the family was labeled matriarchal. If either parent won more than one-third but less than two-thirds of the decisions, the family decision-making pattern was classified as equalitarian.

The most interesting overall finding is that 17 of the 20 black families in the Middleton and Putney study made joint decisions that were classified as equalitarian. When the husband and wife differed, the husband tended to win about as often as did the wife in most of the black families. The findings indicate that, proportionately, more black families (17 out of 20) were equalitarian than white families (13 out of 20).

With reference to social class, middle-class blacks were more equalitarian in family decision-making than any of the other race-class groups studied. Nine out of the 10 black middle-class households resolved their differences in a cooperative, give-and-take way that denoted dominance neither by the husband nor the wife. This was the experience for eight of the 10 working-class black families. A pattern of patriarchal dominance appeared in one of the 10 black middle-class families and of matriarchal dominance in two of the ten black working-class families.

The findings from the Middleton and Putney study are similar to those derived from analysis of the case histories of families in this study. Black families do not constitute a monolithic pattern of relationships; such families vary in behavior by social class as do white families. Research must be sensitive to the variety found in black family life-styles and recognize that there is validity to varying life-styles, that there is no one best family structure for all people in all situations. The family, as well as other institutions, adapts to external as well as internal constraints. Those studying the family must recognize that it is a changing institution and they must take into consideration the qualitative adaptations families make.

Black families are often similar to other families, but they also may differ from white families in specific and fundamental ways due, in general, to their subdominant status in the nation's power structure. These differences should be acknowledged and studied for the information on strategies of adaptation that others may learn whose status, in time, could shift from dominant to subdominant, even as blacks may experience situations of dominance from time to time.

There seems to have been a calculated effort in the United States to doubt, denigrate, and deny the contributions of blacks and other minorities to the culture of this society. This I know because some whites have told me so. More than a quarter of a century ago in 1962, I was called to Washington, D.C., by the Kennedy Administration to serve as Director of Research for Washington Action for Youth—a delinquency-prevention project in the nation's capital that was sponsored by the President's Committee on Juvenile Delinquency and Youth Crime.

I surveyed the distribution of juvenile delinquency in Washington and discovered that two-thirds of the delinquency in that city at that time was committed by youngsters who lived in only one-third of the city's area. The area in which most of the juvenile delinquents lived was impoverished, dilapidated, and racially segregated.

One day, I addressed the Metropolitan Area Crime Council, gave the results of my survey and my interpretation of the findings. In the interpretation, I said, "We are not going to do anything about delinquency in our society unless we do something about poverty; and we are not going to do very much about poverty unless we do something about racial and ethnic discrimination."

A white businessman seated next to me at the head table did not like my remarks and wrote a letter expressing his displeasure. He wrote: "Dear Dr. Willie, You made a very able presentation at the luncheon ... and you exhibit a substantial potential for ... good among your race; ... however, your perspective could stand some small adjustments.... Leaders of your race are never going to pull it up by inculcating in the minds of your people that their plight is caused by whites who 'discriminate' and 'alienate.' ... Ghana, Kenya, Nigeria and all other African nations where the blacks predominate and control are under-nourished educationally [and] impoverished. ... Is there any areas where [Blacks] run their own show where the people are literate and prosperous? ... You have got to do two things. One, you've got to fight for the curtailment of breeding in your low IQ and morally deficient group; and two, you've got to educate all of your race to stop expecting help of any sort. ... When [Blacks] have earned acceptance, they won't have to ask for it. It will come to them. Sincerely, A Suburban White Businessman" (actually, he signed his real name) (Willie, 1969: 6-7).

This letter that doubted, denigrated, and denied the contributions of blacks was written in the 1960s. People were not as wise then as in later years. Yet I received a similar letter in the 1970s after I had addressed the West Tennessee Education Association in Memphis and had endorsed desegregation of the nation's public schools. This time it was a letter to the editor of the Memphis *Commercial Appeal* newspaper. The letter was addressed to the "Harvard educator." The white male letter-writer said: "The first question that comes to mind after reading the remarks attributed to you [in the newspaper] ... is how a possessor of such wild notions could long elude the man with the butterfly net. ... To endorse and promote the forced association of widely disparate races ... is to create abrasive situations in every area of daily existence and to deny human beings the benefits and pleasures of homogeneity. ... History stands as proof that any white nation which crosses its blood lines with blacks sows the seeds of its own destruction. ... It is the white race that has led mankind to its highest levels of achievement. To have race-mixing a sought-after, desired result of education would ultimately lead to genetic changes and condemn civilization to the Dark Ages."

By the 1980s I assumed that my fan letters would be of a different sentiment, that citizens of this nation no longer had the need to doubt, denigrate, and deny the contributions of blacks and other minorities. My assumption was wrong. After an appearance on the McNeil/Lehrer television program of the Public Broadcasting System in the early 1980s to discuss standardized testing as an inappropriate way to assess the teaching competence of blacks and other minorities, I received this letter from San Francisco. It was addressed to "Professor or Doctor or whatever: Charles Willie" and stated these sentiments: "My wife and our two sons are Professors (real ones). They were in your Africa for five years teaching while I was there for electronic-engineering. The Blacks there are extremely stupid but those who are here are stupider to the extreme too! Here you are only good to parade grotesquely with stolen names which belong to White people. You don't see how the Americans are laughing when you tell them your [prestigious] names. Africa needs you and wants you very much. Here our White America doesn't at all!" Then my letter-writer suggested that I should go back to Africa.

There are, of course, whites and other residents of the United States who have sentiments that differ from those expressed by my letter-writers. But too many believe that blacks and their way of life in the United States is a distortion of American culture, a deviation from the mainstream.

My declaration is exactly the opposite: Blacks and other minorities are central to the purpose of this nation. Moreover, they are central to the capacity of this nation to fulfill its purpose. My conclusion is supported by one of the most eminent sociologists in this nation, Robert K. Merton, Professor Emeritus of Columbia University. He said, "It is not infrequently the case that the nonconforming minority in a society represented the interests and ultimate values of the group more effectively than the conforming majority" (Merton, 1968:421). Supreme Court Justice Thurgood Marshall said that "some of the oppressions of the past have been overcome today simply because some of the oppressed had sufficient faith in the Constitution to confront the anomalies in society and to insist that they conform with the basic principles upon which this nation was established" (Marshall, 1973:xii). Former U.S. Secretary of Transportation William Coleman echoed this view when he said, "American whites owe a debt of gratitude to American blacks for making the Constitution work" (quoted in Willie and Edmonds, 1978:3). Of course, when the Constitution works for the minority or the subdominant people of power it also works for the majority.

The significance of the minority (subdominant people of power) to the welfare of the majority is clearly sketched in William Kelley's novel *A Different Drummer,* published in 1959. The story concerns the migration of blacks, all blacks, from a small southern town to the North. Essentially, the story is a lamentation of whites and their fear regarding whether life can be lived without blacks. The high point of the novel is the action by Tucker Caliban, a black man, who decided to cease cooperating in his own oppression. In what would appear to be a self-destructive act, Tucker Caliban asserts himself by tossing salt on his fields, destroying his cattle, and burning down his house. He did all this as means of protest. His action was in accordance with the counsel of an old folk song: "Before I'll be a slave I'll be buried in my grave and go home to my Lord and be free!"

The central and most significant action in *A Different Drummer,* according to Chester Hedgepath, Jr., is "Caliban's destruction of his very means of existence." This action freed both himself and the son of the white plantation owner who was chained to the land as much as the blacks whom he and his family exploited. The son of the white plantation owner had gone north to study at Harvard but could not renounce his way of life and had returned home to collect rents on the land and, in general, to participate in a system of inequality and exploitation even as his father and his father's father had done. When Tucker Caliban decided to cease cooperating in his own oppression, the white plantation owner's son exclaimed: "Who would have thought such a humble, primitive act could teach something to a so-called educated man like myself?" Tucker Caliban's renouncement of his enslavement helped his oppressor to renounce his enslavement too. And so we see in William Kelley's novel that the subdominant people of power who cease to cooperate in their own oppression serve as a corrective to the system established by the dominant people of power (Hedgepath, 1986: 34-35).

Commenting on the responsibility of minorities and other subdominant populations to reform human societies, Richard Korn, a contemporary social scientist, further develops the theme introduced by Kelley in *A Different Drummer*. Korn noted that the majority, the dominant people of power, the inheritors of greatness, tend to waste their heritage. After they have done this, Korn asked, "Who ... is left to keep the flame alive?" His answer, "the oppressed." In the end, said Korn, the bigot can be saved only by his victim (Korn, 1968: 195-196).

I do not wish to romanticize minorities and other subdominant people of power. Actually, they are a reflection of the dominant people of power. They mirror both the worst that a society has been and the best that it could be. Richard Wright wrote this meaningful message about the interdependence of black folk and white folk in America: "The common road of hope which we all have traveled has brought us into a stronger kinship than any words, laws, or legal claims. Look at us and know us and you will know yourself, for *we* are *you,* looking back at you from the dark mirror of our lives!" (Wright and Rosskam, 1941:146).

In this respect, one could assert that Tucker Caliban's self-destructive behavior in *A Different Drummer* reflects the bankrupt southern plantation society in which he participated and the self-destruction inherent in a system of inequality and exploitation. Even so, his willful behavior of ceasing to cooperate in his own oppression ignited the light of freedom in one of his oppressors, the son of a plantation owner. The minority has a beneficial role even under conditions of exploitation and oppression. Because the evil that minorities do tends to live after them while the good is often interred with their bones (to paraphrase Shakespeare's Mark Anthony), I shall devote the remaining portion of this chapter to a discussion of gifts to America from the black experience.

Always there are at least two norms in any social system—the norm of the dominant people of power and the norm of the subdominant people of power. It is well that there should be two norms. For the way of life of the minority identifies customs and conventions that could benefit the majority; and the way of life of the majority identifies customs and conventions that could benefit the minority. All of this is to say that Daniel Patrick Moynihan was wrong several years ago when he said, "it is ... a disadvantage for a minority group to be operating on one principle, while the great majority of the population, and the one with the most advantages to begin with, is operating on another" (Moynihan, 1965:29). It is precisely because minority and majority groups operate on different sets of principles that each group can make a contribution toward social system self-correction. The majority without a minority is incomplete.

Middle-class whites have adopted the idea of individualism, freedom, and autonomy in the family. When there is conflict between the institutional family and an individual member, middle-class whites tend to resolve such conflicts in behalf of the individual because of their fundamental belief in autonomy. Middle-class whites understand individualism as the source of creativity that benefits not only a person but the total society. This is the wisdom of the white middle class that should be shared with others (Willie, 1985:16).

There is a down side to freedom, autonomy, and individualism. When manifested in the extreme, there is little corporate family activity and no sense of a common mission. Feelings of personal entitlement prevail in many white middle-class families. Each family members believes that he or she is entitled to happiness and personal fulfillment. Such feelings can lead to narcissistic attitudes and hedonistic behavior. There is little love and only limited support in a family where these attitudes and feelings prevail. Thus, the freedom that sustains individualism and its creativity sometimes shatters family solidarity among middle-class whites (Willie, 1985:118).

Middle-class black families have a way of life that is almost the opposite of that found among middle-class whites. Among middle-class blacks, maintaining the family in the style to which it has become accustomed is a team effort. Most middle-class black wives and mothers are gainfully employed in the labor force and their wages are a major source of household income. A great stimulus for work by the parents in such families is to equip their offspring with skills and habits of behavior that will keep them from experiencing any deprivations. Thus, middle-class black parents insist that their children get a good education not only to escape possible deprivations but to serve as symbols of achievement for the family as well as for the race. Priming offspring to resist racism and overcome through personal achievement is the main mission of the black middle class.

Celebrations, vacations, and happy times are household affairs that include the extended family in the black middle class. The parental generation does not envy or compete with offspring, and the children honor and are not ashamed of their mothers and fathers. Each generation is expected to stand on the shoulders of the past generation and to do more. All achievement by members in black middle-class families is for the purpose of group advancement as well as individual enhancement. Thus, all family members bask in the reflected glory of any of its successful members. Cooperation rather than competition is the operative concept in black middle-class families.

This corporate activity, as wonderful as it is, has a down side for the black middle class. It stifles experimentation. Family members are urged to adhere to the tried and the true. Because success is a corporate outcome, failure is viewed this way too. Thus, the stress of failure is compounded when one realizes that dishonor has been brought upon the family as well as upon oneself. It is fair to say that the adaptations of middle-class blacks favor the group rather than the individual, including group goals. While black middle-class family members always have a collective cheering squad in the wing, such a group can be quite constraining and may even veto the interests of the individual; inclinations toward personal risk-taking are discouraged and the secure approach is advocated. Indeed, the individual is expected and has an obligation to forego or delay personal gratification for the sake of others in the black middle class (Willie, 1985:72-76). Creativity is limited under these conditions; experimentation is greatly controlled. Individual fulfillment is seen as a self-centered activity and therefore is less valued. What counts in the black middle class is how the family is faring.

Clearly the white middle class that emphasizes individualism could learn something about how to achieve a common family mission and corporate support from middle-class blacks. Such would overcome the fragmentation in family solidarity that is increasingly found in middle-class white families. Likewise, middle-class black families that emphasize group goals and collective effort could learn something about how to achieve freedom, personal fulfillment, and the creativity that flows therefrom. Too much creativity has been stifled in middle-class blacks who have been trained to put family needs above personal needs. And too many individuals have drifted aimlessly in middle-class white families who have been taught to place individual freedom before collective concern. Obviously, the customs and conventions the black middle class has discovered the white middle class has not; and the customs and conventions the white middle class has discovered the black middle class has not. These two groups need each other. It would be a disaster for our society if blacks had adopted the way of life of whites, as suggested by Moynihan; from whence would the source of societal self-correction have come? The complementary functions of black and white families in the middle class also appear in the working class and among the poor. This finding means that at all levels of society blacks and whites have something to teach each other and are therefore interdependent.

In addition to his inappropriate recommendation that blacks should act like whites, Moynihan also described his view of the ideal family. He said, "Ours is a society which presumes male leadership in private and public affairs" (Moynihan, 1965:29). This is a sexist remark. One wonders why the women's movement did not demand an explanation of his sexist orientation when blacks were challenging Moynihan about his inappropriate racial recommendations. To their credit, blacks rejected the Moynihan orientation that men should lead society. Blacks have opted for an equalitarian rather than an authoritarian family. In the black family, neither the husband nor the wife is always in charge (Willie, 1983:156-162).

The gift of the equalitarian or egalitarian family form to America is a common contribution by blacks of all social class levels. New family forms are emerging due largely to changing social circumstances. Andrew Billingsley has stated that "the family is a creature of society" (quoted in Myers, 1982:35). The family form in the United States under greatest attack is the patriarchal structure in which the husband-father is the dominant authority. D.H.J. Morgan has stated, "the patriarchal model of family and society is felt to be inappropriate" today (Morgan, 1975:211). "In most American families," according to Hector Myers, "the pattern of authority and power is differentially assumed by husband and wife in different areas, with different issues, and at different times" (Myers, 1982:57).

Blacks have been pioneers in the development of the flexible family form which distributes decision-making authority between husband-father and wife-mother. My studies and others mentioned of middle-class and working-class black families "confirm the presence of equalitarian decision-making" and reject the notion of female-dominated or male-dominated households (Willie, 1983:159). Furthermore, black parents tend to identify with the future and aspirations of offspring more so than parents in other families who prefer that offspring not forget customs and conventions of the past (Willie, 1985: 154-156, 188-192).

I found that a high proportion of nuclear families among middle-class and working-class blacks were equalitarian in household decision-making (Willie, 1983:15), that the equalitarian pattern of decision-making prevails among whites as well as blacks, but that "more residual practices of matriarchal or patriarchal dominance" are found among whites (Willie, 1983: 161). Therefore, the equalitarian family form is a major contribution by blacks to American society.

REFERENCES

Hedgepath, Chester, Jr. 1986. *Theories of Social Action in Black Literature.*

Heiss, Jerold. 1975. *The Case of the Black Family.* New York: Columbia University Press.

Kelley, William M. 1959. *A Different Drummer.* Garden City: Doubleday.

Korn, Richard. 1968. *Juvenile Delinquency.* New York: Crowell.

Marshall, Thurgood. 1973. "Foreword." In C. V. Willie, B. M. Kramer, and B. S. Brown (eds.), *Racism and Mental Health.* Pittsburgh, Pa.: University of Pittsburgh Press.

Merton, Robert K. 1968. *Social Theory and Social Structure.* New York: Free Press.

Myers, Hector. 1982. "Research on the Afro-American Family." In Barbara Ann Bass, Gail Elizabeth Wyatt, and Gloria Johnson Powell (eds.), *The Afro-American Family,* New York: Grune and Stratton, pp. 35-68.

Middleton, Russell, and Snell Putney. 1960. "Dominance in Decisions in the Family: Race and Class Differences." In C. V. Willie (ed.), *The Family Life of Black People.* Columbus, Ohio: Charles E. Merrill, pp. 16-22.

Morgan, D. H. J. 1975. *Social Theory and the Family.* London: Routledge and Kegan Paul.

Moynihan, Daniel Patrick. 1965. *The Negro Family: A Case for National Action.* Washington, D.C.: U.S. Government Printing Office.

Staples, Robert (ed.). 1978. *The Black Family* (second edition). Belmont, CA: Wardsworth.

Willie, Charles Vert. 1969. *Church Action in the World.* New York: Morehouse-Barlow Co.

_____. 1985. *Black and White Families.* Dix Hills, N.Y.: General Hall.

_____. 1983. *Race, Ethnicity, and Socioeconomic Status.* Dix Hills, NY: General Hall.

Willie, Charles V., and Ronald R. Edmonds. 1978. *Black Colleges in America.* New York: Teachers College Press.

Wright, Richard, and Edwin Rosskam. 1941. *12 Million Black Voices.* New York: Viking Press.

Chapter **9** INTERGENERATIONAL
COOPERATION AND CONFLICT

Of older people in the family, a major difference between
the races is their temporal orientation. My research reveals that
older blacks tend to be oriented to the future and older whites
tend to be oriented to the past. These two orientations have implications for intergenerational harmony and conflict.

There is less intergenerational conflict between older
blacks and succeeding generations in community development
and social action because the older blacks identify with the
aspirations and way of life of the younger members of their
families. In *Children of Crisis,* Robert Coles reports a conversation he had with the father, a minister in a middle-class black
family in the 1960s. The father is a college graduate, a forceful
and sturdy man. When Coles asked the black minister if he
believed the Moynihan Report was for the purpose of collecting
the important facts in a manner that would get congressional
action and help for blacks, the minister replied, "No, I don't. I
rely on what my son says more than my own thinking. ... He is
the coming generation. ... He feels insulted" (Coles,
1968:139-146).

Another example of the older generation identifying with
the younger generation with reference to community development and social action took place in Atlanta, Georgia, several
decades ago. "Daddy" King, Martin Luther King, Jr.'s father,
gathered a small group of older black men (including Benjamin
Mays, then the president of Morehouse College) to take counsel
with his son regarding whether he should return to Montgomery
and risk arrest during the turbulent days of the bus boycott of
which Martin Luther King, Jr., was the appointed leader.
Young King said that he listened to the arguments of a few of
the leaders who were fearful for his safety because they were his
elders whose words commanded respect. But when he replied
that he had reached the point of no return and could not turn

back, his father broke into tears during a moment of silence. Then Martin Luther King, Jr., said, "I looked at Dr. Mays, one of the great influences in my life. Perhaps he heard my unspoken plea. At any rate, he was soon defending my position strongly" (King, 1958). Of Martin King, Jr., Mays said: "I had admired him ever since he entered Morehouse as a freshman; now my respect for him is mounted on wings" (Mays, 1971:268).

And when Martin Luther King, Jr., died, Dr. Mays said: "Fate has decreed that I eulogize him. I wish it might have been otherwise, for, after all, I am three score years and ten and Martin ... is dead at thirty- nine" (Mays, 1971). Here was the older black person wishing that he could have sacrificed his life for the younger black person.

Among whites, it is often the other way around: The older generation tends to hold itself up as a model for the younger generation and insists that the customs and way of life of those who are older should be acknowledged and respected. Because the older generation among whites insists on the preeminence of its customs and ways of doing things, sometimes there are intergenerational strains within the kinship system.

Erik Erikson's paradigm of the eight stages of life indicates how ego qualities emerge through critical periods of development. It is a model of how the dominant people of power in this society conceptualize interaction between age and authority in the social structure. According to Erikson, ego integrity is the final or eighth stage. It is found largely among elders in society and gives both order and meaning to life. One does not approach ego integrity, however, until (in Erikson's words) "the individual know[s] how to be a follower of image bearers in religion and in politics, in economic order and in technology, in aristocratic living and in the arts and sciences." These individuals, according to Erikson, are emotionally integrated and therefore able to accept the responsibility of leadership (Erikson, 1963:269).

Erikson is a great scholar and a great name in the behavioral sciences. One is cautious about challenging his conclusions. Nevertheless, I must respectfully ask: How does learning how to follow the bearers of political images that oppress, economic images that impoverish, and aristocratic living that excludes prepare one to lead? If Martin Luther King, Jr., had followed the bearers of such images as his elders had done, the civil rights movement would not have developed as it did. His elders in the black community knew that this prediction was true, and so they identified with him and his leadership rather than insisting that he identify with the order and meaning to which they had grown accustomed.

According to Erikson and the dominant people of power in this nation, it is proper for the possessor of "ego integrity" (those in the eighth stage of life) "to defend the dignity of [their] own life-style against all ... threats." Even though elders may be aware of the relativity of all the various lifestyles, they nevertheless will defend "the style of integrity developed by their culture or civilization" as "the seal of [their] moral paternity" (Erikson, 1963:268).

This analysis by a white scholar (Erikson, 1963), and the dialogue of black elders with a younger adult member (Martin Luther King, Jr.), illustrate the different practices of dominant and subdominant people of power in this nation. Black elders among the subdominant people of power tend to identify and even defer to the younger people in their community, while white elders among the dominant people of power tend to expect and insist on deference from the younger generation.

According to Micaela di Leonardo, older, middle-class whites have doubts that members of the younger generation can measure up to their standards and older, working-class whites who want to provide better opportunities for members of the next generation are afraid that their upwardly mobile offspring will resent the way of life of their elders and cast them aside as non-assets (di Leonardo, 1984:123).

This intergenerational conflict is not seen as often among blacks because the older generation in both the middle class and the working class expect and even want the younger members of their kinship system to over-achieve the elders. Moreover, they sacrifice or defer their own interests to those of the young to achieve this goal. Older blacks do not set forth their customs and culture as a "moral paternity" requiring emulation. Thus, younger blacks tend to honor older blacks not because of their age and authority, but because older blacks tended to honor the young. It is as simple as that: Respect of the old by the young is a reciprocal response to respect of the young by the old among blacks.

We conclude that there is more intergenerational harmony than intergenerational conflict between older blacks in the family and members of the younger generation because (1) older blacks do not esteem their culture as a model for the young; (2) older blacks respect the aspirations of younger family members and identify with their new way of life; (3) older blacks of all social class levels expect and want family members of the next generation to out-achieve their elders; (4) older blacks make the sacrifices that are necessary for the upward mobility of family members in younger generations by offering financial support, housing accommodations, child-care, and other assistance. These adaptations by some older blacks in the family differ from those of many older whites who tend to esteem their own way of life as the model to which younger generations should conform.

REFERENCES

Coles, Robert. 1968. *Children of Crisis*. New York: Dell Publishing Co.

Erikson, Erik H. 1963. *Childhood and Society* (second edition). New York: W. W. Norton.

King, Martin Luther, Jr. 1958. *Stride Toward Freedom*. New York: Harper & Row.

Leonardo, Micaela di. 1984. *The Varieties of Ethnic Experiences*. Ithaca, N.Y.: Cornell University Press.

Mays, Benjamin. 1971. *Born to Rebel*. New York: Charles Scribner's Sons.

Chapter **10** THE CASE FOR THE BLACK
MALE: A REBUTTAL TO THE
CASE AGAINST THE BLACK
MALE

The black male is a difficult topic to discuss, so much misinformation has been written about him. The case against the black male is being prosecuted in the mass media with white public opinion serving as both judge and jury, and some blacks participating as accusatory expert witnesses. What is strange about this trial is that the accused is not permitted to defend himself. The mass media tend to ignore information that could exonerate the accused.

The *Boston Globe* published an article on black men and black women a few years ago (Reynolds, 1985:B23, B26). It was entitled "Black Men-Black Women: The Expectation Gap." Despite its title, the article really was an assault on the character of black men. Then Bill Moyers trotted out his CBS documentary on "The Vanishing Family—A Crisis in Black America" which highlighted Timothy, an unmarried black father of many children whom columnist George Will called a "paradigm" of guiltless sexual irresponsibility. George Will said "The Timothys are more of a menace to black progress than the Bull Connors were" (Will, 1986:11).

Alice Walker's prize-winning book, *The Color Purple,* made its debut. Now a major motion picture, the book, said *Essence* magazine, reveals truth about black men and black women, and the *New York Review of Books* said Alice Walker called into being a whole submerged world. As you may know, the book begins with a letter to God written by a fourteen-year old black girl who tells how she was raped by her stepfather (Walker, 1982:1). From this point on, the Alice Walker story about black men gets uglier and uglier and becomes, in effect, a stereotype of poor black men as well as a manifestation of self-hatred for black women.

191

Why is maladaptive behavior among black individuals classified as a paradigm or model? When such behavior is found among whites, why is it not referred to as a paradigm or model? As a paradigm or model, maladaptive behavior allegedly impacts upon an entire population group.

In his 1965 report on *The Negro Family,* Daniel Moynihan said, "The white family, despite many variants, remains a powerful agency . . ." (Moynihan, 1965:35). Sociologically, the same may be said of the black family. But neither Will or Moynihan came to this conclusion. Moynihan declared that "White children without fathers at least perceive all about them the pattern of men working" (Moynihan, 1965:35). Sociologically, the same may be said of black children. But neither Will nor Moynihan came to this conclusion. Indeed, without producing comparative evidence, Moynihan concluded that "Negro children without fathers flounder and fail" (Moynihan, 1965:35). The inference is that white children without fathers do not flounder and fail.

The stereotype that there is no pathology among poor whites must be corrected. Writer Ken Auletta has provided a first-hand account of life in Preston County, West Virginia, in the Appalachian area. Preston County is rural and predominantly white. Thirty-one percent of the population is classified as poor. This is three times the proportion of whites in the nation so classified. Nearly 70 percent of the residents have lived in the same house all of their lives, so their poverty is a persisting phenomenon (Auletta, 1982:159). Auletta said the homes in the area are house trailers or wooden shacks, with television antennas sprouting out from most of them. Actually, TV is the sole contact that some of these households have with the outside world (Auletta, 1982:159).

In terms of personal characteristics, the poor white men in this county have an average of less than nine years of schooling. The average mother in Preston County receives welfare and has received it more than a half-dozen years. Auletta called welfare "a way of life" among these people. Being poor is no social stigma in Preston County (Auletta, 1982:160). Incest is common too, and family troubles haunt these poor white people of

Preston County. Auletta said "alcohol, unemployment, ... frustration, and boredom generate violence in the home," of which women are often the victims (Auletta, 1982:160).

Carolyn Chute's novel, *The Beans of Egypt, Maine,* is also about the way of life of the white poor. The opening pages in Carolyn Chute's story about poor whites are not much different from the opening pages of Alice Walker's story about poor blacks.

In both novels, the mother is ill and the man in the house turns to a daughter in the house for sexual favors. The white daughter sleeps in bed with her daddy, not just in the afternoon when her daddy has a pain in his back and has to take a nap but also at nighttime too, according to the book, *The Beans of Egypt, Maine* (Chute, 1985:1-3). And the stepfather forces sexual intercourse upon his black stepdaughter in *The Color Purple* (Walker, 1982:1). There are babies in and out of wedlock and plenty of fussing and fighting in the white households of the poor in rural Maine, according to Chute, and in the black households of the poor in rural Alabama, according to Walker.

The Beans of Egypt, Maine and *The Color Purple* reveal similarities between poor blacks and poor whites. Actually the portraits of the black poor and especially poor black men contained in the *Boston Globe* article and in the CBS documentary are similar to descriptions of poor white men in the social science literature as well as in novels. In my study of *Black and White Families,* I summarize the literature regarding what is known about poor white families (Willie, 1985). Poor white men are as likely to project their frustrations upon poor white women by way of violent behavior as are the poor in any other population. This conversation was recorded between a police officer and a poor white man who is identified as a hillbilly.

Police officer: "Look, you've got four kids. What if they found out you beat up their mother? Why did you do it?"

Hillbilly: "She got out of line and I stomped her."

Police officer: "What would you have done if your father had done it to your mother?"

Hillbilly: "He did it all the time" (Auletta, 1982:160).

Thomas Cottle reports a similar experience of family violence among whites. The interview is with a twelve-year old son:

The Son: "You know what I've been doing for six months? I've been a referee for all their fights".

Interviewer: "Your parents have been fighting?"

The Son: "Just about every night."

Interviewer: "Your dad?"

The Son: "Mother too. Both of them. Screaming, hitting. Breaking furniture. They're all right for two or three nights, then they're back at it."

Interviewer: "What started it?"

The Son: "I don't know. One night, I think maybe it was New Year's Eve, I was in bed and they were fighting. Dad pushed her or hit her and she fell. I waited for a while and then went in. She had this big cut over her eye. I had to push Dad away. Another night I carried Mom into my bedroom. She was barely conscious. Then another night she must have hit him pretty hard because when I got in there his nose was bleeding. It wasn't broken, but he was crying and she was crying."

The Son: "Dad gets awful angry, you know."

Interviewer: "I didn't know."

The Son: "Well, he can. I never saw him hurt anyone, but he's always picked on Mom." (Cottle, 1975:7-8).

The interesting thing about this report in family pathology is that the family is not poor. But the family is white. The father is an automotive executive and has a more than adequate income. Despite the novels, newspaper articles, and television documentaries about poor blacks, comparative social science data indicate that pathology and maladaptive behavior are not limited to poor black men. Indeed, such are not limited to any racial group or social class category. Whites like blacks of all class levels have their share of pathology and so do the affluent and the poor.

The *Boston Globe* article carried this subheadline: "Black Men Are Falling Behind Black Women." *Essence* magazine editor, Susan Taylor, said headlines like this one are a myth because black women are on the bottom of the ladder economically. "They make 92 cents for every $1.00 a black man makes," she said. While *Essence* has published articles on the stresses of black male-black female relationships, Editor Susan Taylor said, "The reality is that there is a war on black people in America," and that neither black men nor black women should "buy into the myth" that one or the other is enjoying some kind of privilege. Taylor concluded that the myth has been cultivated as a way to further pit black men and women against each other (Reynolds, 1985:B23, B26).

The *Boston Globe* included Susan Taylor's contradicting testimony in its case against the black male as a good newspaper should but then immediately ignored the wisdom of her remarks. The reporter continued to build the case against black men. To counter Susan Taylor's statements, the report introduced expert opinion from a few blacks with intimate knowledge of black ghetto and slum life. The first witness was a black lawyer, the president of Boston Black Men's Association. He said black youngsters have no positive black male role models and black boys do not have any goals other than possibly achieving as athletes and musicians. Another witness quoted was a fourteen-year old black male resident of Roxbury. He said that many of his friends had dropped out of school but that they probably would have remained in school if they had a father living with them. These statements described black boys as failures and suggested that black men were contributing to their failure.

Moreover, black boys were described as not aspiring to attend college, never dreaming of becoming a professor or politician, not thinking about a career as a doctor, lawyer, or businessman. Rather, they were characterized as having high rates of unemployment, crime, and incarceration. In summary, black males were portrayed as hanging around the street and getting into trouble. Their problems were described by the *Boston Globe's* reporter as leading to an unbroken cycle of poverty and little upward social mobility.

Mothers were ignored, dismissed, or denied as being of any consequence in the lives of their black sons by the *Boston Globe* reporter. Black wives of black husbands were completely ignored in the article. It was asserted that black boys turn more to their peers for support and direction than to their mothers.

Studies about middle-class black families that I recently reviewed came to conclusions that are opposite to those that were offered by the *Boston Globe* reporter. Annie Barnes said "studies of the black family have primarily focused on the low-income and working-class communities." These studies, she said, have emphasized matrifocality, a concept which describes domestic units dominated by females. Annie Barnes said, "This is a type of family found among [some] lower-class black families in which [the man in the house] appears to be unsuited for steady employment" (Barnes, 1983:55). The error in most studies of black families, Barnes asserts, is "the phenomenon of lumping all blacks together and sometimes comparing them with the white middle class" (Barnes, 1983:56).

Barnes studied middle-class black families in Atlanta, Georgia, and found circumstances quite different from those described by the *Boston Globe*. She found that a majority of the black men and black women in her study had attended college; a higher proportion of black women than black men had graduated from college and gone on to graduate school. But a higher proportion of black men compared to black women had obtained doctoral degrees. She also found that a majority of both middle-class black men and middle-class black women held white-collar jobs but that black women outnumbered black men in these jobs by 12 percentage points. Some of the middle-class families in Atlanta Barnes classified as matriarchal, but they were a minority of the middle-class black families that she studied (Barnes, 1983:60).

Walter Allen studied a sample of middle-class blacks in Chicago. About one-third of the black men and slightly more than one-fourth of the black women in his study had studied in college (Allen, 1983:80). About half of the black men and slightly more than one-quarter of the women held white-collar jobs (Allen, 1983:81). For the most part, Allen discovered that the black wives in middle-class black families reported greater marital satisfaction than their husbands (Allen, 1983:83). Race, however, had little to do with variation in marital adjustment according to Allen (Allen, 1983:85).

Finally, Donald P. Addison reported the results of his study of black middle-class wives in Crescent City, Iowa. In Addison's study, the women found their men to be temperate, industrious, faithful, and trustworthy (Addison, 1983:97-99). Addison said that while the literature on black family life tends to char-acterize black men as "weak, unprincipled individuals with minimum concern for [their] family" (Addison, 1983:100), the black women in his study characterized husbands as "faithful and emotionally strong" (Addison, 1983:109).

One might object to the fact that studies cited have been of middle-class black families only. The *Boston Globe* reporter wrote about poor black families only. If the way of life of middle-class black men is not representative of all blacks, neither is the way of life of poor black men representative of all blacks. Yet, the reporter presented the troubles of some poor black men and their relationships with some poor black women as if they were indicative of the relationships between all black men and black women. Only one-third of the black population is below the poverty line. Thus, stories about poor blacks discuss a minority sector of the black population in the United States.

The mass media commentators and reporters who assert that poor black boys have no male role models, pay little attention to what their mothers say or do, believe they can earn money and be upwardly mobile through professional athletics and music only, and never dream of becoming a professor, politician, doctor, or lawyer, make assertions that are contrary to some of the find-ings reported in this volume.

Actually, black men along with black women, as stated earlier, have contributed to a revolutionary practice in family relations in this nation. The source of this practice, like other good things blacks contribute, has remained invisible or been ignored. The revolution which black men and women have created by rejecting the Moynihan sexist notion of perpetual male leadership is the equalitarian family in which neither partner always prevails. Walter Allen reported that satisfaction ratings increase in families in which power is shared and decrease in authoritarian structures—patriarchal or matriarchal (Allen,

1983:77). The equalitarian black family is a manifestation of this principle and its way of life could benefit all. Therefore, I assert that black men with the help of black women are revolutionizing the power relationship between men and women in the kinship system (Willie, 1981). This new relationship and arrangement is the prevailing pattern now in all USA households, with whites following the lead of blacks. Public opinion specialist Louis Harris found that "a majority of married people are convinced that marriage is no longer an arrangement whereby the husband assumes the breadwinning responsibilities and the wife takes over the household management and childrearing. To the contrary, both men and women are now convinced that a marriage in which both husband and wife work and share the housekeeping and child care is a better one" (Harris, 1987: 129).

Black parents have insisted that their daughters receive an education similar to or better than that provided for their sons as a way of overcoming the discriminatory effects of sexism against women. And black husbands in general have encouraged black wives to enter the labor force and to pursue occupations that sometimes are more prestigious than their own. If measures of satisfaction in marriage increase with the increasing experience of equalitarianism, then this new style of social relations that does not presume male leadership in private and public affairs is something of value to which the rest of society is and should be conforming. Blessed be black men and women who have kept alive the belief in equality in household and other human affairs. Our nation has not recognized equalitarianism in the family as a major contribution to social life in this nation that emerged from the black experience. It has not recognized this because it has been too busy damning black males.

This bit of moral alchemy in which the good things that black males do are transformed into bad things is not new. One of the worse names to attach to a black male is to call him Uncle Tom. Unfortunately, many, including some blacks, have not read Harriet Beecher Stowe's book, *Uncle Tom's Cabin*. It was Tom who sacrificed his freedom so that his master could raise enough money from the sale of his faithful servant to pay off debts and keep the plantation and the other slaves who were Tom's family and friends together until emancipation. No other slave sale could have brought as much money as the sale of Tom. If Tom had escaped to the freedom which was his eternal ambition, debtors would have foreclosed on his master and sold all of the slaves "down the river" to owners who were more inclined to brutalize them. Tom knew this and sacrificed his freedom so that the slave community of which he had been a part could remain together under the protection of a benign rather than a brutal owner.

Tom never made it back to the plantation of his original master as he hoped he would. He died standing up to Legree, the most hated slave owner in the South. Tom was ordered to whip a woman slave. Tom replied, "I beg Mas'r's pardon .... It's what I an't used to, — never did, — and can't do, no way possible." Then he said, "This yer thing I can't feel it right to do; — and, Mas'r, I never shall do it, — never!" Finally, Tom said, "Mas'r, if you mean to kill me, kill me; but, as to my raising my hand agin any one here, I n'ver shall — any one here, I'll die first!" And die, Tom did. A sacrificial death, he died. While the tears and blood flowed down his face, said Harriet Beecher Stowe, Tom exclaimed, "No! no! no! my soul an't yours, Mas'r! You haven't bought it, — Ye can't buy it!" (Stowe, 1852:364-366). Tom understood sacrifice and suffering for the sake of others. His is a marvelous legacy not unlike that of Jesus Christ, Moses, Ghandi, and Martin Luther King, Jr.

How is it that the name of a black man who perfected the practice of sacrificial love has become an appellation of disdain? Sociologist Robert Merton said the moral alchemist transforms what is a virtue for the in-group into a vice when found among the out-group (Merton, 1949). So sacrificial love which is good when found among white men is bad when exhibited among black men, according to some mass media reporters. Thus, acting with courage and sacrifice which are virtues when found among whites is transformed into a vice when exhibited among blacks such as Uncle Tom. People who participate in such racial transformations are appropriately labeled moral alchemists. Black men and women should be honored for discovering and refining the equalitarian family form. Instead they are ridiculed if their families do not act like white families.

There is something strange and even demonic about the case against the black male. Maybe the origin of this strange, demonic behavior is as ancient as the story of the birth of Jesus in an oppressed Jewish family. The Jewish mother, Mary, has been venerated. But the Jewish father, Joseph, has been virtually ignored. And yet it was an act of acceptance and grace for Joseph to accept his wife and care for her child even though he was told that he was not the father. Mary did not earn the right to be the mother of Jesus. But, according to the law of that time, Joseph had the right to divorce a wife who was with child allegedly not his own. Joseph did not respond according to the law. He, a poor and persecuted Jewish man, responded according to the requirements of grace. And for so doing, Joseph has become invisible and virtually ignored when the story of the birth of Jesus is celebrated annually. Black men and especially poor black men exist in the tradition of Joseph — invisible, ignored, and denied. Nevertheless, their way of life is something of value — essential and significant in social organization. The lessons they can teach we ignore at our peril.

REFERENCES

Addison, Donald. 1983. "Black Wives: Perspective About Their Husbands and Themselves." In Constance E. Obudho (ed.), *Black Marriage and Family Therapy.* Westport, CT: Greenwood Press, pp.91-111.

Allen, Walter. 1983. "Differences in Husband-Wife Interpersonal Relationships During the Middle Years of Marriage." In Constance E. Obudho (ed.), *Black Marriage and Family Therapy.* Westport, CT: Greenwood Press, pp.75-89.

Auletta, Ken. 1982. *The Underclass.* New York: Random House.

Barnes, Annie. 1983. "Black Husbands and Wives: An Assessment of Marital Roles in a Middle-Class Neighborhood." In Constance E. Obudho (ed.), *Black Marriage and Family Therapy.* Westport, CT: Greenwood Press, pp.55-73.

Chute, Carolyn. 1985. *The Beans of Egypt, Maine.* New York: Ticknor and Fields.

Cottle, Thomas J. 1975. *A Family Album.* New York: Harper and Row.

Harris, Louis. 1987. *Inside America.* New York: Vintage Books.

Merton, Robert K. 1949. *Social Theory and Social Structure.* Glencoe, Il: Free Press.

Moyers, Bill. 1986. "The Vanishing Black Family." Television documentary.

Moynihan, Daniel Patrick. 1965. *The Negro Family.* Washington, D.C.: U.S. Government Printing Office.

Reynolds, Pamela. 1985. "Black Men-Black Women: The Expectation Gap." *Boston Globe* (September 22), pp. B23, B26.

Stowe, Harriet Beecher. 1852. *Uncle Tom's Cabin.* New York: Pocket Books.

Walker, Alice. 1982. *The Color Purple.* New York: Pocket Books.

Will, George F. 1986. "Dehumanizing Blacks." *Boston Globe* (February 15), p.11.

Willie, Charles V. 1981. *Black and White Families.* Dix Hills, New York: General Hall.

Chapter 11 THE ROLE OF MOTHERS IN THE LIVES OF OUTSTANDING SCHOLARS

Findings in the literature about parental identification suggest that "stronger father identification [is] associated with better adjustment and more masculine sex-role behavior of the son," according to Alfred Heilbrun, Jr. (Heilbrun, 1972:59). Of women who have achieved in science and mathematics and in other areas, including professional athletics and the arts, Henry Biller's review of the literature informs us that "they are likely to have had fathers who did [not] stereotype them and gave them the strength to be able to deal with authority figures.....
[Fathers] ... helped them constructively deal with some of the barriers ... in our society against women achieving...." (Biller, 1976:76).

Not much has been written about mothers and their contribution to career success of their children. It is fair to say they have been ignored or denied. In the award-winning book, *The American Occupational Structure* authored by Peter Blau and Otis Duncan (1967), mothers largely were ignored. Beverly Duncan and Otis Dudley Duncan, analyzing data also collected in the study, reported that a factor favorable to occupational success among white men in two-parent families is a father who himself has been successful in the occupational sphere; "[but] among intact black families...the father's occupational achievement has only a slight influence on the occupational success of his male offspring" (Duncan and Duncan, 1970:168). These social scientists were silent about the effect, if any, of the activities of the mother in two-parent families on the occupational outcomes of offspring.

Much data have been accumulated on maternal deprivation. But such studies are concerned less with achievement outcomes of offspring than with the presence or absence of developmental deficiencies. Even some attempts at positive statements about mothers turn out to be negative: "There is evidence that indicates that father-absent children with competent mothers," according to Henry Biller, "are less likely to have certain types of developmental deficits than are children who have a dominating mother and a passive-ineffectual father." Note that the earlier statements by Duncan and Duncan about the relationship of achievement of children and that of fathers did not mention mothers at all. But the Biller statement characterized dominant mothers as a socialization liability for children when they are present in families with subdominant fathers. Nothing is said about the socialization effect on children of domineering fathers.

Blau and Duncan arranged for the collection of statistics on social mobility in a "Current Population Survey" of the U.S. Bureau of the Census. They developed a questionnaire that obtained information on male respondents and their parents, including marital status of the respondent, items on the birthplace of the respondent, his father and mother, the educational attainment of the respondent's oldest brother (if any), the respondent's several occupations, the occupation of the respondent's father (or mother, if she headed a single-parent family), and for a married respondent the occupation of his father-in-law. To summarize, this study was concerned about the male respondent, and then as a context variable—the education of the respondent's oldest brother but not that of the oldest sister, and the occupation of the respondent's father-in-law but not that of his mother-in-law. In two-parent families, the study ignored the occupational and educational attainments of the respondent's mother (Blau and Duncan, 1967:10-11).

With these data and their omissions, it is impossible to make any determination about characteristics of mothers and their association, if any, with the social mobility of offspring. Thus Blau and Duncan could state only that "father's occupational status ... influences son's career achievement by affecting his education and first job [and] it also has a delayed effect on achievement that persists...." (Blau and Duncan, 1967:40). They could say nothing about the mother's contribution to the offspring's career in two-parent families, the prevailing type.

If Blau and Duncan ignored mothers, Daniel Patrick Moynihan denied them. In his 1965 report to the nation on *The Negro Family,* Moynihan said, "White children without fathers at least perceive all about them the pattern of men working," but "Negro children without fathers flounder—and fail" (Moynihan, 1965:35). Young people, black as well as white, must have had mothers, but their existence and contribution to the educational and occupational success of their offspring is not mentioned by Moynihan. Only fathers or other men count in the career advancement or failure of young people, according to his assessment.

He concludes that "ours is a society which presumes male leadership in private and public affairs. The arrangements of society facilitate such leadership and reward it. A subculture, such as that of the Negro American, in which this is not the pattern, is placed at a distinct disadvantage." Indeed, Moynihan suggests that a family structure other than one that presumes male leadership retards a population "because it is so out of line with the rest of the American society" (Moynihan, 1965:29). He was particularly negative about a matriarchal structure in which there is female leadership or domination. Moynihan's assertion is a general denial of any significance of the contribution of mothers to the career-development of their children, and to the progress of a racial population.

Herbert Wasserman's study of poor black boys in Boston revealed no statistically significant differences in school performance of the sons in two-parent and in single-parent families. His study consisted of a sample of families in the same low-rent housing project, that were similar in a number of background characteristics, including the ages of their male offspring (Wasserman, 1970: 294-298). Although the Wasserman study did not identify a positive effect of mothers on the educational attainment of their children, it suggested the absence of a negative effect. Moynihan gave no evidence to support his contention that black children in single-parent households "fail and flounder." He was convinced, however, that there was "an unmistakable influence" (Moynihan, 1965: 82).

In social science, there ar e agreed-upon canons that prescribe *how* data should be collected and analyzed. But *what* is studied often has autobiographical origins. For example, Blau and Duncan dedicated their book to their fathers "whose occupational achievements," they said, "greatly facilitated those of their [own]" (Blau and Duncan, 1967: v). Believing that their fathers were essential to their success, Blau and Duncan designed a study that had as a primary goal determining the association, if any, of fathers' achievements to those of their sons.

DEFINITION OF THE PROBLEM

I, too, am not immune from insinuating personal history into social science research. Growing up in a sexist society dominated by men that, according to Moynihan, rewards males for being "dominant in family relationships" (Moynihan, 1965: 29), I, too, thought that fathers were the more significant figures that facilitated the fashioning of a child's adult career, until I interviewed in depth my mother and father after I became a professional sociologist.

In my family of orientation, the community at large heaped accolades upon my father—Louis James Willie, Sr.—for the good job he did in providing for his family and in promoting the education of his children. With only an eighth-grade education, my father left his homesite down on the farm in Panola County, Texas, and migrated to the city where he obtained a job with the Pullman Company—first in the Fort Worth district. He later transferred to the Dallas district of the company as a sleeping-car porter. He was a steady worker and remained in the service of the Pullman Company 42 years, until his retirement. He was a thrifty person, who did not squander his earnings. He was respected in the community and was goal-directed. He was an officer of the church, and, for many years, its treasurer.

My paternal grandparents were farmers. Before my paternal grandmother died, she asked my father and his brothers to support the education of their only sister, the youngest child. In part to fulfill the request of his deceased mother, my father left the farm and migrated to the city where he believed he could earn enough money to help send his sister to college. The same year that my father left the farm and moved to the city, he and my mother—Carrie Sykes Willie—married. She and he met as youth delegates to a Sunday school convention in her hometown. They were married for more than 50 years, until his death in the late 1970s.

My mother grew up in Marshall, Texas, a small town also in East Texas near Panola County. My mother was the youngest member of her family and was the only one of several siblings to receive a college education. My maternal grandfather was a blacksmith and my maternal grandmother was a cook in a private household. My mother's father contracted for work at a local college that needed a skilled blacksmith. He requested that part of the funds owed him should be credited to a tuition account for his youngest child's first year of college.

My mother was eager to go to school. She and her mother helped to raise tuition for the subsequent years by taking in laundry. My mother attended college for one semester a year for several years and did not graduate until she was 30 years old.

It was difficult for a married woman to get work in a city school system during the Depression if her husband also had a job. My father, of course, was employed as a Pullman porter. My mother wanted to work as a public school teacher, but the only jobs open to her were in rural counties far from our Dallas home. If my mother had taken one of these jobs, she would have commuted home on weekends only. This arrangement would have increased family finances but weakened family bonds, owing to decreasing interaction between husband and wife and limited surveillance of four boys and a girl coming of age in a city ghetto.

My mother and father decided that she would not work outside the home, given that she could not get a job in the local city school system. Explaining her decision to remain in continuous residence with her family, my mother said she was busy with the development of her "school at home." Her school at home was operated for the benefit of her husband and her five children. My mother believed that if she could raise five good citizens of her community, of her state, and of her country, she would be doing more than if she left them to fend for themselves while she tried to teach the children of others in a distant community. This belief showed her pragmatism and optimism.

My mother and father made a joint decision that he would work for pay to provide the financial resources for the family and that she would work without pay as a homemaker, providing a supportive, learning environment for the family in her "school at home." The school-at-home theme was a manifestation of my parents' belief in education, their orientation to the future, and their ability to transform liabilities into assets.

It is not uncommon for a working-class family to rally around one or two of the smarter youngsters in the household and send them to college. But, when all offspring in a relatively large working-class family with a modest income complete college and four of the five children obtain graduate degrees, something unusual must be happening. Such was the experience of myself and my siblings.

What I had not recognized as a significant contribution to our achievement was the extraordinary capacities of my mother. Her educational attainment was unusual for black women of her background who were born before the twentieth century began. It was higher than that of my father. Moreover, her employment, if the local school system had hired her, would have been as a professional teacher, an occupation also outranking that of my father's as a service worker. Apparently the educational and occupational capacities of my mother enhanced and did not undercut the role of father in the family. This finding is contrary to assertions by some social scientists about the negative effects of a female spouse of achievement who is task-oriented (Moynihan, 1965: 34). In addition, there appeared to be an association between the educational attainment of my mother, a college graduate, and that of her offspring, all of whom are college graduates.

In 1973, three years before *Roots* was published (Haley, 1976), I took my tape recorder in hand and flew from my residence in Syracuse, New York, where I was a university teacher and administrator, to Dallas Texas, to visit with my parents. They were in their early eighties. I wanted to hear from them the specifics of their story—how they managed to do so much for their offspring with so little.

In these conversations I discovered that my father and mother were a team but that she really was the foundation of our family and contributed enormously to the achievement of its members. In unobtrusive ways, she supported and sustained the efforts of her husband and her children. She was the auditor and accountant of family finances, speech writer for her husband, teacher, tutor and story reader for her children, nursemaid for the sick, the purchasing agent and consumer advocate for the best bargain in the marketplace, the director of recreation and celebrant for holidays, the cook, laundry person, disciplinarian, cleaning lady, and a quiet cheerleader for all; she and my father were a team. But without her, what happened would not have happened the way that it did.

Recognizing my mother as a significant contributor to my siblings' and my father's achievement, I have questioned whether or not other mothers have played this fundamental role but have been ignored or denied. In addition to recognizing in adulthood what my mother did for me and my brothers and sister as children, which we did not understand at the time, I also am persuaded to believe that part of my father's in-domitable drive to educate all of his children was, in part, a spill-over from the promise he made to his mother on her deathbed that he would find a way to help send the youngest child in their family to college.

My experience has been that mothers, whether in life or in death, are formidable influences. The thought occurred to me that in my interviews with my parents, I had done more than capture the history of my own family. I had, in the words of the book jacket writer for *Roots,* "rediscovered for an entire people a rich cultural heritage." Indeed my search for the full role of mothers in the achievement of their offspring may speak "not just to blacks, or to whites, but to all people" (*Roots* book jacket, 1976). We can verify these assertions about the contributions of mothers only if we stop ignoring or denying them in our research designs and analyses. Reflecting upon my personal experience caused me to hypothesize that mothers play a significant role in the achievement of many offspring. I was particular-ly interested in the role of mothers in households in which the mother has as much or more education than her husband and in which she worked outside the home or was inclined to do so. Mothers like mine differed from the stereotype of the passive female who needs a dominating male to watch over her. Indeed, Robert Leik's finding regarding interaction within families that mothers are more task-oriented than they are outside the family (Leik, 1972: 265), caused me to wonder whether my mother's contribution to the achievement of her household was nor-mative and not unique.

REVIEW OF THE LITERATURE

A review of the literature revealed an interesting finding about mothers that was similar to my personal experience. James Morgan and associates at the University of Michigan discovered that "an average education attained by children is also influenced by the educational achievement of the mother. The more education the wife has relative to her husband, the more education the children attain.... Where the wife has less education than [her husband], achievement of the children is impeded but not so much as they are advanced when the wife has more education than [her husband]" (Morgan, 1962: 374-375). In the light of this finding, I have been careful to design my social science investigations about career development and social mobility so that they obtain information on mothers as well as fathers.

The study about which I wish to give a partial report is a case analysis of the interrelationship of career-advancement, educational attainment, and the family life of five outstanding black scholars in history, psychology, political science, economics, and literature (Willie, 1984). All of the scholars are male not because of my choice but because the study was of the most outstanding black scholar in each field as determined by vote of their peers. In a sexist society, the most outstanding is likely to be male owing to the extraordinary opportunities that have been accorded to them compared to those accorded women.

CASE STUDIES

John Hope Franklin, Harvard Ph.D., historian, Professor Emeritus of the University of Chicago, former president of the Southern Historical Association, the American Historical Association, and the United Chapters of Phi Beta Kappa, came from a professional family; his parents were college graduates. His father studied and practiced law. However, his practice experienced several reversals owing to racial discrimination, a race riot, and the Depression. When their father was away attempting to establish his law practice in Tulsa, Oklahoma, John Hope Franklin and his siblings remained at home with his mother, who was a school teacher in Rentiesville, Oklahoma— an all-black town of about 2,000 people. His father eventually located the family in Tulsa. Before that happened, young Franklin was in the full care and company of his mother most of the time. Young Franklin accompanied his school teacher mother to school, sat on the back bench in her classes, and was told to be quiet. As he quietly played on the back bench, he also heard her instructions to others and learned to read at an early age. Such early learning gave Franklin a head start.

W. Arthur Lewis, a knight of the United Kingdom with a Ph.D. in economics from the London School of Economics, has been a faculty member in British and American universities. He is Professor Emeritus at the Woodrow Wilson School, Princeton University. Lewis is a former president of both a university and a bank, and he has been elevated by his peers to the offices of vice president and president of the American Economics Association.

Born in the British West Indies to parents who were educated in a two-year normal school for the preparation of teachers in Antigua, Lewis experienced the death of his father, a teacher, when he was only seven years old. His mother gave up teaching after marriage but returned to the labor force as a business woman. She operated a dry goods enterprise after the death of her husband. She supported and sustained five children on the income from this business. All the offspring, five sons, received an education. Some were sent to England to study law, medicine, and economics. Of his widowed mother Sir Arthur Lewis said, "I never found out how she managed to establish and support us; but she did, on the income from the business." In effect, she provided an umbrella of safety and security for the members of her family until they departed from the household to go to college.

Psychologist Kenneth B. Clark received his Ph.D. from Columbia University. Former president of the American Psychological Association, Clark has been an activist scholar, searching for justice and equality. For nearly two decades he served as a member of the powerful Board of Regents that established educational policy for the State of New York. The significant Supreme Court decision of Brown v. Board of Education that outlawed segregated education in the United States was based, in part, on the psychological research findings of Clark.

A loyal member of the faculty of the City University of New York for a third of a century, Clark retired as Distinguished University Professor Emeritus. A member of Phi Beta Kappa, Clark was the first recipient of the Award for Distinguished Contribution to Psychology in the Public Interest.

Clark attributes his success to two women in his life—his mother and his wife. When the marriage between his mother and father broke up, his mother moved with her infant daughter and four-year old son from the Panama Canal zone where the children were born to New York City to be near a sister who already lived there and also to find better educational opportunities for her children. Clark's mother obtained work in the garment district as a dressmaker. She worked and took care of her family during the day, went to school at night, and eventually received a high school diploma.

She insisted that her son be accepted in an academic program rather than being steered to a vocational high school as was customary for blacks in the days of Clark's youth. Clark said his mother insisted on these arrangements because she was not awed by authority; her daring ways, he said, saved him and his sister. She also demanded good grades from her son and told him that he had to go to college but left the choice of college up to him. She told him that he would get good grades or that he would end up in jail. Amused as he reflected upon this, Clark said, "She didn't give me any middle ground." He had some scholarship money and did not have to work his way through college. His mother gave full support. She worked to put him and his sister through college, and she also provided some support for graduate school.

Clark characterized both his mother and his wife as strong women who demanded from him the maximum. Clark and his family of orientation persevered under adverse circumstances and eventually overcame.

Matthew Holden, Jr., a political scientist with a Ph.D. degree from Northwestern University, was born in Mound Bayou, Mississippi, an all-black town. In the Carter administration he was a commissioner of the Federal Energy Regulatory Commission. He has been professor at the University of Wisconsin and now occupies an endowed chair in political science at the University of Virginia. He is a past vice president of the American Political Science Association and has served as an elected member of its Council. In Wisconsin, he was a high public administrator in state government.

Holden remained in Mississippi until the age of thirteen; then his family migrated to Chicago in search of work, because of crop failures on the farm. On the farm, Holden took his turn in the field chopping and picking cotton. He was surrounded by an extended family including his grandparents and several aunts, uncles, and cousins.

Holden's father completed the fifth grade and his mother the eleventh grade. Both worked outside the home. They held semiskilled and laboring jobs in Chicago but wanted their off-spring to achieve more. Going to college for him, said Holden, was as preordained as anything could be. Although Holden worked the fields with his family, they never permitted him to miss school for any reason except illness. Holden believed that his parents' interest in college for him fulfilled wishes that his paternal family had for his uncle who attended college but died before finishing and those of his mother who wanted to go to college herself but was denied that opportunity. Holden's extended family said he was smart like his uncle who died. Family members, therefore, transferred the hopes and ambitions they had for his uncle to him. Holden described his mother as an extremely intelligent woman who always read the newspaper and the Bible. She wanted to go to Rust College in Mississippi and had a patron who offered to send her, but her father would not accept what he called charity. Later, however, he apologized to his daughter, Holden's mother, for not letting her go to college under the available arrangement.

Holden's parents eventually separated after moving to Chicago. He remained a member of his mother's household until he received a master's degree. Of his mother, he said, "I could always count on her." She nurtured him through the doubting years of adolescence and provided a safe and secure shelter to which he could return after his probes into the outside world. There was bread enough in his mother's household but not much of anything else to share. Holden's parents, who were blue-collar workers, supported him through six years of stop-and-go studies at two colleges for a college education. His mother in particular stood by him despite his undistinguished undergraduate career.

Darwin Turner, a specialist in literary criticism, received his doctorate degree from the University of Chicago. A member of Phi Beta Kappa, Turner holds a tenured distinguished professorship of English and is director of the Afro-American Studies program at the University of Iowa. He has shuttled back and forth between administration and scholarship in his career. In recognition of his scholarly attainment, Turner was given the Creative Scholarship Award by the College Language Association and was presented the University of Chicago Alumni Association's Professional Achievement Award. A former member of the Board of Directors of the Modern Language Association, Turner has served as a trustee of the National Humanities Center.

Turner grew up in an extended family of highly educated individuals. His grandfather and grandmother earned degrees for graduate study. In fact, his grandmother, a public school principal, received her graduate degree the same year that her daughter, Turner's mother—also a public school educator—received her graduate degree. Turner's father, a college graduate, also pursued graduate studies, but did not receive a doctoral degree. He shifted to formal training in pharmacy and became a pharmacist.

Turner said his mother and grandmother encouraged him in school. One could say they doted on him. His grandmother offered him a dollar for every A that he received. His mother promised him a car if he was elected to Phi Beta Kappa. Turner does not recall that these promises were kept. But he remembers them as incentives and as statements of expectations.

His family was solid middle class and was able to pay for his education. Turner remembers that his grandmother especially wanted him to go on immediately for the Ph.D. degree after he received his M.A. degree, but he said that he had other things on his mind—getting married and going to work.

Turner grew up in a two-parent household in Cincinnati. However, his father found business opportunities better in Chicago and moved there to establish three pharmacies. His father and mother visited each other often. But Turner remained with his mother and his extended family in Cincinnati. Later while studying for the doctorate degree at the University of Chicago, he and his family of procreation had closer contact with his father.

ANALYSIS OF THE CASES

These case studies, reported in part, do not deny the role of fathers, but they certainly emphasize the contributions of mothers as significantly related to the success of their offspring. After analyzing the lives of these outstanding scholars, one is tempted to hypothesize that the educational and occupational careers of mothers greatly facilitate those of their children. We know this because, unlike in other investigations, we studied the contributions of both mothers and fathers. The mothers in this study gave constant company, care, headstart learning opportunities, partial or full economic support for offspring, including funds for education. They expected good academic performance, had ambitions for the high achievement of their offspring, were patient when the young faltered, provided incentives for good academic work, and expressed hope for success in the future.

The outstanding scholars in this study grew up in different kinds of households. All five experienced two-parent families initially. But three of the scholars saw their families disintegrate before they came of age—one because of death and two because of divorce or desertion. Two of the scholars had intensive interaction in extended kinship units. Even in the two-parent families that remained so, during childhood two of the scholars experienced temporary separations between the parents because of the fathers' work in distant communities. These scholars therefore came of age in a variety of kinship structures, including nuclear families, extended families, and single-parent families. No ideal type or common family form was revealed.

Despite a variety of family structures, the presence and encouragement of mothers were common experiences for all scholars. A similar characteristic of these mothers was their labor force participation. All worked for some period after the birth of children in jobs ranging from unskilled work to business administration and professional activity. The kind of work the mothers perform is less important than the fact that they are available to work, if needed. In four of the households studied, the income of the mothers was essential in providing safe and secure environments for offspring, and educational opportunities for children. Thus, it would appear that expectations and support for young people in the family as well as role modeling were the significant factors that contributed to their success.

Finally, this study of five outstanding scholars confirms the hypothesis set forth by James Morgan and his associates at the University of Michigan (Morgan, 1967). Although the mothers attained varying levels of education ranging from the eleventh grade of high school to certification from a teacher-training school to baccalaureate and master's degrees, in four of the families the mothers received as much, or more, education as their husbands. And, of course, the offspring in all five families received doctoral degrees.

CONFIRMATION OF OTHER STUDIES

Some years ago, I conducted a study of a sample of black poor families and of families slightly above the poverty line to determine how the latter families pulled themselves out of poverty, given that the husbands in all the families were unskilled workers who received low wages. About one-third of all families in the sample had climbed out of poverty largely because of the work of the female spouse. Three out of every four wives in the households slightly above the poverty line were employed, compared with the poor households in which three out of every four wives were not employed. The working wives in the households above the poverty line tended to earn as much as their husbands or more. But the few employed women in the poor households earned significantly less than their male spouses.

A fact possibly related to the earning power of the wives in families above the poverty line was their education. Nearly half of these wives were high school graduates compared with only one-fourth of the wives in poor households. Moreover, a greater proportion of wives than of husbands in households above the poverty line were high school graduates compared with those in the poor households. Thus, in this study, households that had risen out of poverty by their own "bootstraps" did so because of the educational and occupational attainment of the wife (WIllie, 1981).

The findings of this study of poor families and those slightly above the poverty line, and the case studies of five outstanding scholars suggest that Moynihan's assertion that "dependence on the mother's income undermines the position of the father and deprives the children" is in error (Moynihan, 1965: 25).

Studies of black middle-class families reveal the economic foundation of most to be a product of the cooperative work of husband and wife, a genuine illustration of a team effort: "Few, if any, family functions including cooking, cleaning, and shopping are considered to be the exclusive prerogative of the husband or wife." This information leads us to the conclusion, that "probably the best example of the liberated wife in American society is found in the black middle-class family." This is so because "she and her husband have acted as partners out of necessity and thus have carved out an equalitarian pattern of interaction in which neither husband nor wife has ultimate authority" (Willie, 1981). This equalitarian existence that permits full participation of the wife and mother in the family and in other community institutions is beneficial for the personal growth and development of the male as well as the female spouse and presumably for their children as the study of outstanding scholars has revealed. It could be that neither a matriarchal nor a patriarchal family structure is appropriate for the mutual fulfillment of family members—that an equalitarian structure is better for all concerned.

NEED FOR FURTHER RESEARCH

I am mindful that most studies reported here have been of blacks, including black scholars and their families. Their way of life also has been ignored or denied. When acknowledged, the adaptation patterns of blacks have been studied largely as a form of deviance or from the perspective of social problems analysis. This discussion should help us to develop a different perspective on differential adaptations of families in dominant and subdominant racial populations.

With a broader perspective than the one limited to social problems analysis, one is better able to conduct comparative studies of family life, which should be high on our research agenda. I have in progress a comparative study of black and white families in the United States. One of its goals is to determine whether the adaptations discovered among blacks also apply to whites and whether equalitarian patterns of interaction found in the black middle class extend also to other social classes and to these classes in other racial populations. Finally, the comparative analysis seeks to determine whether the contribution of mothers to the achievement of male offspring holds also for female offspring or whether fathers make a more significant contribution to the achievement of daughters (Appleton, 1981: 71-103; Biller, 1974; Hennig and Jardin, 1976).

Meanwhile, I encourage you not to reject or ignore the hypotheses presented because they were derived from the black experience in the United States. What benefits subdominant populations often benefits the dominant population.

REFERENCES

Appleton, W. 1981. *Fathers and Daughters*. Garden City, N.Y.: Doubleday.

Biller, H. 1974. *Parental Deprivation*. Lexington, MA: Lexington Books.

_____. 1976. "The Father-Child Relationship: Some Crucial Issues." In Victor C. Vaughan, III, and T. Berry Brazelton (eds.), *The Family—Can It be Saved*. Chicago: Year Book Medical Publishers, pp.69-76.

Blau, P.M. and O.D. Duncan. 1967. *The American Occupational Structure*. New York: The Free Press.

Duncan, B. and O.D. 1970. "Family Stability and Occupational Success." In C. V. Willie (ed.), *The Family Life of Black People*. Columbus, OH: Merrill, pp.156-171.

Haley, A. 1976. *Roots, The Saga of an American Family*. Garden City, N.Y.: Doubleday.

Heilbrun, A.B., Jr. 1972. "An Empirical Test of the Modeling Theory of Sex-Role Learning." In Ira L. Reiss (ed.), *Readings on the Family System*. New York: Holt, Rinehart and Winston, pp.49-59.

Hennig, M. and A. Jardin. 1976. *The Managerial Woman*. New York: Pocket Books.

Leik, R.K. 1972. "Instrumentality and Emotionality in Family" in Ira L. Reiss (ed.), *Readings on the Family System*. New York: Holt, Rinehart and Winston, pp.257-269.

Morgan, J. and associates. 1962. *Income and Welfare in the United States*. New York: McGraw-Hill.

Moynihan, D.P. 1965. *The Negro Family, A Case for National Action*. Washington, D.C.: U.S. Government Printing Office.

Wasserman, H.L. 1970. "The Absent Father in Negro Families." In C.V. Willie (ed.), *The Family Life of Black People*. Columbus, OH: Merrill, pp.294-298.

Willie, C.V. 1981. *A New Look at Black Families* (2nd ed.). Dix Hills, NY: General Hall.

_____. 1984. *Five Black Scholars*. Cambridge, MA: Abt Books.

PART IV

CONCLUSION

Chapter **12** A THEORETICAL
EXPLANATION OF
FAMILY ADAPTATION
BY RACE AND BY
SOCIAL CLASS

I have tried to describe the ways of life characteristic of black families in different social classes. In many respects this analysis is a continuation of that set in motion years ago by E. Franklin Frazier, who hypothesized that "the social stratification of community ... would provide the most important frame of reference for studying the social changes in the life of [blacks] or any other urbanized group" (Frazier 1968: 141). Stratification among black families was largly ignored by other social scientists in the past mainly because of the small number of affluent blacks and also because of the tendency to stereotype blacks. By his own reckoning in an article published near the mid-point of the twentieth century, Frazier stated that only about one-eighth of the black families in the South, where most black families resided at that time, were able to maintain a middle-class way of life (Frazier, 1968:207). These families, small in number but influential, would have remained invisible had it not been for Frazier's research and publication.

The final trimester of the twentieth century presents a different set of circumstances. No longer may anyone say, "a black family is a black family is a black family." Differentiation among blacks is a fact of life that should be described, explained, and understood. As mentioned in Chapter 1, about 1 out of every 3 black families has an annual income at or above the national median. This affluent population of racial minority families is balanced by an indigent or poor category of about one-third. Notwithstanding the gains in affluent status, black families in the United States still must exist on a median annual income that is 30 to 40 percent less than that for whites. Clearly, differentiation in economic resources exists between the races and among blacks. The analysis in this book has demonstrated that these variations are associated with differing styles of living. This finding is related to another issue discussed by Frazier. His friend and colleague, G. Franklin Edwards, tells us that Frazier maintained a lively controversy with anthropologist Melville Herskovits about Herskovits's claim that "the [black] family continued to be influenced by African survivals;" Frazier disagreed and insisted that "the [black] family was a peculiar expression of response to the American environment" (Edwards, 1968:xvi).

Frazier's belief that blacks had assimilated the cultural ways of the United States placed him squarely in the social theory camp of functional structuralism. According to Walter Wallace, such theorists "define the social in terms of objective behavior relations and seek to explain it by referring to phenomena that are socially generated through characteristics of the participants' environments." In other words, that which is social is a consequence of the behavior of one group toward others (Wallace, 1969:161).

Thus, the way of life of black families and differentiation in life-styles among these families can be understood best by examining the macroenvironmental setting within which they live and the groups with which they interact, rather than by referring back to Africa or to the historical United States and the institution of slavery. Studies of family stability and income support Frazier's situational analysis. For example, in most affluent households there is little difference by race in the proportion of one-parent families. However, single-parent families increase among blacks and whites as their income decreases, with a higher incidence rate among poor blacks reflecting their subdominant situation (U.S. Census, 1969). Delinquent behavior among juveniles also is situationally determined. A Washington, D.C. study reveals that the lowest rate for black and for white populations is found in the same kinds of neighborhoods — those that are characterized by higher income and few broken families (Willie, 1970:265).

The fact, however, that black families and white families exhibit similar overt responses to similar situations does not suggest that there are no differences in adaptations by race. Indeed, the subjective responses of whites and of blacks to similar situations may be quite different, because of their dominant and subdominant positions in the community power structure as majority and minority populations. The effort required of blacks compared to whites to reach the same level of achievement may be unequal, when racial discrimination is factored in. Moreover, a similar experience probably has different meanings for dominant and subdominant populations.

Frazier recognized the minority as a mirror of society and said that the study of blacks could lead to an understanding of the adaptations of other human beings. Particularly did he believe that study of the black family adjustments might lead to "a clearer understanding of the relation of human motivation to culture" (Frazier, 1968:191). But Frazier never extracted from his studies of blacks propositions applicable to other population groups.

Frazier, in effect, abandoned his theoretical position of functional structuralism and the search for commonalities toward the close of his life, when he attempted to explain the consumer behavior of affluent blacks as a function of their alleged isolation from the American social system rather than as a function of the nature of their participation in it. In two of his more polemical essays, written in 1957 and in 1962, he described blacks and especially affluent blacks as "outsiders in American life" (Frazier, 1968:270), who created "a world of make-believe" (Frazier, 1968:255). But earlier, he claimed that "the [black] family had become largely oriented to the values of the American culture." He pointed toward their "conspicuous consumption" as an indicator of commitment to the values of Amercan culture" (Frazier, 1968:207). E. Franklin Frazier, a leading black sociologist and former president of the American Sociological Association, died in 1962 and left unresolved this apparent contradiction — his assertion that affluent blacks were both committed to and isolated from the values of American culture. As a continuation of the study of Frazier, my goal is to resolve the contradiction, if possible.

I think that a structural-functionalist perspective is helpful in analyzing variations of life-styles of families in this society, including both black families and white families. I believe that the adaptations of the affluent are no less deviant than the adaptations of the poor or of the working class. As stated by Robert Nisbet, "all human behavior is normatively directed." Nisbet continues, "It is impossible for human beings to be in continuous association and interaction with one another for long without a culture arising ... norms are the vital core of culture." He describes norms as the ends and purposes in life that are, so to speak, waiting for us in the social order when we are born (Nisbet, 1970:222-224). Ends might be translated as goals. Robert Merton believes that some goals in society transcend class lines (Merton, 1949:137,133). In view of the extended interaction between black and white populations for several centuries in the United States and also the close association between black families of different social classes in black ghettos of the United States, some goals in common must have developed. For this reason the means-ends schema developed by Merton in his essay "Social Structure and Anomie" appears to be an appropriate vehicle for explaining adaptations of families by race and social class. In Table 1, (+) signifies "acceptance," (−) signifies "rejection," and (±) signifies "rejection of prevailing values and substitution of new values." In brackets is the innovative adaptation Type III that Merton classifies as ritualism, which seems to me to be an alternative to his Type II. The ritualization definition by Merton was contaminated by social class concepts. Innovation as used here can appear in any social class and refers to either goals or means.

Merton identifies five kinds of adaptations by individuals to social organization: conformity, innovation, ritualism, retreatism, rebellion. This typology is a conceptual approach to an understanding of the differences in adaptations among affluent, working-class, and poor families.

Merton recognized the value of situational analysis by calling our attention to the fact "that people may shift from one alternative [adaptation] to another as they engage in different spheres of social activities." Thus, he said the categories in the typology "refer to role behavior in specific types of situations, not to personality" (Merton, 1949:133). The adaptations by race and social class then are situationally, not biologically, determined. The situation of blacks in American society, for example, is that of a minority or subdominant population in the power structure that receives an inequitable amount of the nation's wealth. The survival requirements for dominant and subdominant populations differ, and so do those for affluent and poor families. Compassion is a fundamental form of behavior that dominants must exhibit in their interaction with subdominants to prevent rebellion against the existing social order. Courage and endurance are essential among subdominants who would resist and overcome the oppression of dominants. The behavior requirements of groups differ depending on their situation in the social system, their goals, and the methods available to them.

Table 1
A TYPOLOGY OF MODES OF
INDIVIDUAL ADAPTATION
(From Merton 1949:133)

Modes of Adaptation	Cultural Goals	Institutionalized Means
I.Conformity	+	+
II.Innovation	+	−
III.[Innovation]*	−	+
IV.Retreatism	−	−
V.Rebellion	±	±

*Identified as Ritualism in the original table.

Merton states that stability results from adaptation Type I — conformity to both cultural goals and institutionalized means (Merton, 1949:134). This is precisely the adaptation that is manifested by affluent blacks. Far from being isolated from

American cultural values, as Frazier claimed, affluent blacks are central in the maintenance of such values. Former Transportation Secretary William Coleman once said that whites owe a debt of gratitude to blacks for making the U.S. Constitution work (Willie, 1978). It is interesting to note that the most famous black lawyers are constitutional experts. Richard Kluger said that Thurgood Marshall's "record of success as a civil-rights lawyer had begun to turn him into a legend" (Kluger, 1975:18).

The affluent black families analyzed in Part II of this study are conformists to both the cultural goals of this nation and the prescribed means for fulfilling these goals. Their values reflect the philosophy of Thomas Jefferson, one of the founders of this nation, who believed that education should be available to all so that the citizens in a democracy could make moral decisions about governance for the common good; that ability rather than wealth or family connection should be the basis for community leadership; and that democratic decision-making by the people is a virtuous and wise way of arriving at just solutions. The values of affluent black families reflect the U.S. Constitution, the legal norm of our society, and its requirement of equal protection of the laws for all.

Affluent white families, on the other hand, subscribe to democracy as a method of social organization but not fully to its goals. They adapt acording to Merton's Type III. They are innovationists in that they seek to change the goals as a way of frustrating those who might lay claim to their privileged position, but they insist that all use agreed-upon means to achieve power and authority in society, although such means may not be available to or suitable for subdominant people in the power structure who do not have a head start. Because affluent white families are anxious sometimes that others may invade their territory or turf they, in colloquial terminology, try to change the name of the game as a way of eliminating challengers, and they contend that such is fair in a free enterprise system.

H. R. Mencken is an example of an affluent white individual who believed in the method of democracy so much that he attended national political conventions as a news analyst and wrote a book on *Making a President*. Yet, he published a "Proposed New Constitution for Maryland" that, among other undemocratic goals, "advocated creating a grand inquest — a group of outstanding citizens to monitor the conduct of government." A Virginia Law School professor dubbed Mencken's proposed constitution "an honest effort to combine personal liberty and fascism" (Moss, 1980:162). Freedom is a method of social organization; fascism or fraternity are goals. Many white affluent individuals believe in the democratic method but think that society and its institutions should be controlled by an intellectual elite. Those who subscribe to this approach are called innovationists because such a way differs from the vision of American society contained in the Declaration of Independence and the Constitution, our normative documents.

White working-class families appear to be content to settle for a modest place in life. Both mothers and fathers tend to work, usually in clerical or semi-skilled jobs, or in service work. The father or husband in the household sometimes looks upon himself as a failure, although he may be a steady worker. Thus, the parents tend to invest their dreams in their children's future. This is especially true of the mother or grandmother in the household, who is a chief source of emotional support for the children as well as the husband.

There is not much planning for the future in white working-class families. Everything seems to be oriented toward the present. The good life is having a good day, having a steady job, earning enough money to furnish a home and maybe own it, buy tools for a workshop, have a beer from time to time.

Working-class whites do not blame others for their fate. They tend to see themselves as inadequate for the requirements and responsibilities of their time. For this reason they tend not to have a dream of the kind of life they wish for themselves. They more or less drift, enjoying themselves when possible, conforming to the requirements of the situation in which they find themselves, doing what comes naturally, taking little initiative to change things.

Illness and death in white working-class families are nerve-wracking, unsettling experiences. They represent lost opportunities and unfair sentences of fate. They sometimes bring family members together, but they also are the source of escape behavior such as excess drinking and even physical abuse of one's spouse that drive families apart (Levinson, 1978:126-135).

The young who grow up in such households experience a double bind: they are urged to love their parents but not to emulate them. The parents want a better future for their offspring, yet are fearful that their upwardly mobile children may disown them; they are hesitant to urge their offspring to strive for success. The children sometimes are resentful of their misfortune and the desire that parents have to perpetuate family culture and traditions. Education is the social mobility elevator that the children in the white working class sometimes board for movement away from their working-class roots and origin. Education for a few is seen as a great escape (Lewis, 1979: 36-37).

The children may complain, but seldom do their parents. The work of the parents may be unrewarding, but they endure. They may have low self-esteem, but they do not despair. They know how to sacrifice, and they do it willingly, especially for their children. They declare that the world does not owe them a living. If a woman has a man who loves to work, she considers herself lucky, never mind the kind of work her husband does. The white working class pledges allegiance to the flag and tends to accept society as it is. The white working-class family knows hard times. Its members endure hard work, and do not ask for help from anyone. This is how the white working-class family survives, when it does survive. During periods of economic stress, family disintegration increases.

Like the affluent black family, the working-class white family is conformist, and adapts according to Type I — upholding cultural goals and following institutionalized means, believing in self-reliance, accepting the free enterprise system and its opportunities for success or failure. For their circumstances, they blame themselves and not the system. They pledge allegiance to the goals and methods of American society, although the system seems to have left them behind (Wrobel, 1976).

Black working-class families are also innovationists, but their adaptation is different from that of affluent whites, who believe in the institutionalized means but who reject the cultural goal of equal opportunity for all in an open society. The black working class is innovative because its members accept the cultural goals but reject the means for their achievement, largely because these means are unavailable. For the black working class, the opportunity system may be blocked. Its members experience a closed, not an open, society, and must improvise to make their way through. Their adaptation is according to Type II. They strive to achieve, by any means.

The poor are as much a part of society as the members of families in any other social class position. The mainstream values of American culture are well understood by them. Bettylou Valentine (1978:103) said that these values receive general allegiance among blacks. Among poor whites, mainstream values are understood too, so much so, that these families are reluctant to relate to others of a higher status who, they believe, might try to make them feel ashamed of their lot in life (Wilkes, 1977:99). Even though the white poor know that there is a better life, they tend to limit what they permit themselves to wish for as one way of "making life tolerable" and less frustrating (Knupfer, 1953:263). In general, Sally Bould-Vantil found that "the attitudes of the poor … do not differ from the non-poor in terms of their aspirations in the world of work" (Bould-Vantil, 1976:151).

Poor blacks tend to live in urban ghettoes; poor whites may not. Poor blacks appear to have a community support system of kin and friends; poor whites usually have only their relatives to rely upon. Poor whites are proud, and accept their circumstances as a function of fate. Poor blacks are resentful and rage at a discriminating society that they believe has treated them unfairly. Being only one-tenth of the majority population, poor whites are more or less invisible and all but forgotten by others of their race. Being at least one-third of the population of the minority, poor blacks are a sufficient critical mass to demand consideration of their concerns in any social action agenda. Under these circumstances and conditions, one might expect a different pattern of adaptation to social organization by the black and the white poor.

In general, poor whites adapt in a retreating fashion, according to Merton's Type IV. They tend to give up on any hope of ever fulfilling culturally prescribed goals through legitimate institutional means. One might call such families the socially disinherited who have assimilated the goals, rules, and regulations of society but who have found all avenues to them inaccessible. Merton describes their mode of adaptation as that of frustrated and handicapped individuals who cannot cope and who, therefore, drop out. They experience defeatism and resignation, manifested in escape mechanisms such as drinking, gambling, and fighting. It is important to recognize that the retreatism is a way of reducing conflict that arises from internalization of the legitimate goals and means for achievement and the inability to use the illegitimate route because of internalized prohibitions (Merton, 1949:142-143).

There are few structural supports for poor white families, who tend to be isolated from others in rural areas or as invisible residents of the inner city. They are members of few organizations. Family members work when work is available; but the kinds of jobs that they can hold are neither plentiful nor stable. Thus the women in the household in service occupations are sometimes more regularly employed than are their menfolk. The families tend to be stoic and take whatever comes in stride. They do not like to receive charity and boast of the fact that they are not on welfare.

These poor white families are children-centered. Usually, they are large. One could call children the treasure of poor whites. They enjoy seeing them develop the spirit of survival, which includes being tough. Such families have their share of tragedies. One or more members may be victims of homicide; divorce and desertion are frequent; getting into trouble with law enforcement authorities is commonplace; medical problems go unattended and sometimes result in unnecessary deaths.

For these poor white individuals, their family is their world. Others tend to shun them. The mother is the hub of the family. Everything tends to revolve around her. She is the person of wisdom; she is the undisputed authority. She is the person who perseveres, caring for the sick, getting members out of jail, and working when she can. Despite her heroic efforts, nothing seems to be effective. Thus, the poor white family is submissive, tends to withdraw, lacks self-confidence, limits its participation in social organization, and tends to be fatalistic (Knupfer, 1953; Wilkes, 1977; Bould-Vantil, 1976).

The poor black family is rebellious. Their adaptation is Merton's Type V. They press for a modified social structure that will accommodate their concerns and grant them some measure of consideration. They want a society in which there is a "closer correspondence between … effort and reward" (Merton, 1949:145). Seeing that the existing society is organized against them, the black poor veto "business as usual." They do not accept their position as a condition of fate. When they no longer can endure, they riot and rebel, hoping to draw attention to their circumstances, hoping that others will then set things right. Through their rebellion, poor blacks attempt "to change the existing cultural and social structure rather than to accommodate efforts within the structure" (Merton, 1949:379). Merton reminds us, however, that the renegade who "renounces the prevailing values … becomes the target of greatest hostility … " (Merton, 1949:146). This has been the lot of poor black families. The society has resented and raged against them as much as they have resented and raged against society (Geismar, 1973; Jeffers, 1970; Schulz, 1970).

The neat way in which the life-styles by race and social class fit into the theoretical schema developed by Merton for explaining variation in adaptations to social organization suggests that all American families — including affluent, working-class, and poor black and white families — participate in and share a common core of values. Black families are not isolated from the values of American society as Frazier once claimed. Martin Luther King, Jr. contended that blacks were concerned with fulfilling the American Dream. Schematically, the way that black and white families adapt to Amercian society is shown in Table 2.

Table 2
A TYPOLOGY OF MODES OF ADAPTATION
IN AMERICAN SOCIETY BY RACE AND SOCIAL CLASS

Social Class	Black Families		White Families	
	Mode of Adaptation		Mode of Adaptation	
	Cultural Goals	Institutional Means	Cultural Goals	Institutional Means
Affluent	+	+	–	+
Working class	+	–	+	+
Poor	±	±	=	=

Note: + Conformity to goals and means
      – Nonconformity to goals and means
      ± Resistance to goals and means in an aggressive, rebellious way
      = Resistance to goals and means in a passive, retreating way

On the basis of this analysis we may conclude (1) that black families and white families in the United States share a common core of values, (2) that they adapt to the society and its values in different ways, largely because of their dominant and subdominant situations, and (3) that the unique adaptations of racial populations are further differentiated by variations in style of life by social class. Thus, any assumption that the life of blacks in the United States can be understood independently of their involvement with whites appears to be unwarranted. The same may be said of the way of life of whites. Moreover, the life-style of one social class cannot be understood apart from that of other social classes.

Referring to the interdependence of individuals, races, and social classes in the United States, I am reminded of the wisdom of George Bernard Shaw's character Eliza Doolittle, who said that she discovered that the difference between a flower girl and a lady is not so much how she acts but how she is treated. My modified version of her statement is that the difference between individuals, social classes, and races in society is how they act as well as how they are treated. We know this because we have analyzed the intimate details of black family life, using a unique approach of combining data obtained from case interviews with survey research. These two methods enabled us to understand the habits of individuals, the customs of families, the life-styles of social classes, and the adaptations of a race from the point of view of the people studied and also in terms of a logical schema of social theory. The purpose of this book has been to place the discussion of race and social class differentiation among black families in the United States within a theoretical framework.

Further research is needed to compare the rich detail derived from an analysis of case studies of black families by social class with an analysis of case studies of white families by social class.

REFERENCES

Anthropology Today. 1971. Del Mar, CA: CRM Books.

Bould-Vantil, Sally. 1976. *Work and the Culture of Poverty.* San Francisco: R and E Research Associates.

Edwards, G. Franklin. 1968. "Introduction." In *Franklin Frazier on Race Relations,* edited by G. Franklin Edwards. Chicago: University of Chicago Press.

Frazier, E. Franklin. 1968. "The Failure of the Negro Intellectual," "The Negro Family in America," and "Inferiority Complex and Quest for Status." In *Franklin Frazier on Race Relations,* edited by G. Franklin Edwards. Chicago: University of Chicago Press.

Geismar, Ludwig. 1973. *555 Families.* New Brunswick, NJ: Transaction Books.

Jeffers, Camille. 1970. "Mother and Children in Public Housing." In *The Family Life of Black People,* edited by Charles V. Willie. Columbus: Charles E. Merrill.

Kluger, Richard. 1975. *Simple Justice.* New York: Vintage Books.

Knupfer, Genevieve. 1953. "Portrait of the Underdog." In *Class, Status, and Power,* edited by Reinhard Bendix and Seymour Martin Lipset. New York: Free Press.

Levinson, Daniel J. 1978. *The Seasons of a Man's Life.* New York: Ballantine.

Lewis, James. 1979. "The Melting Pot Myth." *Syracuse University Alumni News* 59 (Summer).

Merton, Robert K. 1949. *Social Structure and Social Theory.* New York: Free Press.

Moss, Malcolm. 1980. "Mencken, Politics, and Politicians." In *On Mencken,* edited by John Dorsey. New York: Alfred A. Knopf.

Nisbet, Robert A. 1970. *The Social Bond.* New York: Alfred A. Knopf.

Schulz, David. 1970. "The Role of the Boyfriend in Lower Class Negro Life." In *The Family Life of Black People,* edited by C.V. Willie, Columbus: Charles E. Merrill.

U.S. Census Bureau. 1969. *Trends in Social and Economic Conditions in Metropolitan Areas,* Series P-23, no. 27. Washington, D.C.: U.S. Government Printing Office.

Valentine, Bettylou. 1978. *Hustling and Other Hard Work.* New York: Free Press.

Wallace, Walter L. (ed.). 1969. *Sociological Theory.* Chicago: Aldine.

Wilkes, Paul. 1977. *Six American Families.* New York: Seabury.

Willie, Charles V. 1970. "The Relative Contribution of Family Status and Economic Status to Juvenile Delinquency." In *The Family Life of Black People,* edited by C.V. Willie. Columbus: Charles E. Merrill.

_____. 1978. *The Sociology of Education.* Lexington, MA: Lexington Books.

Wrobel, Paul. 1976. "Polish American Men: As Workers, As Husbands, and as Fathers." Paper presented at American Association for the Advancement of Science, Boston, February 18-24.

APPENDIX

INTERVIEW SCHEDULE
FOR PART II

Note: In addition to the facts that this interview schedule will help you obtain, be sure to ask the interviewee to express his or her opinions about past and present experiences and record these as nearly as possible in the person's own words.

#1 What is the name of the interviewee? Could you list the name of other persons who live here, including family, relatives, lodgers, if any? Write names in this order: Interviewee on first line; spouse of interviewee; unmarried children; oldest first, married children and their children; other relatives; lodgers	#2 What is the relationship of each person to the Interviewee? (e.g., husband, wife, son, daughter, mother-in-law, etc.)	#3 What is the sex of each person? Write M for Male and F for Female	#4 Could you list the year in which the person was born?	#5 Could you list the race of each person? Write in: Black, White, Other Race (list)	#6 Of what nation or country is this person a citizen? Write in: U.S.A. Specify Other
Interviewee					
1.					
2.					
3.					
4.					
5.					
6.					
7.					
8.					
9.					
10.					
11.					
12.					
13.					

#7 With which cultural, ethnic, or nationality group do the members of this house identify? (e.g., Italian-American, Irish-American, German-American; specify others)	#8 What is the highest grade in school *completed* by this person? Write in: correct number and degree, if any. Elementary 1-2-3-4-5-6-7-8-9-10-11-12 College 1-2-3-4 Jr. Hi. Sr. High Graduate 1-2-3-3-5+	#9 What is the marital status of each person? Write in: married, separated, divorced, widowed, single	#10 How many years has this person been married, separated, divorced, or widowed? Write 0 for single people. Reference is to current status	#11 Has this person ever been married? If yes, write # of times YES NO
1.				
2.				
3.				
4.				
5.				
6.				
7.				
8.				
9.				
10.				
11.				
12.				
13.				

FOR EMPLOYED PERSONS ONLY

#12
Was this person *employed* during this last week?

#13
Was this person looking for fulltime work during the past week?

#14
What is the *occupation* of this person? Write in job title or DK (Don't Know).

#15
What *work* does this person do? Write in description of job or DK (Don't Know). (If the kind of work that the person does indicates the job title, fill in the correct occupation for the previous question.)

	A. Full Time	B. Part Time			
	YES	NO	YES	NO	YES NO
1.					
2.					
3.					
4.					
5.					
6.					
7.					
8.					
9.					
10.					
11.					
12.					
13.					

FOR EMPLOYED PERSONS ONLY

#16 What *kind* of organization does this person work for?

a. Fed. Gov't
b. Local Gov't
c. Manufacturing
d. Construction
e. Transportation
f. Utilities
g. Private household (Domestic)
h. Wholesale store
i. Retail store
j. Real Estate
k. Insurance
l. Banking
m. Service work
n. Other (Specify)
o. DK (Don't Know)

#17 Is this the person's usual job?

YES

or

NO

#18 About how many days did each person spend in *bed* because of *illness* last year?

Write in number of days.

#19 In what *state* was this person born? If person was born outside U.S., in what country was he or she born?

Write in name or DK (Don't Know).

#20 How many *years* has this person lived in this city or metropolitan area?

1.
2.
3.
4.
5.
6.
7.
8.
9.
10.
11.
12.
13.

#21
In what state,
city or coun-
try did this
person live
before coming
to this
area?
(Write
"native" for
locally born.)

#22
What is the
religious
preference
of this
person?
Write in:
Denomina-
tion and
Protestant
Catholic
Jewish
None
Other
(specify)

#23
Does this person
attend a church
or synagogue?
write yes or no.

_____
YES   NO
_____

If yes,
how often?
____Weekly
____Monthly
____Holidays only
____Seldom

1._____
2._____
3._____
4._____
5._____
6._____
7._____
8._____
9._____
10._____
11._____
12._____
13._____

#24
Are there any parents or offspring in this family who are not currently in this household? _____ YES _____ NO
If yes, could you give their age and sex, whether or not they are still alive and in what city and state they live and how often members of this household see or visit with them?

Name of Offspring Not at Home	Relation-ship to Interviewee	Name of Parents	Relation-ship to Interviewee	Residence			Visits					
				City	State	Don't Know	Daily	Weekly	Monthly	Yearly	Seldom	Never
1.												
2.												
3.												
4.												
5.												
6.												
7.												
8.												
9.												
10.												
11.												
12.												
13.												

#25
This question has to do with the offspring or dependent children in the household at this time.

Name of Child	Have any of the children listed ever been in trouble with law enforcement or other authorities? If so, what was the problem and what was the outcome? Problem/Outcome	How would you describe the progress of each child in school: Does very well. Does about average work. Has trouble with teachers. Has learning disability. Has trouble with other students. Does not like school. Likes school.	How would you describe the adjustment of each child in the community: Has many playmates. Does not know other children. Gets along well with other children. Has fights and arguments often. Others pick on him or her.	Regarding discipline, how would you describe each child: Follows instructions well. Is rebellious. Looks out for other children. Is agreeable and pleasant. Is a discipline problem.	When this child needs to be disciplined, who does it? Write in mother, father, mother and father, grandmother, grandfather, aunt, uncle Other (Specify)
1.					
2.					
3.					
4.					
5.					
6.					
7.					
8.					
9.					
10.					
11.					
12.					
13.					

#25 (continued)

#26
This question has to do with the offspring who are adult and are no longer at home.

What does this child plan to do when he or she is adult?	How much education will he or she need to hold this job?	Name of Offspring	How old was this person when he or she left home?	Why did this person leave home? Write in: married, work, school, institution, other(specify)	How far in school did this person go? Did he or she receive a diploma or degree? If so, what was it?
1.					
2.					
3.					
4.					
5.					
6.					
7.					
8.					
9.					
10.					
11.					
12.					
13.					

#26 (continued)

What kind of work does this person do?	If offspring is married, what kind of work does spouse do?	When this person was growing up, did he or she ever get in trouble with law enforcement agents or other authorities?	How would you describe the progress of this person in school when growing up? Did very well. Did about average. Had learning disability. Had trouble with others. Did not like school. Liked school.	How would you describe the community when this person was growing up? Had many playmates. Did not know others. Got along well. Had many fights. Others picked on him or her.	When this person needed discipline, who gave it? Write in: mother, father, mother and father, grandmother, grandfather, aunt, uncle, other (specify).
1.					
2.					
3.					
4.					
5.					
6.					
7.					
8.					
9.					
10.					
11.					
12.					
13.					

#27
If you were asked to classify your family, living in the household, would you say it is:

_____ Real Close
_____ Close
_____ Not Close at All

_____ Each person does his or her own thing
_____ Everybody works together for a common goal
_____ We don't see much of each other

_____ We don't do much together

#28
Do you have a regular time for eating dinner or supper in your family?   _____ Yes   _____ No

#29
If the answer is yes, what hour of the day do you usually eat dinner?   _____ PM

#30
Regarding daily family meals, which family members usually eat together? For instance, which family members usually eat breakfast, lunch and dinner together on a weekday like Monday through Friday? Which is typical of your family? What do you do on weekends?

#31

We are interested in what your family does on a weekend day, for instance, on Sunday, from 7:00 a.m. to midnight. Could you give an example of what each family member usually does?

7:00	8:00	9:00	10:00	11:00	12 Noon
1.					
2.					
3.					
4.					
5.					
6.					
7.					
8.					
9.					
10.					
11.					
12.					
13.					

1:00	2:00	3:00	4:00	5:00	6:00
1.					
2.					
3.					
4.					
5.					
6.					
7.					
8.					
9.					
10.					
11.					
12.					
13.					

7:00	8:00	9:00	10:00	11:00	12 Midnight
1.					
2.					
3.					
4.					
5.					
6.					
7.					
8.					
9.					
10.					
11.					
12.					
13.					

#32

We are interested in what your family does on a weekday, say, for instance, yesterday or the day before yesterday. From 7a.m. to midnight, could you tell us what each member of your family usually does? We could start with yourself.

7:00	8:00	9:00	10:0011:00	12 Noon
1.				
2.				
3.				
4.				
5.				
6.				
7.				
8.				
9.				
10.				
11.				
12.				
13.				

1:00	2:00	3:00	4:00 5:00	6:00
1.				
2.				
3.				
4.				
5.				
6.				
7.				
8.				
9.				
10.				
11.				
12.				
13.				

7:00	8:00	9:00	10:0011:00	12 Midnight
1.				
2.				
3.				
4.				
5.				
6.				
7.				
8.				
9.				
10.				
11.				
12.				
13.				

#33

Estimate the household's yearly income from all sources. How much does your family receive a week, a month, or a year?

#33a

Does your family's income come from any of the following sources:
____ wages for work
____ dividends
____ gifts from parents or relatives
____ gifts from friends
____ real estate and investments
____ interest from savings accounts
____ welfare
____ pension or social security
____ unemployment insurance

#33b

What proportion of the income of this family comes from:
____ wages
____ welfare
____ pension or social security
____ dividends or interest
____ gifts
____ Total 100%

COMMUNITY RELATIONS AND FOLKLORE

#36
Are you satisfied or dissatisfied with this neighborhood?

_____ Satisfied Completely
_____ Satisfied Somewhat
_____ Dissatisfied Somewhat
_____ Dissatisfied Completely

Why do you feel this way? _____

#37
Have you ever thought about moving away from this neighborhood?   _____ Yes   _____ No
Why do you want to move or stay? _____

If person wants to move: Where do you want to move? _____

#38
This neighborhood could be classified as a

_____ White neighborhood
_____ Black neighborhood
_____ Mixed neighborhood
_____ Other (write in)
_____ Don't know

#39
This neighborhood could be classified as a

_____ Working class
_____ Middle class
_____ Upper class
_____ Poor
_____ Don't know

#40
Most of the families in this neighborhood

_____ Have well-behaved children
_____ Have children that get into trouble
_____ Don't know

#41
In this neighborhood _____ the police do a fine job of enforcing the law
_____ the police are unfair
_____ the police do not care about enforcing the law
_____ Don't know

#42
Do you own or rent this dwelling unit? _____ own _____ rent
(If home is owned): About how much would you estimate this dwelling would sell for? $_____
(If home is rented): What are the weekly $_____ or monthly $_____ payments?

#43
How many rooms are there in this dwelling unit used exclusively by this household?
_____ Kitchen _____ Bedroom _____ Living Room _____ Dining Room _____ Other (specify) _____ Total

#44
How would you describe this dwelling unit? _____ a room _____ an apartment _____ a single-family home
_____ a flat _____ a duplex _____ Other (specify)

#45
Do you have a television? _____ Yes _____ No

#46
If yes, what kind of programs do you watch? _____

#47
About how long do you watch television each day? _____

#48
About how long do the children watch television each day? _____

#49
Do you have a radio _____ Yes _____ No

#50
Where do you hear about news? _____ TV _____ radio _____ paper _____ relatives or friends

#51
Do you get a daily paper? _____ Yes _____ No

#52
Do you get any other publications or magazines? _____ Yes _____ No
If yes, which? _____

#53
Do you have a telephone? _____ Yes _____ No

#54
What I like best about this neighborhood is _____

_____

#55
What troubles me most about this neighborhood is. _____

#56
About how many people in this neighborhood do you know? _____ Five to ten _____ Forty to fifty
_____ Ten to twenty _____ One to five
_____ Twenty to thirty _____ None

#57
This neighborhood has a reputation as _____ a dangerous area _____ in between safe and dangerous
_____ a safe area _____ uncertain

#58
Why do you describe the neighborhood this way? _____

_____

#59
If you had the power to change this neighborhood, what would you change? _____

_____

#60
If you had the power to change this city, what would you change? _____

_____

#61
Which person or persons would you turn to for help in an emergency or to deal with a problem you could not handle alone? If possible, tell us the name of the person you would turn to, what he or she does for a living, how this person is known by you, and why you would turn to him or her for help. _____

_____

#62
We would like to get an understanding of how decisions are made in this household and who influences the decisions that are made. Could you please tell me who usually has the most influence on some of the following decisions? (If there are no children in the household now, whom do you remember having the most influence when children were present?)

CHECK ONE THAT HAD MOST INFLUENCE

DECISION	Mother	Father	Mother Father Equal	Grand-mother	Grand-father	Other Specify	Does Not Apply or Don't Know
a. Helping children with homework							
b. Teaching children manners							
c. Taking care of sick children							
d. Deciding what to eat for meals							
e. Cooking							
f. Assigning chores to children in the home							
g. Helping children to decide how to spend money							
h. Going to school to talk with the teacher							
i. Deciding to move into this house							
j. Helping children to find part-time work							
k. Helping children to decide on adult occupations							
l. Deciding what job each spouse should take							
m. Deciding on what political candidate to vote for							
n. Deciding what school to send children to							
o. Deciding on what church or synagogue to affiliate with							
p. Deciding on what political party to join							
q. Deciding on what car to buy							
r. Deciding on what furniture to buy							
s. Deciding on the number of children							

#63
What kinds of organizations, if any, does your spouse belong to?

A. Religious or Church Connected   E. Voluntary or Service
1.   1.
2.   2.
3.   3.
4.   4.

B. Lodge or Secret Society   F. Neighborhood Improvement
1.   1.
2.   2.
3.   3.
4.   4.

C. Recreational or Social   G. Social Action/Civil Rights
1.   1.
2.   2.
3.   3.
4.   4.

D. Political   H. Business, Professional or Work Ass'n
1.   1.
2.   2.
3.   3.
4.   4.

#64
What kinds of organizations, if any, do you belong to:

A. Religious or Church Connected   E. Voluntary or Service
1.   1.
2.   2.
3.   3.
4.   4.

B. Lodge or Secret Society   F. Neighborhood Improvement
1.   1.
2.   2.
3.   3.
4.   4.

C. Recreational or Social   G. Social Action/Civil Rights
1.   1.
2.   2.
3.   3.
4.   4.

D. Political   H. Business, Professional or Work Ass'n
1.   1.
2.   2.
3.   3.
4.   4.

Note: What are attitudes and opinions of your family members about participation or the lack of participation in community groups. Obtain information on reasons for participating or not participating.

#65
What kinds of organizations, if any, do the children in this household belong to?

A. Religious or Church Connected E. Voluntary or Service
1.   1.
2.   2.
3.   3.
4.   4.

B. Lodge or Secret Society   F. Neighborhood Improvement
1.   1.
2.   2.
3.   3.
4.   4.

C. Recreational or Social   G. Social Action/Civil Rights
1.   1.
2.   2.
3.   3.
4.   4.

D. Political   H. Business, Professional or Work Ass'n
1.   1.
2.   2.
3.   3.
4.   4.

Note: What are attitudes and opinions of your family members about participation or the lack of participation in community groups. Obtain information on reasons for participating or not participating.

#66
This question has to do with the kinds of things people in this household do when they are not working. You may indicate who in the household does it — you, another adult, or children (if applicable), and how often the activity is engaged in.

Person in the household
who engages in the
activity _____

Activity	Frequency
Vacation trips	
Attend professional athletic games	
Attend large dances in clubs or in ballrooms	
Attend house parties at others' homes	
Attend large conventions	
Read books for pleasure	
Sit and talk with family member	
Sit and talk with friends	
Play cards	
Go to the movies	
Invite people over for dinner	
Invite people over for a house party	
Go to dinner in a restaurant	
Go to dinner in the home of a relative or friend	
Go bowling	
Play tennis	
Go swimming	
Read newspaper	
Watch TV	
Listen to the radio	

#66 (continued)
Person in the household
who engages in the
activity

Activity	Frequency
Attend club meetings	
Fix up the house	
Repair car	
Garden	
Sewing or knitting	
Go shopping	
Go to concerts	
Go to lectures	
Visit museum	
Jog or walk	
Fish or hunt	
Camping	
Do volunteer work in the community	
Do volunteer work at the church or synagogue	
Do volunteer work at the school	
Go to school and study	
Other (specify)	

#67
What were the happy times that the members of this household have shared during recent years? When were they and what was done?

#68
What were the sad times that the members of this household have shared during recent years? When were they and what was done?

#69
If you were to sum it up, what would you say this household is trying to accomplish in life?

#70
Have they accomplished this?

#71
If not, what have been the barriers to this accomplishment?

#72
Please discuss briefly the grandparents in this family, including their work, education, interests, socioeconomic status, and how they related to their offspring. Were there unique family values to which they subscribed?

#73
Please discuss some of the places you lived as a child, including neighborhoods, schools, and playmates, if any, and racial experiences.

#74
Please discuss any other facts about the grandparents in this family. Indicate relevant family history, privileges, and adversities of the past and how these were handled. What were the living conditions, honors, opportunities of the grandparents in this family?

#75
What, if any, were the aspirations of the grandparents in this family for their offspring? What did they do to help or hinder the implementation of these aspirations?

#76
Were there any circumstances external to the family that helped or hindered the progress of the grandparents in this family?

INDEX